Cecelia and Fanny

CECELIA
AND
FANNY

∼

The Remarkable Friendship
between an Escaped Slave
and Her Former Mistress

Brad Asher

THE UNIVERSITY PRESS OF KENTUCKY

Scholarly publisher for the Commonwealth,
serving Bellarmine University, Berea College, Centre
College of Kentucky, Eastern Kentucky University,
The Filson Historical Society, Georgetown College,
Kentucky Historical Society, Kentucky State University,
Morehead State University, Murray State University,
Northern Kentucky University, Transylvania University,
University of Kentucky, University of Louisville,
and Western Kentucky University.
All rights reserved.

Editorial and Sales Offices: The University Press of Kentucky
663 South Limestone Street, Lexington, Kentucky 40508-4008
www.kentuckypress.com

15 14 13 12 11   5 4 3 2 1

Library of Congress Cataloging-in-Publication Data

Asher, Brad, 1963–
  Cecelia and Fanny : the remarkable friendship between an escaped slave and
her former mistress / Brad Asher.
    p. cm.
  Includes bibliographical references and index.
  ISBN 978-0-8131-3414-7 (hardcover : acid-free paper) —
  ISBN 978-0-8131-3415-4 (ebook)
  1. Larrison, Cecelia. 2. Ballard, Fanny Thruston. 3. Slaves—Kentucky—
Louisville—Biography. 4. Slaveholders—Kentucky—Louisville—Biography.
5. Fugitive slaves—Canada—Biography. 6. African American women—
Kentucky—Louisville—Biography. 7. Women, White—Kentucky—
Louisville—Biography. 8. Friendship—Case studies. 9. Louisville (Ky.)—
Race relations—History—19th century. 10. Louisville (Ky.)—Biography.
I. Title.
  F459.L853A22 2011
  305.8009769—dc23
                        2011018437

For Sue and Mom

Contents

Illustrations

Preface

I first became interested in the life of Cecelia Reynolds, later Cecelia Holmes, still later Cecelia Larrison, when I discovered a collection of letters that Mrs. Frances Thruston Ballard had written to her, an escaped slave living in Canada. Why, I wondered, would an ex–slave mistress write to a former slave?

The collection, found at the Filson Historical Society in Louisville among the papers of the Ballard family, consists of only a handful of letters, five in number. They are all from Fanny (Frances T. Ballard's nickname) to Cecelia. The letters had been collected by Fanny's son in the late 1890s. The son, Rogers Clark Ballard Thruston, was one of those obsessive, detail-oriented researchers who populated so many of the nation's local historical societies in the waning years of the nineteenth century, without the likes of whom so much of the nation's past would have been lost.

It seemed odd that Cecelia's side of the correspondence was missing. That would have been the half originally in Fanny's possession, and as I came to know and appreciate Rogers Clark's attention to detail, it seemed to me that he would have preserved them if they had existed. I concluded that Fanny most likely had thrown them out, while Cecelia had held on to Fanny's letters to her for fifty years. Obviously, Fanny's side of the correspondence had been much more valuable to Cecelia than Cecelia's had been to Fanny.

Rogers Clark, I think, had wanted to mine the story of his mother's relationship with Cecelia for his own literary purposes. He wrote a preface to the letters that laid out the backstory of Fanny's ownership of Cecelia, the slave's escape, and how he eventually came into possession of the letters. Cecelia, who had returned to Louisville after the Civil War, turned to the family of her former mistress for assistance after a series of financial and family disasters in the 1890s. Rogers Clark helped her and, discovering she still had his mother's letters in her possession, bought them from her. In terms of fodder for Rogers Clark's literary efforts, the letters evidently proved disappointing, for he never got beyond the preface he wrote in 1899. He would go on to write books on the history of the American flag and the lives of the signers of the Declaration of Independence, but Fanny's letters sat unutilized in the archives of the Filson, of which Rogers Clark served for many years as president.

By themselves, Fanny's few letters provide only hints of Cecelia's life in freedom. To flesh out the stories of both women required delving into the archival records of their families. Cecelia's second husband, William Larrison, had served in the Union army during the Civil War, giving Cecelia a claim on a government pension as a veteran's widow. The process of applying for that pension entailed an investigation of the claim by Pension Bureau examiners, an investigation that filled in some of the gaps in the lacunae-laden story of her life. Other gaps were filled by the appearance of Cecelia's household in public administrative records—census documents, tax rolls, death records, and the like. But many gaps remained, holes in her life that had to be papered over with squishy terms like "perhaps" and "most likely," based on what historians have discovered about other people in similar circumstances at the time.

Fanny, whose life followed the common nineteenth-century trajectory for women as she filled the roles of daughter, wife, and mother, likewise did not leave an extensive paper trail. The Ballard Family Papers at the Filson contain some business correspondence and some memorabilia from her reign as Queen of May, a social honor bestowed upon her when she was just thirteen years old. The men in her life left caches of personal papers, as the rich and prominent are wont to do, but in most cases these yielded precious little insight into Fanny's own life.

In short, with no voluminous correspondence, no decades-long span of diaries, the lives of Fanny and Cecelia cannot be told in the full detail that the life stories of other "ordinary people" have been, stories that benefited from such extensive records. No life is completely documented, and the ordinary life is documented only in fragments. Fanny and Cecelia thus cannot be known in the way one knows the subject of a three-inch-thick biography, but piecing together the archival fragments of their lives allows them to be known by the contours of their intertwined life paths and to illuminate broader themes about womanhood, slavery, and family life in nineteenth-century America.[1]

Are they worth knowing? With so many books on slavery, slaves, and slaveholders, why add another to already overloaded shelves? First, the history of slavery remains heavily weighted toward the rural plantation. But Fanny and Cecelia lived in cities all their lives, and urban life put different twists on the master/slave relationship. Second, the story of slavery and race relations in Kentucky remains underexplored. As a border state, it does not fit comfortably into the history of either South or North. Third, the historical rupture that was the Civil War still serves as the conventional endpoint for stories of slavery or the conventional starting point for stories of freedom. But for Fanny and Cecelia, the war was neither start nor end. Their lives straddled the watershed of the war and were reconfigured by it, as they learned to navigate President Lincoln's "new birth of freedom."

Chapter 1

Eight Minutes from Freedom

In far western New York State, the short but powerful Niagara River divides the United States from Canada. For fugitive slaves seeking to escape bondage, that international boundary marked the frontier between slavery and freedom. About midway through its course, at Niagara Falls, the river plummets spectacularly over a 170-foot precipice. At the base of the Falls, in the years before the river was bridged, it took a competent ferryman just eight minutes to row the quarter mile across the churning waters from the American side to the Canadian side.

In the spring of 1846, when she was fifteen years old, Cecelia journeyed to Niagara Falls with her mistress, twenty-year-old Fanny Thruston. Fanny and her father, Charles W. Thruston, had traveled from Washington, D.C., for a holiday at the Falls. The Thrustons resided in Louisville, Kentucky, but Fanny had spent the winter with relatives in the capital. Cecelia, as Fanny's personal maidservant, accompanied the Thrustons on the trip. She had been with Fanny over the winter in Washington, and since Fanny and her father would be returning directly home from the Falls, it made sense to bring the slave girl along. In his succinct retelling of his mother's trip to Niagara, Rogers Clark wrote simply, "One fine day Cecelia was missing. Investigation showed that she had gone to Canada." Lodged in a hotel at Niagara Falls, Cecelia must have known that freedom lay just across the river, eight minutes away.[1]

Crossing that border wouldn't be like crossing the Ohio River from Louisville into southern Indiana. As a slave in a border city, Cecelia knew the geography of freedom, and she knew that slave catchers still operated north of the Ohio, that courts in free states sometimes returned runaways to their owners. Sympathy for fugitive slaves was scant in most parts of southern Ohio, Indiana, and Illinois, and networks for apprehending escaping slaves and returning them to captivity functioned with frightening efficiency. But crossing into Canada—the promised land of so many runaways' dreams—meant freedom, plain and simple.[2]

Why had the Thrustons taken the risk? Why bring a slave girl so tantalizingly close to the border where the temptation to flee might be overwhelming? No doubt they did it because they did not perceive it as risky. They had little reason to suspect Cecelia of harboring thoughts of freedom. She had been in the family since infancy; surely her loyalties rested with the certainty and stability of the only life she had ever known, not with some untested and abstract notion of freedom. Besides affection for her mistress and the rest of the Thruston family, her own family ties—a mother and a brother back in Louisville, still Thruston family slaves—would keep Cecelia from entertaining subversive thoughts. Many other Southern slaveholders made similar calculations. While Southern men traveling alone might forego the services of their slaves while on a business trip, Southern women and those traveling for leisure with large families were more reluctant to do so.[3]

In Washington, Fanny had wintered with the family of Thomas Sidney Jesup, a career military officer who served as the quartermaster general of the U.S. Army. Jesup had married a Thruston family cousin, Ann Croghan, and the Jesups had spent much of the summer and fall of 1845 at Locust Grove, a well-known Kentucky estate near Louisville owned by Ann's parents. When the Jesups returned to Washington in December, Fanny went with them, doubtless to help celebrate the engagement of her second cousin, Mary, to a prominent young Washingtonian. Mary was twenty years old, the same age as Fanny, and the wedding would have offered ample opportunity for Fanny to see and be seen in Washington society. In such a milieu, she would have required the services of Cecelia. Mary Jesup wed in January, but scarcely three months later, on April 24, 1846, Ann Croghan Jesup—Mary's mother and Fanny's hostess—died after a short illness. The trip to Niagara—which probably took place soon after Ann Jesup's untimely death—may have been intended as a balm for Fanny's grief.[4]

The Thrustons' choice of destination was by no means unusual; thousands of antebellum travelers, including many Southerners, came to Niagara every year. An 1846 guidebook estimated that twelve thousand to fifteen thousand visitors made the trip annually, and while Northerners typically outnumbered Southerners, genteel urbanites from Virginia, Louisiana, and Kentucky—like the Thrustons—were easy to find. One Richmond-based traveler in 1845 found himself in the company of more than a dozen other sojourning Southerners; they all stayed in the same wing of the same hotel, which was promptly dubbed Southern Hall. Awed by the scenery and the "truly Elysian" climate, another Virginian gushed, "The wonder is that Southerners do not spend the entire summer at the Falls."[5]

The Falls stand just about midway along the thirty-five-mile course of the Niagara River, which drains Lake Erie into Lake Ontario. The Niagara was "a full-grown stream at the first moment of its existence," one nineteenth-century traveler wrote, "and . . . no larger at its mouth than at its source." At the Falls, an island—Goat Island—divides the river, separating by yards the American Falls on the U.S. side from Horseshoe (or Canadian) Falls across the international boundary.[6]

The opening of the Erie Canal in 1825 and the development of the railroad in the next decade helped transform Niagara into the antebellum period's most popular vacation spot. By the mid-1840s, three railroads served Niagara from nearby cities, steamboats brought passengers downriver from Buffalo and Lake Erie and upriver from Lake Ontario, and stagecoaches ran to and from the Falls "in all directions." In 1846, the Thrustons' journey to the Falls from the capital probably took only three or four days. As one Southern traveler to Niagara remarked, "With what rapidity one travels now-a-days!"[7]

English writer Charles Latrobe, commenting in the 1830s on the ease of travel to Niagara Falls, griped that "the forest has everywhere yielded to the axe. Hotels, with their snug shrubberies, outhouses, gardens, and paltry embellishment, stare you in the face."

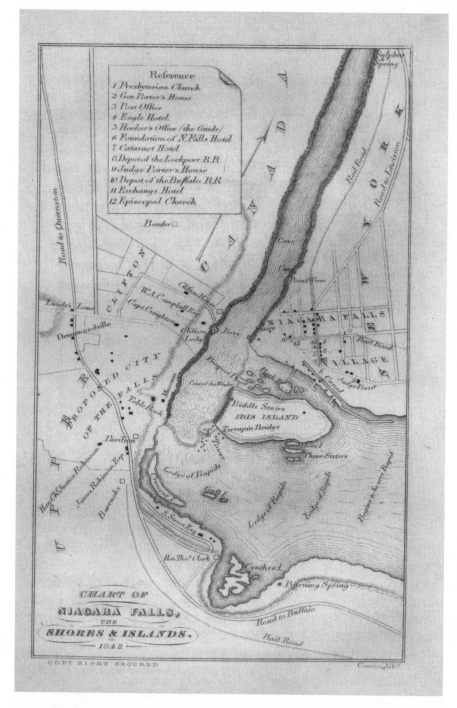

Map of Niagara Falls, 1842. (J. W. Orr, "Pictorial Guide to the Falls of Niagara," Niagara University Library, Niagara Falls, N.Y.)

Travel was now so convenient that one could leave Richmond and arrange a meeting in Niagara with a friend from Quebec "with a moral certainty of meeting at the very day and hour specified, by taking advantage of the improvements of the age, and the well-arranged mode of conveyance by steamers, railroads, canals, and coaches. In short, Niagara is now as hacknied [*sic*] as Stockgill Forge [Force], or Rydal-water," two aqueous attractions in England's Lake District.[8]

Latrobe was not the only dissatisfied visitor. As America's first overhyped tourist destination, Niagara Falls disappointed more than a few travelers upon first viewing. "[I have] seen Niagara and felt—no words can tell what disappointment," wrote one woman in the 1830s. Conditioned by guidebooks and magazine articles to expect unparalleled majesty and awe-inspiring grandeur, this tourist found the "two great cataracts" to be a mere "feature in the landscape." For some guidebook authors, this was a natural consequence of the *way* in which people visited the Falls. "Don't attempt to 'do' the Falls in a day or even two days," one Southern traveler counseled. Another traveler criticized the haste of casual tourists at the Falls. Too often, they jumped down from the train or coach and hurried to catch their first glimpse, "and this view may in all probability be one of the least attractive." Disappointed, they "wonder at the eulogium bestowed by other travellers, who have used more time and discretion." They then "jump into the first car that leaves, and—praise the Falls, *because every one else does*."[9]

Most antebellum visitors to the Falls, however, could not understand any reaction short of awe. The Englishman John Barham, who visited in the fall of 1845, wrote that he had "heard of persons being disappointed with Niagara: to me it appears, that if bad taste may be considered a species of insanity, such persons ought to be regarded as maniacs." The majesty of the Falls overcame even the jaded Latrobe, for whom the convenience of travel to the Falls had made them hackneyed. "You may have heard of individuals coming back from the contemplation of these Falls with dissatisfied feelings. To me this is perfectly incomprehensible."[10]

Charles Dickens felt himself drawing near to the Creator at the Falls. Frances Trollope, the mother of novelist Anthony Trollope, wept and was "violently affected" by the Falls. Many confessed that the wonder was simply beyond words—and then proceeded to try to put it into words anyway. "The scenery is grand beyond description," a Southern visitor wrote. James Stuart, in his 1833 travelogue, wrote, "Such words as grandeur, majesty, sublimity, fail altogether to express the feelings which so magnificent a sight, exceeding so immeasurably all of the same kind that we have ever seen or imagined, excites." John Barham compiled a variety of writings on Niagara when composing his own guidebook, borrowing the words of others, he said, to make up for his own "inability to convey in words a just idea of this the most stupendous cataract on the face of the globe."[11]

As awestruck tourists groped for words to describe their Falls experience—grand, majestic, magnificent—one word recurred in their reminiscences more than any other: sublime. The sublime was that which inspired awe or uplifted the spirit, and sublimity was the most sought-after quality by the antebellum middle class. Niagara delivered in spades. "The sensation which fills the soul is overwhelmingly sublime," a Virginian wrote in 1845. In recommending two particular vistas, Barham declared that they "combine more of the beautiful and sublime" than any other views of the Falls. "The effect of the Falls upon the beholder is most awfully sublime," he wrote. James Stuart stated that "the mind is wholly absorbed in the contemplation of a spectacle so sublime." Another traveler attempted to characterize the distinction between the Falls on the Canadian side and those on the American side. The Canadian aspect, he wrote, "is beautiful, inclining to the sublime." The American was "sublime, inclining to the beautiful."[12]

Fanny and her father left behind no accounts of their feelings about the Falls, so we cannot know whether they experienced the spiritual uplift that came from such a powerful and direct communion with the majesty of nature. Given the escape of Cecelia, however, it seems doubtful that they harbored many positive memories of Niagara.

Of course, slavery was illegal in New York, as it was in the other Northern states, so the idea of slaveholding sightseers touring Northern vacation spots with their bondmen in tow seems a little odd. Many modern Americans tend to think of the institution of slavery as peculiar to the South, but slavery was never content simply to rest isolated in the Southern states, and slave owners were never content to have their property rights respected only at home. As citizens of the nation coequal to Northerners, slave-owning Southerners felt that they should have the right to take their property—including their human property—with them wherever they traveled.

There were risks, of course. Throughout the antebellum period, freedom-seeking slaves and their abolitionist supporters sporadically challenged the legal rights of slaveholders traveling in free states to retain their bondmen. The outcome of these court cases depended partly on the sympathies of the presiding judge and the depth of abolitionist sentiment in the surrounding community. But the underlying legal issue in these cases was whether or not a Southern traveler intended to establish residency in the North or was merely passing through. If the slave owner was intending to relocate to the Northern state, then he could not retain his slave property. If the slave owner was just a casual visitor—a "sojourner," as the legal profession put it—then the master/slave relationship was maintained. As one Pennsylvania judge reasoned when denying a slave's claim to freedom, to grant a bondman freedom just because a master liked to visit a Northern vacation spot in the summer months would be "a denial of the rights of hospitality."[13]

Prior to the mid-1830s or so, a kind of implicit agreement had been worked out between North and South over the issue of whether the master/slave relationship persisted in areas where slavery was illegal. In Northern states, sojourning Southerners were exempted from state laws banning slavery. In Southern states, if a slave sued for freedom based on a previous extended stay in a Northern state, arguing that the slave relationship had been dissolved by the master's residency in that state, Southern courts not infrequently freed the slave. Courts thus viewed slavery as an issue of "comity"—of respecting the laws of another jurisdiction.

New York, in fact, was especially hospitable on this issue. Its so-called nine months law allowed a Southern slave owner to pass three-fourths of a year in the state without jeopardizing his slave property rights. New York's commercial classes had no desire to alienate the large number of Southern planters and merchants who did business in New York City—and then journeyed on to spend money at Saratoga, Niagara, and other "watering holes" in the state.[14]

Fanny and her father were obviously sojourners, so they may have felt that their right to own Cecelia was not legally at risk. At the time they visited Niagara, however, the preexisting legal landscape was changing all across the North. The change had begun, unsurprisingly, in Massachusetts—New York's boisterously abolitionist neighbor—in 1836. In that year, the Massachusetts Supreme Court decided the case of *Commonwealth v. Aves*, ruling that slaves coming into Massachusetts were free to leave their masters since no law in Massachusetts allowed masters to hold slaves. Slaveholders were forbidden to forcibly restrain or retain their slaves. Slaves could *choose* to remain in slavery and return to a slave state, but they could not be forced to do so. Under the *Aves* doctrine, once a slave set foot in Massachusetts, his or her bondage ceased. (Ironically, the *Aves* rule did not apply to runaways—because state law was trumped by federal fugitive slave law—but only to those slaves who traveled with their masters.)[15]

It took a few years for the legal doctrine enunciated in the *Aves* case to have an impact in New York. The antislavery movement in New York—never as strong or as aggressive as that in Massachusetts—had to contest continually with the Southern-friendly commercial interests in New York City. Abolitionist sentiment was growing, however, particularly in the upstate "Burned-over District," which had been "scorched" by revivalist preachers in the 1830s, and in 1841 antislavery advocates successfully petitioned the New York legislature to repeal the nine months law.[16]

Nobody directly tested the repeal, however, until 1852. In that year, a Virginia woman named Juliet Lemmon brought eight slaves with her to New York City, intending to secure passage to New Orleans with the eventual destination of Texas. Mrs. Lemmon was clearly in transit, sojourning in a free state while en route from one slave state to another. Nonetheless, Louis Napoleon—a "colored citizen" of New York—filed a writ of habeas corpus on the slaves' behalf, requiring Mrs. Lemmon to produce the slaves in court. The Lemmons' lawyer argued for the right of sojourners to pass through a free state without losing their property rights, but the court rejected the plea. Under the terms of the 1841 repeal of the nine months law, the judge declared, the Lemmons' slaves were free when they touched New York soil. The court liberated the slaves in November 1852, and the former bondmen promptly fled to Canada. The Virginia legislature then financed an appeal of the case to the New York Supreme Court, which approved the trial court's decision in 1860. "Comity does not require any state to extend any greater privilege to the citizens of another state than it grants to its own," the court ruled. "As this state does not allow its own citizens to bring a slave here, *in transitu*, and to hold him as a slave for any portion of time, it cannot be expected to allow the citizens of another state to do so."[17]

When the Thrustons traveled to Niagara with Cecelia, therefore, they trod on shaky legal ground. Had Cecelia known about the changing legal landscape, had a lawyer been willing to take her case, had a sympathetic judge ruled in 1846 the way the judge in the *Lemmon* case ruled six years later, she would have stood a good chance of securing her freedom in a New York courtroom. Given that daunting set of conditions, however, Fanny and her father doubtless felt that their property rights were secure enough.

If lawyers represented little real threat to the Thrustons' hold over Cecelia, another group loomed larger, especially in the minds of Southerners. As abolitionist agitation and sectional tension increased, Southern travelers began to view the North as honeycombed with abolitionists and free blacks who had no other purpose in life but to "steal" Southerners' slave property. An 1851 article in the *Southern Literary Messenger* recalled fondly the time when Northern resorts welcomed Southerners, a time when "the southern gentleman might take with him his dark body-servant Sam, without fear of having him stolen by the philanthropists of the North."[18]

The town of Niagara Falls had a local African American community; many of them worked as waiters in the hotels and steamboats, as porters, or as ferrymen. Barham noted during his 1845 excursion that the ferryman who took him across the river was black. The Canadian villages—St. Catharines, Niagara, and Queenston—on the other side of the river also had their own African American communities. None of these communities were especially large; the 1840 U.S. census reported just 241 African Americans in all of Niagara County, and the 1850 enumeration found just 317. About that same number lived among the scattered settlements in Canada. Free blacks, former slaves, and fugitives congregated in these towns and villages, building their own institutions and offering aid to newcomers. Many of them took an interest whenever traveling Southerners brought their slaves with them.[19]

Historians have begun to recognize in just the last few decades the crucial role played by such local communities of free blacks in the functioning of the Underground Railroad. The view that a runaway slave's path to freedom was paved by a well-organized network of (mostly white) "conductors" is mostly seen now as the product of Southerners' prewar paranoia about an abolitionist conspiracy and abolitionists' postwar preening about their role in destroying the "peculiar institution." Historians now see the Underground Railroad, far from being the well-oiled machine of lore, as a pastiche of local people, many of them African American, scattered in many communities, who helped fugitives along, prevented their recapture, and assisted other slaves to claim their freedom. These local communities made the Underground Railroad work. Local activists in Niagara Falls could have directed Cecelia to sympathetic ferrymen and provided her with Canadian contacts, moving her toward the promised land.[20]

In 1847, about a year after the Thrustons' visit, Niagara's black community did try to help a slave in a situation very similar to Cecelia's. A traveling Alabama couple toured the Falls in July with slave girl in tow. As the Alabamans prepared to leave, several local African American men attempted to liberate the girl. The slave owner, aided by various others, rebuffed the attempt by force, and a near riot resulted. In this case, the local squad of liberators was unsuccessful, and master and slave departed together on the train. Repercussions for the black community followed. A group of whites—described in one account as "a few drunken Irishmen . . . and several wicked young lads"—descended upon the houses of some African Americans in Niagara. Things turned ugly, shots were fired, and the mob ended up burning at least one house to the ground.[21]

Press accounts of this incident show two very distinct points of view regarding efforts to help sojourning slaves claim their freedom. Establishment newspapers—hostile to abolitionism, friendly to Southern business interests, and disapproving of social disorder—painted the incident as an assault upon an innocent man. The *Buffalo Republic* reported that the black community "determined even against the wishes of the female slave, to attempt to set her free. . . . No wish was evinced by the slave, to be set free, on the contrary, she expressed a desire to return with her master home. But the rioters appeared to want to force her away from her master." The *Buffalo Commercial Advertiser* wrote that "between twenty and thirty colored persons, as had been previously arranged among themselves, rushed to the cars and attempted to take by force the object of their sympathies. . . . They were resisted by the conductor, engineer, and others." The *Buffalo Express* told a slightly different version, stating that the local black community attempted to "kidnap some one or two colored servants, of Southerners, visiting at the Falls." The "kidnapping" triggered a house-to-house search that resulted in a gun battle between those seeking the slave and those trying to conceal her. "We understand the servants were forced away from their masters contrary to their wishes or desires."[22]

For Southerners, such incidents merely confirmed their worst suspicions about the determination of abolitionists and free blacks to "steal" their property. The newspaper accounts reflected the fear that such disorder would harm Niagara's business interests. The *Express* noted that local "citizens have endeavored to inspire visitors from the south with the belief that . . . their rights and property shall be protected from molestation." The *Republic* pronounced itself "gratified that no considerable or respectable portion of the population at the Falls, countenanced this violence, but came promptly to the rescue. . . . Whatever may be our opinion of the evil of slavery, we cannot but regard such an interference of a mob with the private rights of the citizen, as dangerous in the extreme, and think it should be promptly put down." One editorialist glumly concluded, "A few more such riots will turn the tide in favor of the Clifton House [a rival hotel] on the Canadian side."[23]

The abolitionist press portrayed the incident in a very different light. In their accounts, the aspirations of the slave girl to be free took center stage. Far from an attack on the property rights of an innocent tourist, it was a bold attempt to rescue an oppressed waif from unjust bondage. In the *True Wesleyan*'s account, the girl made contact with one of the "vast number of colored waiters" working at the Cataract Hotel. "The girl made known her situation to one of them and stated that she was wretched beyond description because of the cruel treatment of her master and mistress. She wished him to convey her to the Canada side." An article in the *Pennsylvania Freeman* described the Southerner visiting the Falls as "having with him a woman he claimed as a slave, contrary to our laws. He kept her secluded (some say confined) under circumstances to render the belief that she was illegally restrained of her liberty." When master and slave made their way to the railroad car, escorted by the hotel landlord, "a colored man . . . asked her if she wished to go back to the South." This man was knocked down by those escorting the slave and her master and when several other blacks moved in to offer support, "a row followed in which several colored persons were badly injured." A letter writer to the *Freeman* who was at the Falls during the incident said that the girl "was desirous of enjoying the blessings of as much freedom as the laws of the land would admit of, and a little more than her master was willing she should enjoy. She made her wish known, and with the aid of the colored people at the Falls, made a desperate attempt which terminated in quite a mob."[24]

This 1847 "race riot" made plain a couple of points. First, there was a community of activists in Niagara Falls dedicated to helping enslaved Africans claim their freedom. Second, they did so in the face of local hostility and at significant personal risk. The different perspectives of the press on the incident, however, raise a third point: that of how the Thrustons calculated the risk when they brought Cecelia north. The Thrustons, like the establishment newspapers and Southerners generally, perceived the threat that a slave might escape as primarily *external* to the master/slave relationship. It was the result of abolitionist agitation, of "kidnapping" by antislavery fanatics, of unlawful assaults on established and legally protected rights of property. In Rogers Clark's telling of his mother's story, Cecelia's flight was blamed on "abolitionists and run-away negroe slaves" who were "always lurking along our Canadian border." These people's "main object in life was to allure away from their masters such body and maid servants as the southern people chose to take with them to places of resort along the border."[25]

According to slaveholders, many postemancipation Southerners, and an earlier generation of historians, slaves would have been content with slavery if not for the machinations of this group of extremists, obsessively bent on destroying slavery as an institution. "Serpents . . . had crept into the garden and subverted paradise," wrote one historian. "Nor was it a spontaneous, unorganized campaign, for the abolitionist power had established an intricate and widespread network of agents and agitators who busily plotted the overthrow of the regime." The historical literature on slavery is full of examples of masters who, not accepting that their slaves wanted to run away, claimed that they were enticed away. In one well-known incident in 1855, abolitionists in Philadelphia intercepted John Wheeler, the U.S. minister to Nicaragua, with three of his slaves. Told they were free by virtue of standing on Pennsylvania soil, the slaves left Wheeler's service. Wheeler then sued the abolitionists for kidnapping his slaves against their will, claiming that the three servants had been happy with their state. One of the former slaves appeared in the courtroom and forcefully debunked Wheeler's claim that she had been content with slavery.[26]

Many years later, Cecelia herself buttressed Rogers Clark's view that his mother had been the victim of abolitionist aggression. When Cecelia appealed to him in 1899 for financial assistance, Rogers Clark asked her why she had run away. "Lord, Mr. Rogers, I didn't run away!" Cecelia replied. "Them niggers up there jest took me away." No desire on her part to seek freedom, no initiative in breaking her bonds, complete passivity—with her words, Cecelia painted a picture of slavery as Rogers Clark wanted to see it. This was no doubt the response expected from a former slave asking favors of a former master. The five intervening decades between her escape and her conversation with Rogers Clark give the lie to the story, however. Cecelia's subsequent life and letters to Fanny show little regret at having achieved freedom and less desire to return to slavery.[27]

The question of Cecelia's motivations lays open the risk that went unperceived by Fanny and her father. Their decision to have Cecelia accompany them on the trip to Niagara spoke to their belief in Cecelia's willing acceptance of her slave status. That Cecelia nurtured aspirations independent of her owners, and that these included freedom, no doubt came as quite a shock. The risk that a slave might escape, in other words, was less related to external factors—like abolitionism—and much more related to factors *internal* to the slave herself. Because the Thrustons could not know Cecelia's heart, they were caught unawares.

Herein lies the critical distinction between the differing press accounts of the 1847 affray in Niagara. For those writers sympathetic to the abolitionist cause, the Alabaman slave girl initiated the actions of the local black community by making known her desire to be free. She was the agent; the local community merely responded with sympathetic aid to her plea.

For the modern generation of historians, this issue of agency has completely altered prevailing interpretations both of the institution of slavery as a whole and of the Underground Railroad more narrowly. This new understanding has changed the view of slavery from a totalizing institution of control to a highly contested struggle between masters and slaves; it has changed the view of emancipation from a "gift" bestowed by Lincoln and the Union army to a "taking" by a mass movement of African Americans who fled to the sanctuary behind the army's lines and created new facts on the ground; and it has changed the view of the Underground Railroad from a tightly organized web of primarily white conductors helping desperate and destitute fugitives to a loose coalition of local cells of activists— mainly African American—who reached out opportunistically to help slaves who, for the most part, had already been the agents of their own liberation, fleeing bondage on their own initiative.[28]

So what were Cecelia's motivations? The Thrustons had presented her with an opportunity; what feelings prompted her to act? To try to understand Cecelia's feelings, one must consider her situation as Fanny's personal maidservant. The two young women had grown up under the same roof; Cecelia had entered the Thruston household as an infant. As Cecelia's role in the household shifted, however, from being one of several house servants under the overall control of Fanny's father to being directly under Fanny's control, her relationship with Fanny no doubt also shifted. The familiarity that had existed between them as children decreased, replaced by the hierarchical formality of the mistress and the slave.

As Fanny attained the age to enter society, Cecelia would have spent even more time in personal attendance upon her young mistress, helping fix her hair, assisting her with dressing, and passing on gossip learned from servants in other households. No doubt Cecelia knew—from bedroom chatter with Fanny—that her mistress was a desirable marriage prospect. Maids often took as much interest in fashions, suitors, and parties as their mistresses. But Fanny's entrance into society represented the threat of change for Cecelia. If Fanny married, she was likely to set up housekeeping in a new place with her new husband, an upheaval that would affect Cecelia as much as Fanny herself. Not only would it separate Cecelia from her mother, but who knew how the new husband would treat the household slaves? Cecelia may also have realized her own value on the market. She had been trained in household service, and good domestics fetched a good price. She may have considered herself loyal to Fanny, but how much could she count on Fanny's loyalty to her, especially if Fanny got married? Would there be a place for her in the new household, or would she be just a valuable financial asset? These thoughts and doubts bred a feeling of restlessness within Ce-

View of the Landing on the American Side by William Bartlett (1840). Before the Niagara River was bridged, tourists descended a steep staircase to embark on rowboats that ferried them across to the Canadian side. This was Cecelia's most likely escape route. (New York State Library, Albany, N.Y.)

celia. All slaves probably knew this feeling—the uncertainty, the lack of control over one's own life, the fear of separation from one's family, the desire to settle oneself for one's own benefit, instead of serving the master's whim. By bringing Cecelia to Niagara, Fanny and her father had given the slave girl the chance to act on those feelings.[29]

Still, she must have been tormented by doubt. She couldn't simply walk down to the ferry landing below the Falls, pay her fare, and cross the river, could she? She probably had no money, and after having lived a life under regular surveillance, she must also have thought that in any case she would never get away with it. As Frederick Douglass remarked about his own flight from slavery, "No man can tell the intense agony which is felt by the slave when wavering on the point of making his escape."[30]

Most probably, Cecelia made contact with the free African American community in Niagara Falls. It could provide answers about *how* to escape bondage, but it was Cecelia herself who ultimately had to make the choice. Freedom waited for her just eight minutes away, but behind her lay the only life she had ever known. Behind her, too, lay her mother and brother, still enslaved. In front of her was perhaps her only chance to help free them from bondage. She would probably never have another opportunity like this: Kentucky, after all, was a long way from Canada.

Sometime in late April or early May 1846 (the exact date cannot be determined), she made her choice. She crossed the river and cast her lot for freedom.

Chapter 2

Fanny: Learning to Be a Slave Owner

It took Fanny and her father a little time to discover that Cecelia had fled. When they did, it must have seemed incomprehensible. Why would this slave, so kindly treated, so much a part of the family, have absconded? When, years later, Fanny's son wrote about Cecelia's escape, he described his grandfather as "very angry" and Fanny herself as "quite annoyed," but that anger and annoyance were not directed so much at Cecelia as at those they blamed for seducing her into running away. According to Rogers Clark, Fanny and her father successfully made contact with some of the people who aided Cecelia in her flight, but their attempts to contact Cecelia herself were rebuffed. Cecelia's conductors feared, according to Fanny's son, that "the slave might be induced to return to her former mistress." Eventually, Fanny packed up Cecelia's clothes and effects—along with a sum of money—and handed them over to someone who knew Cecelia's whereabouts. However, "the scoundrel pocketed both money and effects and poor Cecelia never saw either." (Exactly how Fanny or her son learned about this theft is unclear.) Eventually, having been betrayed by a slave and fleeced by a con artist, the Thrustons returned to Louisville.[1]

Cecelia's escape ended Fanny's first foray into slave ownership. She had received Cecelia as a coming-of-age gift from her father some five or six years previously, when Fanny was approximately fourteen and Cecelia about nine years old. Fanny's older brother Sam received a manservant at about the same time. Writing down his family's history many years later, Rogers Clark remarked that "it was the custom among the slave-holders to give to each son upon arriving at a certain age, generally about 16 or 17 years of age, a negroe boy of about the same age, who was his especial property and body servant. Each daughter, upon arriving at the age of 14 or 15, likewise received a negroe girl, of about her age, to be her especial property and lady's maid." Having grown up in a slaveholding household, Fanny was no doubt accustomed to the presence of slaves and her general authority over them. Before coming to possess Cecelia, however, Fanny had never been a slave owner herself or borne an owner's specific responsibilities.[2]

While a personal servant made life easier and was no doubt a wonderful luxury, the gift of a slave also helped groom a young master or mistress for the more extensive responsibilities of slave ownership that would come with the establishment of an independent household. Despite being culturally conditioned from early childhood to view themselves as members of a master class, slaveholders' children still had to learn how to manage slaves; it was a crucial part of their adolescence. Throughout their childhood, they absorbed lessons on slave management from family stories, from parental advice, and from direct observation of their parents' actions. A slave of one's own, however, provided direct hands-on experience. Making Cecelia Fanny's personal property helped draw the line between childhood and adulthood. As children in the same household, Fanny and Cecelia may have grown up more as companions than as mistress and slave. As one of several house servants under the general authority of Fanny's father, Cecelia would have come only tangentially under Fanny's control. But when Fanny became her mistress, Cecelia became directly subject to her authority. An aspiring slave mistress had to learn to "set a tone" in dealing with slaves if she were to run an efficient household. Cecelia was expected to "know her place," and Fanny was expected to teach her.[3]

Such were the cultural expectations thrust upon Fanny with the "gift" of Cecelia. Unfortunately, it is almost impossible to know Fanny's attitudes toward slavery during the time when Cecelia was her property. Nothing in her sparse collection of papers addresses Cecelia's escape or even mentions slavery until later, when Cecelia contacted her. But that early silence is in itself revealing of her ac-

Charles William Thruston (Fanny's father), ca. 1855.
(Filson Historical Society, Louisville, Ky.)

ceptance of the institution as a "cultural necessity," as her son described it. It was simply part of her status quo, and she never found
cause to question it. In addition, she had before her the powerful
example of her father, who no doubt coached her on slave character
and slave management, using his own experience and his own family history to drive home the lessons. Indeed, Cecelia's escape was
probably more galling to Charles Thruston than to Fanny. He had
vastly more experience than his daughter at managing slaves, and he
did not like it when one slipped through his fingers. Rogers Clark
characterized Charles Thruston as a lukewarm supporter of slavery,
one who viewed it as a necessary condition of life in a Southern state
but who hoped it "would be some day abolished." Until "someday"

came, however, Charles William Thruston behaved like most Southern slaveholders—he disciplined his slaves if they misbehaved, he pursued them if they ran away, and he disposed of them when they no longer served his purposes.[4]

Thruston was a well-to-do retired businessman of fifty years of age when he journeyed to Niagara with his daughter. In his earlier years, he had some difficulty deciding on a profession. His mother wrote in 1824, when Thruston was twenty-eight, "Charles is at a great loss to know where he had best settle himself." The family owned a small plantation near the river town of Westport, just up-river from Louisville, and his mother urged the rural life of a gentleman farmer on her son. But Charles William eventually settled on a different course. He had largely grown up in the town of Louisville, and by the mid-1820s it was clear that Louisville was destined to be the great commercial hub of Kentucky.[5]

Situated at the Falls of the Ohio, the only barrier to navigation between Pittsburgh and New Orleans, Louisville enjoyed natural geographic advantages. When the river was low, the Falls forced boats to stop, offload their cargo, transport it overland to a point below the Falls, and then reload it to continue on downstream. That was good enough to give Louisville a head start over most of its nearby competitors, but in 1814 the future of Louisville's river trade came to town in the form of the steamboat *New Orleans*. At first, the consensus was that steam offered a faster way downriver, but conventional wisdom in town said the *New Orleans* could not make it back upriver. Conventional wisdom was soon proved wrong.[6]

Two-way river traffic triggered Louisville's economic takeoff. The hauling, warehousing, wholesaling, insurance, and banking businesses that formed the heart of the city's economy all boomed. Population tripled between 1810 and 1820, and almost tripled again in the next decade. Louisville rapidly shouldered its way past its Kentucky river-port competitors and by 1830 surpassed its land-locked Bluegrass rival, Lexington.[7]

So Charles William Thruston rejected his mother's advice and embarked on the life of an urban entrepreneur. In 1826, in partnership with his uncle, he opened a ropewalk and bagging factory. It

Map of Louisville, 1832. Charles William Thruston's ropewalk was at 5 Water Street, close to the public wharf. The Thruston home was located away from the bustle of the business district, on East Walnut Street in the less developed southern end of town. (*Louisville City Directory*, 1832, University of Louisville Archives, Louisville, Ky.)

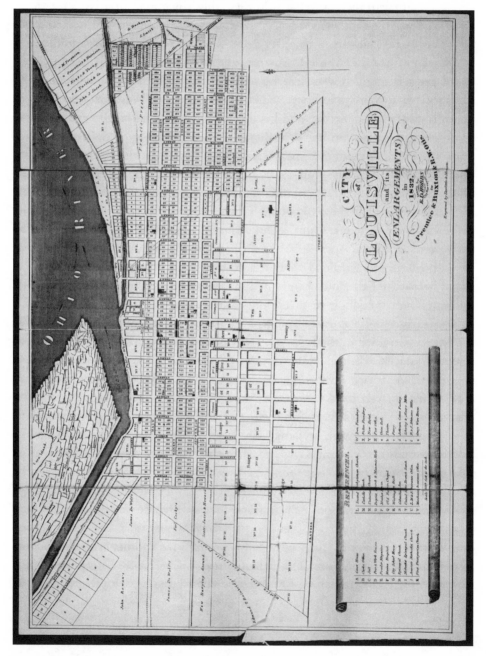

was an auspicious time to do so. As the Chesapeake-based economy of tobacco—the Southern cash crop during the colonial period—exhausted itself, post-Revolution Southern planters moved west and embraced cotton cultivation. Aided by the invention of the cotton gin, Southerners expanded into new territory in Mississippi and Alabama, expanding the realm of slavery with them.[8]

Kentucky, too far north to grow cotton, nonetheless benefited from the cotton boom. Cotton planters needed rope and bagging to bale their cotton, and Bluegrass planters responded by expanding their cultivation of hemp. Kentucky planters referred to hemp as a "nigger" crop, because they felt that slaves were ideally suited to the hard work of tending the fiber. With the expansion of hemp cultivation came the growth of the hemp-processing industry, turning the fibers into rope, bagging, cheap cloth, and rough floor coverings. The heart of the Kentucky hemp-processing industry lay in Lexington and Fayette County. Already by 1810, Fayette County had five bagging factories and thirteen ropewalks. But Louisville, benefiting from its location on the Ohio River, had its share of factories as well. In 1832, the River City had four such establishments, including Charles William Thruston's.[9]

Ropewalks were long narrow buildings. Thruston's factory was about 26 feet wide and 570 feet long. Making rope was essentially like spinning yarn. A worker with a bundle of hemp around his waist twisted the fibers together and attached them to a hook on the "whirl." A second worker then spun the whirl while the first played out more hemp from the bundle as he walked backward the length of the building. The spinning motion of the whirl twisted the fibers together into rough rope. When a worker's bundle of hemp was exhausted, the end was removed from the whirl hook and rolled onto a reel, the worker keeping the cord taut by walking back up the length of the building as the rope rolled onto the reel. The ends of successive batches of hemp were twisted together on the reel to make one continuous length of rope. Further steps—"warping" the yarns and "laying the cordage"—followed to smooth and straighten the rope.[10]

Like other rope makers in Kentucky, Thruston used locally grown hemp and slave labor to produce his twine, rope, and bag-

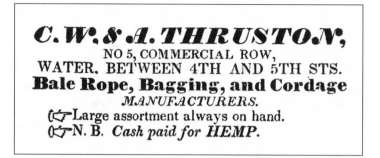

C. W. & A. THRUSTON,
NO 5, COMMERCIAL ROW,
WATER. BETWEEN 4TH AND 5TH STS.
Bale Rope, Bagging, and Cordage
MANUFACTURERS.
☞Large assortment always on hand.
☞N. B. *Cash paid for HEMP.*

Ropewalk advertisement, 1832. Charles W. Thruston went into the business with his uncle Alfred in 1826. He would later buy out Alfred's share of the business. (*Louisville City Directory*, 1832, University of Louisville Archives, Louisville, Ky.)

ging. Between 1826 and January 1837, when he quit the business, Thruston bought some thirty-one slaves, ranging in price from $150 to $800, most of whom were intended for work in the ropewalk. All but four of these slaves were men or boys. Sixteen of them were younger than twenty years old when Thruston bought them; slave children proved themselves excellent workers in ropewalks and other hemp-processing plants across the state. One Lexington rope factory employed no fewer than eighteen boys between the ages of eight and fifteen. Thruston's operation was about as large. When he sold the business in 1837, he had a total of twenty-seven slaves working in the factory.[11]

In addition to his slave purchases, Thruston also hired several slaves from his neighbors. The "hiring-out" system, which was especially common in urban settings, allowed slave owners to earn money from their "surplus" slaves by renting them to someone for a period of time. Advertisements featuring slaves available for hire or seeking slaves for hire appeared regularly in Louisville's newspapers. "Any person having a male slave about 16 or 18 years of age, of good character, smart and active, and of genteel appearance, that wishes to hire him out for one year, or longer, in the city of Louisville, can hear of a person that will give a liberal price by applying at this office," ran one ad in the *Louisville Public Advertiser*. Slaves might even be hired out to large public-works projects. In 1828, for example, the *Advertiser* ran a notice seeking "500 Negroes" to work on the Louisville and Portland Canal. "Liberal wages will be given; every possible effort will be made to render them comfortable, by furnishing good lodgings and wholesome diet, and to preserve their health by working them moderately."[12]

The hiring-out system was a necessary adjustment in the institution of slavery given the growing complexity of urban economies. Slaveholding industrialists needed to be able to regulate the supply of labor based on demand for their products. Hiring contracts allowed them to manage the size of their workforce within the context of an overall labor system that relied on lifetime chattel slavery. Thruston made frequent use of hiring contracts to fill his labor needs. For $65 to $80, he could hire a slave for a year, saving himself the large expense of purchasing an extra hand. Thruston's papers contain eleven contracts for eighteen slaves during the period in which he owned the ropewalk. Rogers Clark, who collected his grandfather's papers, indicated that this represented only a selection of the hiring contracts found in Thruston's correspondence.[13]

The hiring contracts specified the length of time the slave would be under Thruston's authority—generally for the remainder of the calendar year in which the deal was struck. Sometimes Thruston paid the fee for the slave in advance; sometimes he paid after the term was up. The contracts also usually contained some type of boilerplate language requiring Thruston to provide food, clothes, and medical care to the slave, and specifying that Thruston was responsible for any taxes assessed on the slave property and for returning the slave in good condition. Some of the contracts were struck with family members or acquaintances—for example, with the Croghan family (cousins), Alfred Thruston (uncle), and the Churchill family (in-laws)—while others seemed to be strictly business deals between unrelated parties.

Industrial slavery worked well for Thruston, and his rope business prospered. In addition, as Louisville grew, his urban landholdings appreciated. The 1830 tax assessment listed real and personal property, including twenty-two slaves, totaling more than $18,000.

"I flatter myself that I am adding a little to a little," he wrote to his half brother in St. Louis. With a good income, Thruston could buy slaves for domestic service rather than industrial use. The female slaves he bought probably worked in the house rather than the factory. Thus Cecelia and her mother, Mary, came into the household in 1831. In November 1846, Thruston indulged himself. He bought forty-five-year-old Jack for $550. Jack became Thruston's personal servant.[14]

Thruston followed standard operating procedure when managing his human property. Long before Cecelia, for example, he had problems with slaves running away. All slaveholders encountered this problem at some time or another. Slaves ran for any number of reasons. Sometimes they were making a break for freedom, trying to take advantage of Kentucky's long border with free states. At other times, their intention was merely "time off" from slavery—they might disappear only for a few days or weeks, "lying out" until they calculated that it was safe to return. Slaves ran away from cruel treatment or to avoid punishment. Some ran away because they feared an impending sale. Others ran because a previous sale had broken up their families, and they wanted to see their loved ones again. When the slave John fled Thruston's service in 1827, for example, Thruston speculated that he was headed to St. Louis to visit his sister Catherine, who belonged to a Mr. Coleman there. "You will do me the favor of enquiring and if he is there please send him back by the first boat," Thruston wrote to his half brother John O'Fallon, who lived in St. Louis. "He is a slippery fellow."[15]

When his slaves did run away, Thruston was not inclined to accept their departures with resignation. He used all available means to apprehend his runaways. He took out advertisements in newspapers announcing the slave's escape and likely destination. "Ran away from the subscribers, living in Louisville, on the 19th Nov. last, a negro man, named ANDREW JONES," began one such notice. The ad went on to describe Jones's appearance and stated that he had run away with his wife and four children. "His wife is named MARIA, 28 or 29 years of age, large, likely and well made; . . . usually talks loud and distinctly." The ad then described each of the children, who

$300 REWARD.

RAN AWAY from the subscribers, living in Louisville, on the 19th Nov. last, a negro man, named *ANDREW JONES*, forty years of age, five feet ten or eleven inches high, tawney complexion, likely and well made, most of his jaw teeth out, and by trade a plasterer; he has a pleasant countenance when spoken to, and is plausible and intelligent. He took with him his wife and 4 children. His wife is named MARIA, 28 or 29 years of age, is large, likely and well made; probably weighs from 160 to 170 pounds; usually talks loud and distinctly, and had, when he left, a thick coat of hair. Her two eldest children are boys; the eldest is black and about 7 years old; the second has a tawney complexion, and is about 5 years old; the third child is a black girl, between three and four years of age; and the fourth child is a black boy, two years old. The above described negroes will probably endeavor to reach Canada. Previous to their departure, a pass was given to the woman, with leave of absence for 12 days, under the impression that they were going to Frankfort, to which place they spoke of going in a Dearborn wagon to be drawn by a bay horse about 15½ hands high. There can be little doubt that they have forged free papers in their possession.

The above reward will be given for the said negroes, if taken out of this State, or $100, if taken in Kentucky.

C. W. THRUSTON,
J. W. ERICK,
dec 16—1488w   COLEMAN DANIEL.

The Mercury, Pittsburgh; Republican, Cincinnati; Journal, Detroit; Democrat, Indianapolis; Bulletin, Columbus; will publish the above seven weeks, weekly, and forward their accounts to this office.

Advertisement for runaway slaves, 1830. Charles William Thruston's advertisement regarding Andrew Jones and his family helped spread the word among the white community to look out for the escaped slaves. (*Louisville Public Advertiser*, December 16, 1830.)

ranged in age from seven years to just two, in similar detail. "The above described negroes will probably endeavor to reach Canada. Previous to their departure, a pass was given to the woman, with leave of absence for 12 days, under the impression that they were going to Frankfort. . . . There can be little doubt that they have forged free papers in their possession." A reward of $300 was offered if the fugitives were captured out of state, $100 if they were apprehended before they left Kentucky. To spread the word, the notice was to be printed in papers in Cincinnati, Columbus, Indianapolis, Pittsburgh, and Detroit. The hunt for Andrew Jones and family was a joint project between Thruston and two other slaveholders, J. W. Erick and Coleman Daniel. Most likely, the Jones family had been split up among the three owners, and the attempted escape was a bid to gather the family back together and put themselves beyond recapture.[16]

Kentucky's legislators aided the state's slaveholders in their efforts to apprehend runaways and to prevent slaves from absconding in the first place. Gripped by fear of an abolitionist conspiracy, the state's lawmakers increased the penalty for inducing slaves to escape—first from a fine of $50 to $500 in 1830, then from $500 to imprisonment in 1846. Recognizing the role of the Ohio River as the boundary between bondage and freedom, Kentucky law forbade any African American—slave or free—from ferrying another African American across the river, unless the passenger's owner had given explicit consent. The state required ferryboat operators to post $3,000 bonds to guarantee their cooperation in scrutinizing black passengers. Misjudgment could result in the impoundment of the boat. In 1823, legislators imposed on steamboat masters the job of checking that any black passenger either had free papers or a master's consent before boarding. In 1838, the state further restricted slave mobility, barring slaves from traveling on mail coaches anywhere in the state without the express written permission of the slave's owner.[17]

In addition to publicly advertising a slave's escape, Thruston at times hired slave catchers to pursue his escapees, granting them power of attorney to act in his stead wherever the slave might be found. So when Maria—Andrew Jones's wife—and the children still had not been apprehended several weeks after their escape, Thruston appointed Louisvillian William Clark on January 4, 1831, "to apprehend seize take confine imprison or otherwise for me a negro woman slave belonging to me together with her four children, who absconded and fled from me on or about the 19th day of November last."[18]

In general, slave catchers divided into two groups: amateurs and professionals. The latter group charged by the day and by the mile to track a slave. As the Kentucky legislature steadily increased the fees paid to those apprehending fugitives, the enticement to specialize in slave tracking also increased. Amateur slave catchers, on the other hand, might be slave traders, overseers, merchants, or other travelers either seeking financial reward or willing to do a favor for a slaveholding employer or acquaintance. William Clark most likely fell into the latter category.[19]

Thruston also pursued redress in the courts to retake runaways who might have successfully made it into free territory. His papers contain a legal memorandum, for example, regarding Baldwin Jones, a slave who Thruston claimed escaped from his service. More precisely, Thruston claimed that the "boy was stolen by a white man calling himself Peter Mandeville." The memorandum speculated that Baldwin had procured free papers that attested to his release from slavery. Therefore, the lawyer counseled, Thruston would need the Kentucky secretary of state to make an authorized copy of the statutes that allowed slavery in the state of Kentucky to prove in court that his ownership of Baldwin was legal. In addition, as Baldwin was expected to try to prove he was free, it would be "expedient to produce another witness to the fact of his being a slave and of his being the property of Mr. Thruston."[20]

In addition to his slaves running away, Thruston had other discipline problems. To these he again responded like most slaveholders, using physical punishments to control his unruly slaves. The lash was probably the most common form of punishment, but Thruston's use of the whip is not documented in his papers. Some other punishments are, however. A bill in his business papers from 1832 shows that on April 17 he purchased two "Negro yokes" for $3 and in August paid 50¢ more for "putting yoke on Negro." In November 1834, he was similarly billed 50¢ by a local blacksmith for repair of a "Negro collar." These devices—intended both as punishments and as restraints on movement—were commonly used among American slaveholders.[21]

In an urban environment, Thruston could also call upon the municipal power to help discipline his slaves. While in the country-side power over slaves tended to be vested exclusively in the slave-holder and the wider white community, in the cities there was a greater reliance on public force. An owner could, for example, send a slave to the city jail with a note detailing how many lashes to administer. This corrected the slave and spared the owner the often unpleasant task of whipping. Thruston seems to have taken advantage of this option at least once, for his papers contain a receipt for payment of the costs of holding a "Negro boy" in jail for eight days in the summer of 1836.[22]

Finally, Thruston occasionally deployed the ultimate weapon against unruly slaves: selling them. The most egregious example involved a slave named Wesley. In 1832, Thruston and his business partner/uncle bought Wesley and two other boys (including Wesley's younger brother) for $1,100 when Wesley was twelve years old. About two years later, Thruston's uncle sold his share of the business, including his half interest in the ropewalk's slaves, to Thruston. Soon after, Thruston began having trouble with Wesley. The papers do not reveal exactly what sort of trouble, but we know that Wesley was disciplined. The "Negro collar" mentioned above was most likely used on him, or so surmised Rogers Clark. When Wesley—whom Rogers Clark branded "incorrigible" and a "hardened sinner"—did not straighten up under correction, Thruston sold him in 1836.[23]

Unfortunately for Thruston, Wesley was returned in October 1837 with a rather scathing note from the buyers. Wesley was warranted as sound, the note read, "which has turned out *not to be the case*. Mr. Hawes [the buyer] has repeatedly returned him to you but at your request has continued to try him to ascertain if his complaint was temporary or *constitutional* it has showed itself to be the latter. . . . [We] will expect you to make a proper allowance for him from the general cost of the negroes purchased from you."[24]

Thruston's difficulties with Wesley continued for ten more years before Thruston delivered the harshest blow of all, short of death. It was in September 1846, just months after Cecelia had fled to Canada. He sold Wesley to Arterburn Brothers, a well-known Louisville slave-trading outfit, for $600. "It is now . . . understood between the parties," the bill of sale read, "that the said Arterburns are to take the said boy Westley [sic] out of the State that is to some of the Southern States and their [sic] sell him and it is understood that should said boy be sold . . . at any other place or places they forfeit for the same Five hundred dollars to be paid to me."[25]

The interstate slave trade between the Upper South and the Lower South had become a big business by the mid-1840s, and Arterburn Brothers had emerged as one of several large Louisville firms specializing in this trade. The 1843–1844 city directory listed eighty-four traders who specialized in human trafficking, and Louisville had several public slave pens where slaves were kept before being sold south. Being sold "down the river" to the southern cotton and sugar plantations was the most oft-expressed fear of Kentucky slaves, and slave owners often used the threat of a sale to keep slaves in line.[26]

The growth of the trade created an image problem for those Southerners defending the institution of slavery from abolitionist attacks. These attacks focused relentlessly on the auction block, the forced sale, and the breakup of slave families. Slaveholders tended to deny how prevalent slave traders were in Southern communities and insist that the traders dealt only with a very small number of slaves. Traders even became useful scapegoats, as slaveholders blamed them—particularly the "lowly class" among them—for many of the reported abuses of slavery, thus absolving themselves of guilt. Despite their reservations about the trade, however, slave owners like Charles Thruston still needed a market for their "unruly" or "surplus" bondmen, and so they conquered their qualms.[27]

Of course, masters sold slaves not just as a disciplinary measure but also because of simple economics. Thruston was not immune to the vagaries of the market for his products, and as he saw the bagging and rope market deteriorating in the late 1830s, he did what any smart investor would do: he cashed out. "Fearing that the rope and bagging business would not be profitable for some time to come," he wrote to his half brother, "I was induced to sell 27 hands employed therein at $900 each payable in five years with interest from the date . . . ; I likewise rented my ropewalk and bagging factory for the same length of time payable in the same way at $800 per annum. I shall not engage in any business immediately. In the course of the year I shall have about $20,000 in money which I may invest in the exchange business."[28]

Thruston could hardly have timed his exit from the rope and bagging business any better. Beginning in 1836, the Bank of England restricted the flow of gold to the United States. At about the same time, the demand of British manufacturers for American cotton declined. The double whammy of tight international credit and declining demand for its principal export sent the American economy into a tailspin. Banks refused to make loans, and merchants, farmers, and manufacturers faced bankruptcy. In April 1836, Thruston saw the writing on the wall. Banks in Louisville, he complained to his half brother, were not lending money.[29]

Thruston opted to sell the slaves working at the factory and rent out the property some months later. In a cogent demonstration of his business acumen, he watched the new owners of the ropewalk fail, while his own fortunes remained secure. "I can say what few can in this country," he boasted to his half brother. "What I have is my own, I owe nothing of any consequence and not likely to do so." Thruston's 1836 tax assessment valued his real and personal property, including twenty-seven slaves, at $34,350. Four years later, while much of the rest of the nation still floundered, Thruston's finances remained buoyant. His property, now including just twelve slaves (Mary and Cecelia among them), had an assessed value of $35,025.[30]

His former slaves, those workers who had helped build his fortune through their labor in his factory, did not fare so well. When the new owners of the ropewalk went bankrupt, Thruston's old workers were sold at auction. "They became scattered," Rogers

Clark wrote later, "father, mother, and children going to different and new masters."[31]

Thruston's attitude toward slavery may in fact have been the benign "someday-it-will-be-abolished" view described by his grandson. But that institution made behavioral demands upon him as a slaveholder. He had to act like a slaveholder, disciplining his slaves and correctly valuing his financial assets, including the human ones. Fanny and her brother Sam—hearing his words and watching his behavior—would have learned the appropriate lessons: slavery might someday come to an end, but until that time came slave ownership required prudent and responsible management.

Children learn not just from example, however. Children also derive lessons on what to expect and on what is expected from them by hearing family stories and lore about the family's past. This was true to an even greater degree in the antebellum period, when formal education outside the home was limited and parents played a greater role in shaping their children's education. The Thruston, Clark, and Churchill families from whom Fanny descended were all early Kentucky landowners who left their imprint on the history of the state. Their trove of family stories included tales of beautiful, dark-haired women, of star-crossed lovers, of patriotic warriors, and of land schemers. It also included a grim tale of the betrayal and murder that claimed the life of Charles William Thruston's own father, a tale that likely shaped his view of the nature and character of slaves.

Charles William's father was also named Charles. This Charles— Charles M. Thruston—had migrated to Kentucky from Virginia in the 1780s with his two older brothers, Buckner and John. Their decision to leave Virginia stemmed largely from a family quarrel over land between the brothers and their father, who likewise was named Charles. A soldier turned minister turned patriot turned Southern planter, this Thruston patriarch—named Charles Mynn Thruston—hailed from Gloucester County, Virginia, and was quite a colorful character. In the 1930s, a novelist even queried his descendants about his love life in hopes of writing a historical novel about him.[32]

Charles Mynn served in the French and Indian War, helping to evict the French from Fort Duquesne. After his military service, he studied for the ministry and led a parish in his home county for several years before taking a church in Frederick County. Then came the agitation of the 1770s and the problems between the colonies and the mother country. At first, Charles Mynn was content to stay in the pulpit, whence he preached resistance to the Stamp Act. When hostilities commenced, he spoke out in favor of the rebellion and even tried to procure arms and ammunition for the colonials. Finally his revolutionary sentiments got the better of him. As one county history tells it, after delivering a sermon one Sunday, "he threw aside the gown and seizing the sword raised a volunteer company [and] they marched off to join Washington in New Jersey."[33]

In battle with a Hessian force near Perth Amboy, his arm was shattered by a musket ball, and he was carried from the field. He was promoted to colonel, but unfortunately, the men needed for his regiment could not be raised. Left with no soldiers to command, he retired from the service. His actions, however, earned him a lasting nickname, "the fighting parson." In his later years, he moved south to New Orleans and became a wealthy sugar planter with extensive slaveholdings.[34]

The origins of the quarrel between the fighting parson and his sons long predated the excitement of the Revolution. Buckner, John, and Charles M. were the offspring of Charles Mynn's first marriage, to one Mary Buckner, who died in 1765 leaving behind a substantial land inheritance. Over the years, the fighting parson sold away his dead wife's lands and invested the money in his own name in lands to the west, including a portion in Kentucky, which was then the far western province of the colony of Virginia. Almost every Virginian with any money wanted a piece of Kentucky, and Charles Mynn was no exception. By the late 1760s and 1770s, Kentucky was being hailed by hunters and surveyors as a land of promise; one preacher in the 1780s even compared it favorably to heaven. Speculators large and small wanted in on the action, and by the end of the Revolutionary War, Charles Mynn Thruston had accumulated a good sized chunk of Kentucky. What he had apparently neglected to notice was that the money he had used to acquire the land was technically supposed to be the boys' inheritance from their mother.[35]

When his sons reached maturity, they challenged the old man—who had married again and fathered a second set of offspring—on his dishonorable practices. This set off a "family quarrel which lasted for three generations," according to Rogers Clark, the family historian. Ultimately, it cost the elder Thruston forty thousand acres to buy a little family peace. In October 1787 the old patriarch granted John, Buckner, and Charles M. forty-one thousand acres of western lands, reserving one thousand acres for himself. Shortly thereafter the three boys emigrated from Virginia to Kentucky.[36]

They came as part of a flood of settlers from the Old Dominion. During the 1780s, upward of seventy thousand people moved to Kentucky, most of those coming in the last five years of the decade. Most came from Virginia, but Pennsylvania and North Carolina contributed their share, too. The 1790s saw even more dramatic growth, with the population almost tripling to 220,955 by 1800. The Thruston boys—like almost everyone else in Virginia, it seemed—had caught Kentucky fever. John settled near Beargrass Creek and became a farmer until his early death at age forty. Buckner became a lawyer and then a judge, and was eventually elected U.S. senator from Kentucky. He ultimately resigned from the Senate to accept a federal judicial appointment in Washington, D.C., where he lived until his death in 1845. Charles M.—Fanny's grandfather—became a merchant and set up shop in Westport, just up-river from Louisville.[37]

In Kentucky, Charles M. fell in love with the lovely Frances Ann Clark, the fourth and youngest daughter of John and Ann Clark. She, too, came from Virginia; indeed, the Clarks had begun migrating from Virginia into Kentucky even before the Thrustons. The Clarks were an illustrious group. One of Frances's brothers was George Rogers Clark, who came to Kentucky for the first time in 1774 as part of a military surveying expedition and thereafter joined his future with that of Kentucky's, leading the defense of the frontier settlements during the American Revolution. All told, five of Frances's six brothers served as officers during the Revolutionary War, and Frances's brother William later teamed up with Meriwether Lewis to explore the Louisiana Purchase.[38]

Soon after they met, Frances Clark, who also went by the nickname Fanny, and Charles M. Thruston were engaged. Before they were married, however, Charles M. needed to return to Virginia to finalize his business affairs there. Unfortunately, things did not go well in Virginia, and the young man's return to Kentucky was long delayed. As luck would have it, his letters explaining the delay to his beloved went astray. Fanny, heartbroken that Charles would abandon her on the Kentucky frontier, soon found consolation in the courtship of a local doctor, James O'Fallon. The good doctor's wooing apparently helped heal her wounded ego, for when he proposed marriage she accepted him. They were married in 1790.

Charles M., who had finally gotten his business affairs in order, heard the news at a dinner party held in honor of his imminent departure to Kentucky. According to a 1943 letter by Rogers Clark Ballard Thruston to a relative seeking genealogical information, a traveler passing through, invited to the table, revealed over dinner that he had just come from Kentucky. "Of course that was an added interest to the individual and he was asked what news he had. He said that there was little except that the great black-eyed beauty of Kentucky, Fanny Clark, had just married James O'Fallon. . . . Charles Thruston fell over in a faint at the news and was in a desperate condition for several weeks."[39]

Charles M. eventually recovered and made good on his intention to return to Kentucky. He was despondent, but he might have taken heart had he known of the troubled state of his former betrothed's marriage to Dr. O'Fallon. The "marriage was not a happy one," Rogers Clark reported, and by 1793 it had disintegrated. In June of that year, O'Fallon was thrown from his horse and killed, leaving Frances with a two-year-old son, John, and another baby on the way. She was nineteen years old.[40]

Suddenly Charles M. came back into the picture. The reconciliation did not go smoothly at first. She was convinced he had jilted her; he was just as certain she had wronged him by hastily marrying O'Fallon. Eventually some unnamed "community elders" intervened, and the couple came together at last. The two were married in January 1796. The union quickly produced a son, another Charles

Mynn, born in December. But there was already a Charles Mynn Thruston—a cousin—living in Louisville, so in time this latest Charles Mynn dropped the "Mynn" and became Charles William Thruston, in honor of his mother's brother. In 1798, a daughter, Ann Clark Thruston—to be known as Nancy—arrived. After such a rocky beginning, the couple's fortunes seemed to be looking up. But Frances, despite her beauty and esteemed local lineage, was not very lucky in love. Before her daughter's third birthday, she would be widowed a second time. "Poor Fanny is an unfortunate girl," lamented one letter writer.[41]

The couple had settled on about five hundred acres near the town of Westport, which Charles M. thought had a good chance of besting Louisville in the competition to be the commercial hub of Kentucky. Charles M.'s mercantile business took him away to Virginia and Maryland once or twice a year, where he bought goods to supply his own store. Usually on these trips he took along his trusted manservant, Luke, "whom he indulged a great deal," according to Rogers Clark's disapproving analysis of the situation. This generous treatment caused Luke to misbehave and become unruly, banking that his master's fondness for him would spare him punishment. As Charles M. planned his next buying trip back east, he told Luke that the slave would not be going along. Further, he threatened Luke that if he misbehaved while Charles M. was away, the slave faced a sound thrashing when the master returned. Luke did misbehave in some unspecified fashion and, fearing his master's promised punishment, ran away.[42]

He did not run far, for his intention was to avoid punishment, not to escape. Slaves had a term for this; it was called "lying out." Slaves who were lying out might stay away only a short time or absent themselves for weeks or even months. They lived by hunting, fishing, pilfering, and by using their connections with neighboring slaves to procure food and shelter. Few communities in the slave South were completely free from sporadic bouts of vagrancy by the slaves of neighboring plantations—vagrants who earned the planters' ire for lurking about and "causing mischief."[43]

The difficulties of lying out forced many of the slaves to return to their master's service on their own. Others tried to strike a bargain with the master in order to improve their conditions upon returning. This was probably Luke's intent. By absenting himself, he was hoping to use his master's fondness for him to negotiate a return to his previously privileged position. These negotiations were always uncertain from the slave's point of view because the owner enjoyed such an enormous advantage in legal and coercive power. A slave had to calculate well how the master might respond to demands if such negotiations were to end favorably. In Kentucky, and likely elsewhere, slaves often sought out a minister or other white acquaintance who might serve as an intercessor with the master. Luke may have been thinking of a similar strategy.[44]

Whatever his line of thinking, Luke reappeared on the night of December 8, 1800, disrupting a family dinner honoring the fourth birthday of young Charles William Thruston. Luke entered the kitchen, stole a leg of mutton and a kitchen knife, and then disappeared again. The cook reported the disturbance to the master, who decided it was time to put an end to Luke's foolishness. Luke had clearly miscalculated Charles M.'s reaction to his misbehavior and prolonged absence. There was snow on the ground, so the master had no trouble following Luke's trail out into the night. He brought along the birthday boy, the four-year-old's hand firmly clasped in his father's. The trail led into a field where the corn shocks were stacked. Approaching a particular corn shock, the master called out for Luke to show himself. When the slave did not emerge, Charles M. stepped forward and began pulling down the shock. Luke apparently abandoned all hope. Not only had he disobeyed his master, but he had also run away, stolen food from the master's kitchen, and now run away again. He certainly faced punishment: probably the lash, but perhaps something worse. Luke leaped out of the shock, kitchen knife in hand, and stabbed his master fatally in the chest. As Charles M.'s lifeblood trickled away in front of his traumatized son, Luke disappeared anew into the woods.

Once again, Luke did not run far. "Something," wrote Rogers Clark, "held him close to the spot." The Thruston papers contain no information on Luke's antecedents, but judging from other historians' research on runaways, the most likely "something" was family ties of one kind or another. The killing of a white master galvanized the community, of course, and Luke was soon apprehended. Thruston family tradition held that he was the first person in Kentucky hanged by verdict of a jury, but Rogers Clark, unable to find confirmation of that bit of family lore, discounted it. Luke may have been the subject of some form of legal proceeding, but it was not one that yielded any official records—nor was its outcome in any serious doubt.[45]

Luke's violence, although unusual, was certainly not unheard of across the South. Although murdering a master meant that the slave almost certainly forfeited his own life, it was not unusual for Southern courts to have a murder case on the docket in which a slave had killed an owner. In Kentucky, an infamous 1844 case involved the slave Richard Moore, who choked his abusive mistress to death. He fled north but was soon arrested and put on trial. Though the citizens of Lexington, where the trial took place, generally knew of the abuse Moore had suffered, none came to his defense, and he was publicly hanged.[46]

The boy whose fourth birthday celebration was cut short by his father's violent death left no mention of this event in his personal papers. His grandson, however, recalled that Charles William "never forgot the incident." One wonders what he told his children and grandchildren about it, what lessons he derived from it about the best way to manage slaves and about the character of African Americans. There is little in the way of direct evidence, but some indirect evidence exists in the tone and style of Rogers Clark's description of his great-grandfather's death.[47]

Luke was a slave who was "indulged a great deal," who "presumed on his master's fondness for him," according to Rogers Clark. As the young Charles William grew up to own slaves himself, he must have interpreted "indulgence," undue fondness, or gentleness of treatment as mistakes to be avoided. Such misplaced sentiments yielded only disorder, betrayal, and death. He also must have formed a vision of slaves as inherently untrustworthy. No matter how many years of loyal service they had performed, they remained unpredictable creatures of passion who could turn on their benevolent masters at any moment.[48]

In Charles William's view, slaves could be—indeed, had to be—managed. While they could not be trusted, they could be made obedient; though they were incapable of exercising self-discipline, they could be controlled. Very much like recalcitrant children, slaves had to be guided, directed, taught appropriate behavior. The difference between slaves and children, of course, was that slaves never grew up.

Again, there is no evidence of young Fanny Thruston's view of slaves or slavery in the years leading up to Cecelia's escape. Yet she doubtless knew her father's history, knew of her grandfather's violent end, knew of her father's bleak view of slave character. Did she share it? Her father's dark view would have been tested everyday against Fanny's actual life experience of interacting with slaves and of growing up with Cecelia. In one of the letters that passed between them, Fanny fondly referred to Cecelia as the "companion of my childhood." Perhaps the bonds of intimacy that existed between them—at least in Fanny's recollection—countered the lessons about slavery that Fanny learned at her father's knee.[49]

But then how could Fanny explain Cecelia's flight? Perhaps it was easier to blame meddling abolitionists than to peer into Cecelia's heart and know her desire for freedom, because then both Fanny and her father could be right about Cecelia. She had not betrayed Fanny's affection; rather, she had been led astray by ill-meaning men. Cecelia had not lashed out in passionate and unpredictable violence as Luke had, she had only followed—gullible and childlike as she was—her momentary desire for the sweet promises of freedom falsely pledged by outside agitators. Cecelia's flight both confirmed Charles William's bleak view of the slave character and drove home to Fanny her father's lessons about the dangers and difficulties of being a slave owner.

Chapter 3

Cecelia: Learning about Being a Slave

Cecelia learned about slavery from the same sources as Fanny—family stories, parental advice, and direct observation. However, it is much more difficult to piece together the elements of Cecelia's education—given the lack of documentation—than Fanny's. In contrast to the vivid family history of the Thrustons, very little is known about Cecelia's family.

Cecelia entered the Thruston household on October 4, 1831, in the arms of her mother, Mary. Cecelia was just an infant, listed as five months old on the bill of sale. Her mother was seventeen. Mother and infant together cost Fanny's father $400. Mary was brought into the household to care for Charles William Thruston's four young children. Sam, the oldest, was six years old; Fanny was five; Mary Eliza was two; and O'Fallon was only ten months old. With an infant of her own, Mary would be the perfect caregiver for young O'Fallon.[1]

Thruston purchased Cecelia and her mother from a slave dealer named William Cotton. Cotton was an early participant in the interstate slave trade—the business of moving slaves from the Upper South to the Lower South. In the first seventy years of the nation's life, an estimated 1 million enslaved people were moved south and west from the Chesapeake states into the expanding regions of cotton cultivation. Some slaves moved when their masters migrated, but about two-thirds of them were relocated by sale. When William Cotton was building his business, the interstate slave trade was not yet an established institution in which large slave trading firms controlled much of the traffic. It was still predominantly a face-to-face business built on "informal networks and chance encounters," as one historian wrote. It "was a practice without a name or a center."[2]

Cotton owned a slave depot in New Orleans and a residence in Nelson County, Kentucky. In general, he spent the summer and early fall in Kentucky and other states of the Upper South, buying slaves and gathering groups together for shipment south. The best time to purchase slaves was after the harvest was in, when there was less work for them to do. The slaves were moved south by boat or on foot, usually in coffles—long lines of slaves chained together to prevent escape—during the fall. Slave-selling season generally fell in the winter and early spring, after the planters had been paid for their harvest, so they had ready cash, but before planting and the heavy labor began. The fact that Charles Thruston bought Mary and Cecelia in October may have meant that Cotton was readying them for shipment south when Thruston came shopping for a nanny.[3]

No records indicate where Cotton procured Cecelia and her mother. It is possible that he purchased them in Virginia and brought them over to Kentucky, since Cecelia's death record lists her birthplace as Virginia. Some census forms, however, give her birthplace as Kentucky. Neither do the records reveal anything certain about the identity of Cecelia's father. Instead, the bill of sale for mother and infant offers mute testimony to the breakup of Cecelia's family. Whoever her father was, he was not included in the transaction that brought Mary and Cecelia into the Thruston home. This was perhaps the first lesson of slavery that Cecelia had to learn, though as an infant she could not have comprehended it. Slave families faced a cruel difficulty in their efforts to stay together. Slave marriages and parental relationships had no legal standing; they existed at the whim of the owner, and could be destroyed just as lightly. But that was not the entirety of the lesson; there was a corollary to the fragility of family life under slavery. That corollary, embraced by the slaves themselves, stated that family connections needed to be preserved and protected to the greatest extent possible under the extreme conditions of servitude. Cecelia doubtless learned this lesson from her mother, and would have heard its variations repeated in the countless slave stories about family breakups on the auction block. She would have learned this, too, in the stories of runaways that circulated within the slave community. One of the most common reasons given by slaves for running away was either to reunite with family members who had been sold off or to short-circuit a master's planned sale of a family member.[4]

Mary's family life, disrupted by sale, had to be rebuilt, and it appears that Cecelia's mother did just that after she entered the service of the Thrustons. The evidence, however, needs to be pieced together carefully, and the final conclusion about what happened must be viewed with uncertainty, given the scanty historical record. The piecing-together of the story of how Mary restitched her family life begins in 1899, when Rogers Clark wrote the brief history of his mother's relationship with Cecelia. In that history, the story of Cecelia and Fanny veers off into an anecdote Rogers Clark tells of his early adulthood. One hot summer day in 1877, an old black man showed up on the doorstep of the Thruston home. The man said his name was Adam, but "I had never seen him before and had never heard of him as one of the old slaves." Rogers Clark gave the old man a little money so he would go away, but money was not what Adam was after. At Adam's request, Rogers Clark, then just nineteen years old, fetched his mother from upstairs. "She did not recall any old slave named Adam but laid aside her sewing and went down to see him." Upon seeing Adam, Fanny recognized that "he was the father of Cecelia, her maid . . . who had run off from her over thirty years before."[5]

Was this Adam Cecelia's father? Not, most probably, in the biological sense. It seems unlikely that Fanny would have known Cecelia's father—particularly by sight—unless the slave man had been a regular presence in the Thruston household after the Thrustons had obtained Cecelia. Yet the slave lists available for Charles William Thruston do not show any adult male slave named Adam in the household. Of course, the records could be missing or the old slave known as "Adam" in 1877 could have been known by another name entirely during the 1830s. So it is possible that Adam was Cecelia's biological father and that, while the family had been broken up by sale, Cecelia's mother and father both resided in Louisville.

It seems more likely, however, that Adam was—to use modern terminology—Cecelia's stepfather. In 1831, when Charles Thruston purchased Cecelia and her mother, he did own a slave named Adam, but Adam was only a ten-year-old boy. Thruston had purchased Adam—along with two other young slaves—from his sister-in-law in January 1831, about ten months before buying Mary and Cecelia. As Adam matured, he and Mary may have begun a relationship, perhaps deep enough for him to be considered Cecelia's "father." Whether Adam and Mary ever "married" cannot be determined, but it is possible that at some point they regarded themselves as married. Adam may have even been the father of Cecelia's brother, Edward, who was born about 1836.[6]

This version of events contains its share of implausibility, too. Adam would have been quite young—just sixteen years old—when Edward was born. And Rogers Clark's estimate of Adam's age in 1877 is woefully off the mark if this version of Adam's story is correct. Rogers Clark pegged the old man's age at eighty-six years. But if the Adam who showed up on the doorstep in 1877 is the same Adam who was just a boy when Cecelia was bought, then he would have been only in his midfifties. Slave age, of course, is difficult to pinpoint with certainty, and Rogers Clark gave no account of how he arrived at the higher figure.

Neither version of Adam's story is completely supported by the evidence. And other versions are possible: Adam might have been a slave from outside the Thruston household who had a fondness for Cecelia and came to be known as her "father," or perhaps Fanny was entirely mistaken about Adam's identity but the old slave elected not to correct her. Such uncertainties, the inevitable result of a scant and scattered historical record, bedevil all efforts to reconstruct slave biographies. But that is not sufficient reason to disregard entirely the evidence that does exist.

Rogers Clark's brief history clearly states that Fanny recognized that there was a relationship of some kind between Adam and Cecelia. Fanny branded it as a paternal relationship, which at least suggests that there was some sort of relationship between Adam and Mary, Cecelia's mother. The exact nature of that relationship cannot be determined with any degree of certainty, but it is not implausible to believe that Cecelia's mother, having had her first family torn asunder by sale, began to reconstitute some semblance of a family life with Adam under the Thrustons' roof. The precise details of that family life, however, must remain sketchy, the product of educated guesswork rather than hard evidence.

Mary and Adam probably never set up housekeeping together. Adam would have been purchased for work in the ropewalk, while Mary and Cecelia worked as house servants. This was a common practice in families of the Louisville commercial class. Opulent homes might even have three or four servant rooms under the main roof. As a laborer, on the other hand, Adam did not live in the master's house. He may have lived in the slave quarters in the back of the house. Many urban slaveholders—including many prominent Louisvillians—housed their slaves in separate outbuildings to the rear of the master's house. Given the proximity of the slave quarters to the master's residence, these facilities would often be cleaner and better maintained than slave quarters on rural plantations. Nonetheless, architecturally, urban slave quarters—like their rural counterparts—reflected the control of the master and the subservience of the slave. Typically, the outbuildings faced the master's house and the roofs sloped in toward the yard, not toward the outside world. These quarters would be hemmed in on the sides by high brick walls, creating the effect of a closed compound. The whole idea was to isolate one's slaves from outside contacts. Still, proximity to the Thrustons' house would have made regular contact between Adam and Mary relatively easy.[7]

It is also possible, however, that Adam may not have resided near the main house. Factory owners like Thruston had little desire to house thirty to fifty workers on their own property. Adam, therefore, may have lived nearer the ropewalk itself. That might explain why Fanny did not recognize him by name; he was not one of the slaves who lived in the household. Adam may even have "lived out" once he got to a certain age. Living out was a freedom granted by some urban factory owners to their industrial slaves, allowing the slaves to seek their own housing in the city. As early as 1828, the

Louisville City Council reported that bondmen were "renting houses, and residing therein." The councilmen declared such arrangements "a great public nuisance." If Adam was living out or living in quarters near the ropewalk, of course, his courtship of Mary was made that much more difficult. Nonetheless, despite the logistical difficulties and the burdens of bondage, Adam and Mary somehow maintained a relationship.[8]

By watching her mother and Adam, Cecelia may have begun to learn a second lesson of slavery: that despite the legal privileges of absolute power over slaves, a master's control was never complete. That lesson held true even on isolated rural plantations; the master's power over the slaves was continually undercut by slaves' assertion of their own autonomy. Indeed, much of modern slave historiography has been devoted to showing the varied and creative ways slaves on the plantations struggled for a portion of control over their own lives. But that truth was even more evident in the commercial and industrial cities of the slave South, where slave masters' control was tempered not only by the slaves' exercise of personal autonomy but also by the increasing demands for free-flowing commerce and information in an urban environment.[9]

Urban life demanded that slavery in the cities develop into a very different institution than the plantation slavery of the countryside. The historian Richard Wade made this point more than forty years ago in his book on urban slavery. Unlike in rural slavery, women slaves tended to outnumber men, because the greatest demand in the cities was for female house servants. Unlike in rural slavery, urban slave populations fluctuated over time based on market conditions for slaves, whereas slave populations in the countryside showed steady growth during the antebellum period. And unlike in rural slavery, the peculiar institution became steadily less important to the life of the city over time. There were fewer slaves and fewer slaveholders—the vitality of the institution in the cities was sapped by the time of the Civil War.[10]

From the slave's perspective, the most important difference between life in the city and life on the plantation was the busyness and bustle of urban life, which created a little extra space for slaves to exercise control over their own lives. Unlike a rural plantation, an urban household could not pretend to self-sufficiency. The need for contact with other people inevitably eroded the master's control in the city. The architecture of the urban slave quarters, for example, might seek to create an enclosed compound isolated from contact with the world outside. But the alleys that ran back of the houses served as passageways for communication between slaves living with different masters. Free blacks, whites, and slaves all found opportunity for social intercourse in the alleys, despite masters' attempts to restrict it.[11]

The development of the practices of hiring out and living out—both far more common in the cities than in the countryside—gave some slaves the opportunity to live and work outside the direct surveillance of the master. It is clear that the hiring-out system contained room for negotiation between slave and master. Slaves might approach certain owners and ask to be hired by them or attempt to dissuade potential hirers by denigrating their own fitness or work ethic. By such tactics, slaves sought to exert what little control they could over their working conditions. The loosest form of hiring out came when a master allowed slaves to hire their own time: that is, find their own work and negotiate their own wages with an employer, in exchange for turning over some or all of those wages to the master. Adam probably never hired his own time, as this privilege was limited to a relative few who had the most marketable skills. Nonetheless, it was not unheard of for slaves to hire their own time in Louisville. One slave named Jim, a carpenter, not only hired himself out but began to place other hired slaves in different jobs around the city, acting as an employment agent and taking a portion of the other men's pay as his commission. At one point, Jim was earning $200 per month, while paying his master only the agreed-upon sum of $20 per month.[12]

Cities also allowed some degree of social autonomy for slaves. In 1856, the *Louisville Daily Democrat* mocked the pretensions of the fancy-dressed slaves who held their own New Year's Eve ball. About four hundred bondmen—many of them hired out for work at the Falls City Hotel—attended the year-end revelry. Blacks also found it easier to learn to read in the city, as contact with greater numbers of people in a greater variety of situations increased opportunities to gain literacy. Black churches, all-black neighborhoods, groceries that doubled as grog shops, whorehouses—all these experiences and institutions were available to urban slaves to a degree impossible for slaves in the countryside. As Wade wrote, "On any day in every city, slaves could be seen away from their master's supervision and still not at work. . . . In every part of town, slaves of different masters got acquainted, struck up friendships, mingled with free blacks, and came to know a fragment of the white community. These contacts were an inseparable part of urban life."[13]

Working in the ropewalk, Adam thus enjoyed some degree of personal autonomy as he grew from boyhood to manhood free from the omnipresence of the master. In some ways, Adam's situation may have been preferable to Mary and Cecelia's. Living in the master's house meant always being subject to the master's beck and call. House slaves lived a life of continuous surveillance. Constant service to the members of the master's household, from youngest to eldest, was expected of domestic slaves. Cecelia, growing from infancy into girlhood, must have observed something of the interstices of independence that existed within the bounds of slave life as she watched her mother and Adam strike a spark together.[14]

There were advantages, of course, to being a house slave. They were often better fed than other slaves, as they got first crack at the master's leftovers. They were also usually better dressed, since part of their role was to serve visitors and guests, and therefore they had to look presentable. They also had superior quarters by virtue of being housed in the master's residence, whereas the outbuildings on the alley were often more shoddily made.[15]

Mary's principal task was to care for the Thruston children. Charles William Thruston had married Mary Eliza Churchill, the daughter of a local plantation owner, in 1824. By 1831, the couple had four children. Since white women of the master class tended to view domestic tasks as demeaning, it was clear by 1831 that Mary Eliza was going to need some help. Mary was probably not the sole domestic slave in the Thruston household. Although it is difficult to

Mary Eliza Churchill
(Fanny's mother), undated.
A daughter of the promi-
nent Churchill family, she
married Charles William
Thruston in 1824. She died
in 1842. (Filson Historical
Society, Louisville, Ky.)

distinguish between slaves bought for labor in the ropewalk and those bought for domestic service, it is known that Charles William had purchased at least two other female slaves—those most likely to work as domestics—in the years before he bought Mary and Cece-lia. Even if she was not alone, Mary probably had other tasks around the household beyond childcare, doubtless assisting with the never-ending routines of preparing and serving the food, making and washing the clothing, cleaning the house, and rendering personal service to the master or mistress. As early as five or six years of age, Cecelia, too, would have begun performing simple household chores; by age eight or nine, she would have been an integral part of the household workforce.[16]

Cecelia's education and upbringing would have thus been over-seen not just by her mother but by Mrs. Thruston as well. When it came to slave children, owners considered themselves "surrogate parents" who meted out discipline and rewards as they thought best. Childhood under slavery was thus marked by a constant tension be-tween the masters, determined to exercise power over their "prop-erty" independent of the child's biological parents, and the parents themselves, who tried to retain authority over their own children. This tension provided a daily echo of the lessons Cecelia was learning about slavery in general: that while the master's claims to control were total, slaves could learn how to blunt, turn back, or refute those claims.

Learning to be a house slave could be a difficult business. The possibilities for transgression were legion; one historian's list of offenses includes "malingering, performing chores poorly, violating rules of racial etiquette, and appropriating items belonging to the owning family." A misstep in any of these areas brought on serious risk of physical punishment. One young slave girl was clocked by her mistress with a heavy stick of wood for blackening her eyebrows with fireplace ashes. The slave girl, who had seen her mistress blacken her eyebrows, was considered guilty of mocking her superiors.[17]

Henry Bibb, a Kentucky slave who later escaped to Canada and published his memoirs, worked as a house slave in his youth. He wrote about how difficult it could be to please the mistress of the house with his service. He performed all sorts of tasks, including building the fires, scrubbing the floors, washing clothes, polishing furniture, and shooing the flies away from his mistress while she napped. Yet, he recalled, his only rewards were frequent scoldings and getting his ears boxed. How often the Thrustons had to resort to physical punishment to train Cecelia in the art of domestic service—or how severe those punishments were—cannot be known with certainty. There is very little in the archives documenting domestic life within the household.[18]

The domestic chores in a nineteenth-century household were onerous, tedious, and labor intensive. The common judgment of most historians of slave-owning families is that white women did not perform much of this labor themselves, as they tended to view such domestic exertions as beneath them. "Keeping house" involved less accomplishing household chores oneself and more directing the slaves to do them.[19]

A good house slave not only performed her assigned tasks efficiently but also succeeded in looking presentable and adhering to the rituals of racial subordination within the home. The house slave helped represent the slave owner's status and style to the public. Interaction with guests made house slaves part of the "public face" of the household. Failure to show deference to white people—whether by appearance, behavior, or speech—reflected badly on the master and could result in punishment for the slave.[20]

It bears repeating that whether these historical generalizations applied in the specific case of the Thrustons and Mary and Cecelia—or the degree to which they applied—is impossible to determine with certitude. Mary's performance as a domestic servant must have been satisfactory or the Thrustons would not have retained her for the many years they did. Cecelia, too, must have learned her lessons adequately, or she would not have been much of a "gift" to give young Fanny.

Although the documentary record does not reveal much about life inside the Thruston household, certain events were recorded that allow tentative conclusions about how the relationship between Fanny and Cecelia developed over the years. These events altered the roles of Cecelia and Fanny in the household and, no doubt, changed their relationship. The first event was a tragedy that occurred just a little over a year after Mary and Cecelia came to the Thruston house. Little O'Fallon, barely two years old, died. The cause of his death is unknown; the only indication of it in the family's records is a small folded paper containing the beads he wore around his neck with the notation that his mother saved the beads when the boy passed away. Barely had this blow been endured, however, when another struck. Two and a half years after O'Fallon's death, in May 1835, six-year-old Mary Eliza died. What had been a bustling family of six became a battered family of four.[21]

These awful events carried significant risks for Mary. Slaves caring for children often bore the brunt of their owners' ire when their charges got hurt, sick, or died. One slave woman in Kentucky, for example, was whipped by her master, a Methodist minister, for "letting" the minister's young daughter fall against a hot stove. And in 1812 a Christian County jury convicted a slave of murder for the accidental overdose and death of a child under her care. The mistress of one Virginia slave deliberately burned the nursemaid with a hot iron after the baby left in the maid's care hurt his hand. Again, such brutality may not have pertained in the Thruston house during this dreadful time; no records show whether Mary was in any way held responsible for the deaths of the young children under her care.[22]

The deaths of the youngest children certainly changed Mary's position in the household. Purchased as a nursemaid, she had no charges left to attend. The fact that the Thrustons kept her on as a domestic slave probably illustrates Mary's value to Fanny's mother. The deaths of O'Fallon and Mary Eliza probably changed Fanny and Cecelia's relationship as well. Fanny went from being the big sister to being the little girl again, and Cecelia was suddenly the girl in the household closest in age to her. The two probably grew closer, and Cecelia may have spent a good deal of her girlhood in the company of Fanny. No doubt it was these years that Fanny recalled when she wrote of Cecelia as the "companion of my childhood." While there was never any doubt about Fanny's place in the master class, during the girls' childhood the horizontal bonds of companionship may have temporarily obscured the vertical bonds of the mistress/slave relationship.[23]

Some two years after the death of Mary Eliza, a different sort of tragedy struck. This blow fell on Mary and Cecelia's family but probably passed virtually unnoticed by Fanny and her family. This tragedy was the result not of disease but of economics and the property relations of slavery. Somehow, despite the restrictions of bondage, Adam and Mary had pieced together a shared life. In 1837, however, the shrewd business judgment of Charles William Thruston ripped that life apart. In that year, fearing for the future of the rope business, Thruston had sold out to Henry Hawes. As a laborer in the ropewalk, Adam was included in the transaction. The change in ownership perhaps mattered little. After all, the ropewalk was in Louisville, and if Adam had been living out, then a change of master would not necessarily have affected his relationship with Mary. But Mr. Hawes's economic fortunes turned sour in a hurry. Adam was one of the slaves sold after Hawes went bankrupt during the Panic of 1837. On the auction block, Adam—just sixteen or seventeen years of age—was sold to an Arkansas planter and moved south.

Eventually, he would marry again and raise another family in his new home.[24]

Cecelia would have been old enough in 1837 to understand the lesson imparted by Adam's sale. At six years of age, she probably understood the meaning of the auction block and the threat it posed to slave families. And she probably came to understand that no matter how much "wiggle room" slaves were able to conjure within the bounds of slavery, ultimately the master held the upper hand. When the Panic of 1837 closed down around Mr. Hawes and his newly purchased ropewalk, Cecelia watched the man she knew as her father disappear forever. The forcible dissolution of her mother's relationship with Adam may have brought the reality of slavery home to young Cecelia unlike anything that had happened to her before. The physical punishments she had faced up to that point likely fit into the category of "education," and may have come from her mother as much as her mistress. Her mother may have endured physical punishment as well, which doubtless underscored her subservience to the Thrustons. Yet the sale of Adam would have emphasized the lack of control that slaves had over their own lives in dramatic fashion. The companionate relationship Fanny and Cecelia had enjoyed no doubt began to change as Cecelia recognized the vulnerability of her own family in the slave system.[25]

In 1840, a vastly more important change came to Fanny and Cecelia's relationship: Fanny was made Cecelia's owner when Charles William Thruston presented the slave to his daughter as a gift. Fanny's entrance into slaveholding coincided with her formal entrance into Louisville society. The two events went hand in hand, signifying her passage into maidenhood. Her social debut announced her entrance into the marriage market. The gift of the slave would prepare her for her duties of running the household once she did marry.

The twin events affected both Fanny's and Cecelia's lives. Both girls must have found the social whirl giddying, filled with parties and beaux. For Cecelia, the vicarious excitement of being close to Fanny must have been bittersweet. As a house slave, Cecelia probably had limited opportunity for courtship herself. And, as the recent example of her mother's relationship with Adam showed, any beau who came courting was ultimately under the control—as Cecelia herself was—of the master. Fanny's entry into society doubtless drove home to Cecelia the insurmountable difference between herself and her former childhood companion.[26]

Indeed, Fanny's rise in status from childhood playmate to owner was intended to affect her relationship with Cecelia. The gift of Cecelia was meant to give Fanny direct experience with slave ownership. As a white person and member of a slave-owning family, Fanny had always had authority over the Thruston slaves, but her authority was a reflection of her mother's authority and, ultimately, her father's power. Becoming a slave owner herself meant that Fanny held primary authority over Cecelia. The gifting of Cecelia to Fanny was intended as a type of apprenticeship, a way of getting her used to having complete authority over another human being. Fanny was not yet running a household, merely a busy social calendar, but becoming a slave owner thrust new responsibilities upon her.[27]

In her former situation, Cecelia was one of several house slaves. Mrs. Thruston probably exercised the most direct command over her, although she would have had to obey any member of the family and, of course, virtually any white person. Nonetheless, Mary probably still continued to wield a good deal of influence over her. As Fanny's personal maid, however, Cecelia's relationship with her mother no doubt attenuated. She probably moved from sharing sleeping quarters with her mother to sleeping on the floor of Fanny's room, ready to attend to whatever Fanny needed during the night. In fact, Cecelia's role as Fanny's maid raised the bar for Cecelia's performance higher than it had previously been. A good lady's maid served as wardrobe manager, hairdresser, messenger, go-between, and confidante. Cecelia helped Fanny present her public self and, perhaps by gathering and passing on gossip from servants in other households, helped her manage her private life as well. As one house servant among many, Cecelia had had the opportunity to recede into the background; as Fanny's maid exclusively, such opportunities arose less frequently.[28]

The relationship between Cecelia and Fanny took another turn just two years after Fanny became Cecelia's owner. In February

1842, Fanny's mother—Mary Eliza Churchill Thruston—died. Since Louisville's vital records do not exist that far back, the cause cannot be pinpointed. The only death notice is a two-line announcement in the *Louisville Daily Journal* requesting friends and relatives to attend the funeral service. Charles William Thruston himself, never one to pour out his emotions in correspondence, did not mention his wife's death in the letters from this period to his half brother in St. Louis. Her mother's death elevated Fanny to chief mistress in the household. Alongside her father, she would have now found herself—as the oldest white woman under the Thruston roof—responsible for much of the household management. That meant, in essence, slave management. Fanny's relationship with Cecelia no doubt moved further toward the formal hierarchy of mistress and slave.[29]

As Cecelia grew older, she probably participated to some degree in the social networks that joined slaves, free blacks, and some whites in the urban environment. This would have improved her understanding of slavery, as stories of family breakups, beatings, and escapes—both successful and failed—circulated through the community. By the time she reached fifteen years of age, when she journeyed with Fanny to Washington and then Niagara, she probably had seen, heard, and experienced enough to understand the subtleties and the ambiguities of these lessons.[30]

She had learned from the breakup of her biological family and the subsequent breakup of the relationship between her mother and Adam that those in the master class could cut away ties to family and community whenever they chose. But she had also learned the importance of preserving and protecting those ties and that, with persistence, creativity, and effort, family could be rebuilt and community relations restored.

She had learned from the development of her relationship with Fanny that there were insurmountable differences between whites and blacks. Whites lived better, ate better, enjoyed better health, and had more leisure time and educational opportunities. But she had also learned that her life could be much worse. She had to be aware of the relative privilege of her life compared to the lives of other slaves. There were substantial material and educational rewards to being a house servant as opposed to being a laborer in a factory or on a farm or plantation, especially if that plantation were in the Deep South.

She had learned from punishments both verbal and physical—those inflicted upon her and those she knew about—that the master class demanded obedience and subservience. But she had also learned that its control did not—could not—reach everywhere. There were places within the totality of the master/slave relationship where one could cheat the masters of their expectation; no matter the humiliation to which one might be subject, there was a piece of one's soul that they could not touch, an inner life they could not understand. Slaves had to nurture that spark to survive the rigors of bondage.

And she had no doubt learned that there were places to the north where slavery did not exist, where one could be free from the relentless power of the master class. But she had also learned that getting there was difficult, that crossing the Ohio River was not enough, and that fearful repercussions might follow failure.[31]

The tensions and contradictions within these lessons existed together in the mind of every slave. For millions, the "pull" factors—family ties, fear of punishment, habits of obedience—outweighed the "push" factors and kept them in bondage. For several thousand others, the push factors reached a tipping point that impelled them to try to break their bonds. For Cecelia, that tipping point probably came with the trip to Niagara Falls. Opportunity to act on her feelings of restlessness—opportunity that was denied to millions of others—persuaded her to step into that rowboat to begin her eight-minute journey to freedom.

Chapter 4

Fanny: A Woman's Place

When Fanny returned to Louisville from Niagara Falls, not much in her life had really changed. She was still the daughter of a wealthy, well-connected father, returning home to the city where she had been born, to the house on Walnut Street where she had always lived. With the escape of Cecelia, she had lost a personal maid but not the service of slaves. According to the 1847 tax list for Louisville, Charles W. Thruston still owned eleven slaves—a number that would shrink but never fall to zero over the coming years. Perhaps, Fanny felt, she might have even gained something from Cecelia's flight—a bit of wisdom in the ways of slaveholding.[1]

At twenty years old, Fanny was in the full flower of her maidenhood. She was a desirable marriage prospect, and her social calendar no doubt filled quickly. With Louisville's economic takeoff in the 1830s, the social lives of the city's elites had blossomed with parties and balls. Wealthy families competed with each other in opulent shows of hospitality. "Set suppers are all the fashion and they purchase everything that will cost the most money," wrote one young female partygoer to a cousin of Fanny's in 1832. "Mrs. Pearce supper was most splendid. It is supposed the ladies table cost 5 hundred dollars independent of the one for the gentlemen which it is said was equally as handsome." That winter, this young socialite reported, there was an apparent "mania for dissipation" as two and three parties a night were held among the city's wealthy. "You have no conception of the number of parties given this winter. . . . It appears as if the people have done nothing but give parties."[2]

Fanny had made her debut in Louisville society in 1840. In the middle of her thirteenth year, she was crowned the Queen of May. This gave her the most prominent role in the large semipublic celebration that attended the coming of spring. There were concerts and plays, parties and a parade—all presided over by the young May Queen. Among Fanny's few preserved papers are the letters of homage written to the Queen by the various young men's societies of Louisville. The Kosciuzko Cadets, for example, wrote "Her Majesty" to "acknowledge with gratitude the honor your Majesty has confer'd upon them by commanding their services on the First day of May next." According to Rogers Clark, the year his mother was named Queen was "said to have been the grandest such celebration ever witnessed in Louisville."[3]

In 1846, when Fanny and her father returned from Niagara, the city was really hitting its economic peak. Louisville had begun as a merchants' city, but during the 1840s manufacturing began to take root. When Charles Dickens paid a brief visit in 1842, he wrote of buildings blackened by the soot from coal-burning businesses. The city's population, which had been 10,341 in 1830, grew to 43,194 in 1850. River traffic was soaring: the Louisville to New Orleans run ranked first in terms of passenger and freight traffic of all the western rivers. Louisville's "wharves were lined with steamboats from every river point," recalled A. J. Webster, reminiscing about his midcentury boyhood in the city. "Its streets echoed with the rumble of six-mule team 'Conestoga' wagons loaded with the farm products of the up-county 'hinterland.'"[4]

By the 1850s, Louisville was larger, dirtier, more diverse, and more divided than the Louisville of Fanny's early childhood. The late 1840s saw an influx of immigrants from Germany and Ireland to the city. While in the rest of the nation the Irish—fleeing famine in their homeland—outnumbered the Germans, in Louisville the opposite was true. In 1850, the census showed more than 7,500 city residents born in Germany, compared to just over 3,000 Irish. While Louisville had long had a proportion of foreign-born residents, the upward spike in immigrant numbers in the 1840s sharpened class and ethnic tensions between "natives" and "newcomers." The predominant character of these newcomers contributed to these tensions. The Irish famine migrants were desperately poor and willing to take any unskilled work on offer. In so doing, they competed directly with the slaves and free blacks in Louisville, who had long occupied that economic niche. The Germans, by contrast, contained a higher proportion of well-educated liberals and radicals fleeing the failures of the 1848 revolutions that had swept across Europe. Their rationalism, anticlericalism, and political radicalism offended many in the conservative and pious Louisville establishment. The class of people who did not regularly attend church, editorialized the *Louisville Daily Courier*, increased "with every new infusion of the foreign element. . . . These make each Sunday a Saturnalia, and with all their might are attempting to Europeanize our population." Worse, in the paper's view, was that it seemed to be working. Attracted by the novelty, many of the city's American citizens were trying to adapt themselves "to enjoying German music and Lager beer, and Hockheimer and Bremen cigars."[5]

Ethnic nativism took a political turn with the formation of the American Party, known more commonly as the Know-Nothings. The focus of the Know-Nothings was to prevent Catholics and the foreign-born from holding public office, thus saving the country from falling under the control of the church and the pope. The party steadily gained adherents in Louisville and by mid-1855 was a strong presence in local government, with vociferous editorial backing from two of the city's four daily newspapers. On an election day in August 1855, the party's anti-immigrant rhetoric culminated in a horrific riot by Know-Nothing mobs who stormed through German and Irish neighborhoods burning homes, beating unlucky bystanders, and shooting those who tried to fight or flee. "Bloody Monday" left at least twenty-two dead (probably many more) and a vast amount of property damaged.[6]

As a daughter of the urban elite, Fanny was no doubt shielded from much of the violence and ethnic tension that racked her city. Nonetheless, as a pious and respectable member of that elite, who frowned on drinking, card playing, and Sabbath breaking, she probably had some sympathy for the criticisms directed at the city's new residents.

Fanny may also have noticed the upside of the city's growth more than its downside. For while class and ethnic tensions were on the rise, so was the cultural and artistic sophistication of her city. Traveling circuses came to town, and Louisville had its own horse track. Literary societies, theatrical performances, dancing schools: all testified to the growing refinement of the Falls City. "Its theatre patrons were responsive to such artists as Booth, Barret, and Salvani, and the never-to-be-forgotten voices of Jenny Lind, Brignoli, and Parepa Rosa," A. J. Webster recalled. Perhaps more than any one cultural event of those years, the three shows by Jenny Lind in 1851 signaled the city's vibrancy and wealth. Tickets were auctioned off for each show and went for as much as $175. A local newspaper labeled Lind "the greatest of all vocalists," delivering tones so pure they were "almost angelic in their sublime sweetness and harmony."[7]

It was in this context of political, economic, and cultural change that Fanny had to negotiate her own transition from maiden to woman. Courtship was no longer just a matter of a closed circle of established local families cementing kinship links. The field was more open, the expectations were different, the importance of romantic love was on the rise. The historian Ellen Rothman has written that nineteenth-century American women of a certain social class "made only one truly fateful choice in their lives," the choice of a husband. While men were "not born to assume any preordained occupational role," Rothman wrote, and hence might move from farmer to merchant to lawyer, a woman knew that she was really "preparing for the one career open to her: to be a man's wife and mother to his children. Once she made her choice, her options were suddenly, irrevocably gone."[8]

As she contemplated her marriage prospects, therefore, Fanny really faced the defining moment of her young life. To aid her in this transition Fanny had a large group of prominent friends and family members in Louisville and its environs. Although her mother had died four years before, her mother's fifteen brothers and sisters gave

Frances (Fanny) Thruston Ballard, undated. As a young slaveholding bride, one of Fanny's principal tasks was to manage the household slaves. (Filson Historical Society, Louisville, Ky.)

Fanny a surfeit of aunts and uncles and cousins, and she made frequent trips to Spring Grove, her Grandfather Churchill's estate south of Louisville. It was these people—including, of course, her father—who would help guide her through the perilous passage to womanhood and then on to wife and mother.

Fanny had several suitors during these years. Shortly after her mother's death in 1842, she met Andrew Jackson Ballard. He was eleven years her senior, a local lawyer who knew Charles William Thruston professionally. He was also a great whist player, and whist, a card game akin to bridge, was one of Charles William's delights, so he invited Ballard over to play. Some years later Ballard recalled that at his first meeting with Fanny he was so tongue-tied he did not speak to her.[9]

They would not see each other again until the summer of 1845. One Sunday morning, as Fanny prepared to go to church, she found Ballard and her father playing cards. Fanny, a pious member of Christ Church Episcopal, was offended by card playing in and of itself and doubly offended by card playing on Sunday morning. "Shocked she certainly was," Ballard recalled, "for her countenance betrayed it. I well remember its mournful expression. She remained but a moment and left, no doubt, as I then thought, blaming me for her Father's profaning the sabbath." Ballard himself did not understand the girl's religiosity. "I had done nothing which . . . a correct religion would condemn," he wrote later. Still, he found himself feeling oddly guilty for the reproachful look Fanny had given him.[10]

Fanny's mother evidently had been the guiding force in her daughter's religious upbringing. Charles William Thruston's name made no appearance in the Christ Church registers during his lifetime. Indeed, next to Mary Eliza Thruston's name in the roster of communicants, the register specifically notes: "Husband not a communicant." As for Ballard, he remained outside the church until the 1870s.[11]

After catching Ballard at cards that ill-fated Sunday, Fanny would not have close contact with him again for two years. Although he was a frequent visitor at her father's house, Ballard by his own admission did not run in the same social circles as the Thrustons. Fanny had many admirers and was "often courted and addressed," Ballard wrote, so she paid little attention to him. Indeed, although Ballard had a distinguished pioneer lineage, his current station in life had little to recommend him as a beau. His ancestors, like the Thrustons', had been Virginians. Andrew Ballard's father, James Ballard, emigrated to Kentucky around 1780 with his father and brother. James's brother, Bland W. Ballard, soldiered with George Rogers Clark in the campaign for the Northwest during the Revolution, gaining a reputation as an Indian fighter. This reputation reached legendary status during the famed Ballard Massacre of 1788. When a party of Delaware Indians attacked the family's cabin along Tick Creek in Shelby County, Bland fired six shots in defense of the family home and is said to have killed six Indians. Bland's marksmanship saved his own life, but the Indians shot and killed his father, two brothers, and one young sister, and tomahawked his stepmother. Bland later served with distinction in the War of 1812.[12]

Andrew Jackson Ballard, undated. The son of a Kentucky pioneer family, Ballard became a lawyer before marrying Fanny in 1848. (Filson Historical Society, Louisville, Ky.)

Andrew's father, James, had been gone the day of the massacre—most likely having joined neighboring men on a punitive attack against an Indian raiding party—but he returned to cultivate his farm in Shelby County until his death in 1849. At the time of his death, his personal estate, which included twelve slaves, was valued at just shy of $8,000. His real estate holdings amounted to five hundred acres of land—perfectly respectable, but definitely a step or two down the economic ladder from the Thruston family.[13]

Andrew, born in 1815, evidently had little desire to follow in his father's footsteps. In 1835, he quit classes at a local seminary and began to read law under a locally prominent lawyer, George Bibb. He passed the bar and began practicing in Louisville in 1837. His tax assessments during those years hint at a young man trying to establish himself in the city's competitive legal environment. In 1838, the tax assessor listed no property for the young lawyer. In 1844, he had obtained one small piece of property in a less than prime area of town valued at $384.[14]

Regarding his relationship with Fanny, it was not until the spring of 1847 that Ballard made his move from a friend of her father to an admirer. He saw Fanny anew at a party at her Grandfather Churchill's. "It was the first time in my life I had ever endeavored to engage her in conversation," he recalled later. They took a walk together, and although Fanny seemed happy and talkative, Ballard thought he saw something deeper in the young girl's spirit. There was "something which told of dissatisfaction with the circumstances that then surrounded her, that she had longings of the heart and aspirations of the soul which had never yet been realized." Ballard, full of nineteenth-century romanticism, pondered deeply his feelings for Fanny. As with all good romantics, he convinced himself that he had loved her from the first. After all, he reasoned, why had her look of reproach when finding him playing cards on Sunday filled him with regret? "No event of my past life had caused such bitter, such painful regrets," he wrote. As he reflected upon their incidental meetings around town, he remembered emotional stirrings that he could not explain. "I certainly never intended to love her for love is involuntary," he wrote. "I now know I could not have loved another, I now believe I then loved her."[15]

As he began to court Fanny in earnest, Ballard faced rivals. One was an old friend of his, the overeager Mr. Logan, who visited Fanny in company with Ballard at Spring Grove, her grandfather's plantation. As the two men were returning to Louisville, Logan declared to his friend his love for Fanny. Ballard refused to be the go-between; "I told him of my extreme repugnance to become the confidant and adviser of any one in an affair of love." Nonetheless, he did offer Logan one piece of advice. Given Fanny's position in society, Logan was bound to have rivals. He should not put off declaring his feelings to Fanny. "He had everything to lose and nothing to gain by postponement," Ballard wrote. But as it turned out, Logan had everything to lose by rushing into a confession of his feelings. A month or so later, he and Ballard again paid a call on Fanny. Logan's passion was so great that he "transcended all propriety in the undisguised exhibition of his love for her," Ballard recalled. Fanny recoiled, clearly avoiding him and displaying her "annoyance at his attentions." And thus there was one fewer rival with whom Ballard had to contend.[16]

Two months later, Ballard and Fanny met again, this time at Paroquet Springs, a then-popular spring and spa about eighteen miles from Louisville. They were each in the company of friends and had not apparently arranged the meeting, for they spent several days engaged in entirely separate activities. Finally, though, Ballard invited her for a walk, and then awaited her response with trepidation. She at first declined, then changed her mind and decided to accompany him. They went to the grave of a certain Mrs. Lynch, "a lovely Being whom Heaven had permitted for a few brief years to mingle with mortals and while she was still young had translated to a world of bliss." In modern dating practices, a walk to a gravesite might seem a little odd, but for the nineteenth-century romantic, it was fittingly "sublime." It linked the traditional female virtues of purity, beauty, and emotional sensitivity with the romantic notion that such virtues routinely took a beating in the broken and vice-ridden world in which women had to live. Women worth having, in other words, were too good for this earth. After a few moments contemplating the "sublime virtues and pure nature of her whose mortal remains were then beneath me," Ballard wrote, his thoughts were "diverted from the Dead to the Living" and "to the enrapturing visions which the dawning future then presented to my view."[17]

After several more meetings, Ballard finally openly pledged his love to Fanny on September 16, 1847, asking her to marry him. She kept him waiting four days for an answer, but then she "requited all my doubts, fear, and anxieties, all the dreadful anguish I had suffered, by saying she loved me. She promised to marry me—unconditionally, unreservedly promised."[18]

Fanny's father was strongly opposed to the marriage, as were several other members of the family. Ballard may have been a fine companion with whom to while away a few hours playing whist, but Charles William had his doubts about the man's fitness as a son-in-law. It probably had less to do with Ballard's economic station than with his behavior. Rogers Clark wrote later that his father was "dissipated" as a young man, an old-fashioned way of saying he drank too much. Fanny had plenty of admirers, and the old man obviously thought she could do better than a struggling lawyer who liked his liquor. Ballard was not deterred. "Can it be that these bright and lovely visions are never to be realized—that these wild and joyous hopes of my heart are ever to be disappointed[?] I cannot—I will not believe it. I have crossed the Rubicon." Even if she called off the engagement, he wrote, he would still love her. "She might *break*, but she cannot *change* my heart." Although he was not hopeful that he would succeed, he told Fanny he would seek a personal interview with her father to gain his agreement to the match.[19]

Two weeks later, he wrote that he had met her father on the street and that he had seemed "more than usually friendly." He also confessed that he hated being stranded in the limbo between rejection and acceptance. He did not like to see her in company with others, he wrote to her, because he shrank "from the fixed gaze and cold speculations of those who suspect my feelings and wish to discover the secret of my heart."[20]

Fanny's female relatives, meanwhile, tried to promote other suitors whom they thought better matches. They suspected the depth of Ballard's feelings for Fanny, worried perhaps that he might be seeking attachment to her family's fortune and social status rather than to Fanny herself. Ballard did what he could to maintain his connection to his beloved. He wrote her a note regarding one proposed beau, whom he said might meet some people's criteria of a "safe match" but whom Ballard described as "somewhat eccentric." He desisted from further commentary, observing that he was "too generous even by inuendo [*sic*] to deal unkindly with a rival." He signed off with a determined "Believe me constant."[21]

By January 1848 the proposed engagement was in serious trouble. Fanny wrote to Ballard that experience had taught her that "love's sceptre could be dexterously wielded by prudence alone," a sign that she was beginning to heed her relatives' warnings. Ballard was aghast. He accused her of never truly loving him. "Would a pure, an ardent love have ascribed to me sentiments so much at variance with all I have ever either written, said or done[?]" He challenged her to look into her heart to decide if she truly loved him and, if not, "if the past has been but a dream, let me awake to the reality, awful and overwhelming though it be."[22]

Less than a week later, Fanny repented and expressed her undying love for him. It set his troubled heart at ease, and he thanked her for "all that is bright and glowing and cheering in the future." With Fanny's doubts erased, Ballard made a promise to her and to her family to mend his ways. He swore to stop drinking and stop playing cards. Eventually, the family's resistance gave way, and Fanny and Ballard were married on April 27, 1848, on the Churchill estate.[23]

Still, family suspicions about Ballard persisted. Less than a year after their marriage, Fanny took a trip to Savannah, Georgia, where she evidently received reports that, in her absence, her husband had relapsed into his bad old habits. She wrote him two accusatory letters, and he bristled defensively. "My dearest Fanny do you not think that a little more confidence in your husband . . . a little more reliance on his undying love would grace your letters and occupy your thoughts, just as well as the accusations you bring against him." He called it "unmanly and humiliating" to have to respond to such accusations from any source, and it was "doubly painful" when they came from his own "beloved wife." "I will never play cards because I hold my promise to you sacred," he wrote. He then went on to caution her about corresponding too openly with her female relatives who, he felt, were biased against him.[24]

It is worth asking why these details of Fanny and Ballard's courtship and marriage survived in the archival record. Obvious reasons are that Fanny was a member of a prominent family and that her son later served as president of the local historical society. But not much else of Fanny's correspondence survived. Beyond these "letters of tender interest," as Fanny labeled them, and some mementos from her reign as the Queen of May, the remaining fifty years of her life are represented in the archives only by a scattering of letters and a smattering of receipts relating to various memorials she purchased for deceased members of her family. There must have been more documents at some point, but either she or her son discarded them. There was more involved than just a desire for posthumous privacy in the decisions about what to keep and what to throw away. Indeed, suspicion of "prying eyes" would have seemed to demand that these "letters of tender interest" be discarded as well. More than likely, these letters survived because they recalled the pivotal event in Fanny's life. For an upper-class woman, the transition from daughter to wife was one of the most significant in life—and thus worth preserving.[25]

The importance of a "good match" and "true love" shines through in the story of Fanny and Andrew's courtship and marriage. Students of American courtship have noted that couples in the colonial period focused on the "suitability" of marriage partners more than love. The late eighteenth century viewed romantic love with caution. Romantic love could not be trusted; it was self-indulgent, fleeting, and the mark of an immature personality. By the 1830s, however, Americans had shifted to a companionate idea of marriage and, with it, attached an increasing importance to romantic love. At least among the middle classes, romantic love was becoming the critical prerequisite for marriage. Historians studying couples' letters have found a general decline in the discussion of practical matters, such as governed courtship in the colonial period, and a general increase in the discussion of love and romance. Ballard's letters and reminiscences, with their fine dissections of feelings, their focus on the powerful emotional force of his love for Fanny, and their small dramas of suspicion, betrayal, and redemption, obviously fit neatly into this schema. The prevailing theme of courtship among the middle classes was intense emotional introspection and detailed interpretation of one's partner's inner life and true feelings. Moreover, as was the case with Fanny and Andrew, this unpeeling of social conventions and revelation of the true self was most often carried out via love letters.[26]

The dramatics within the Ballards' courtship—Fanny's doubts, Andrew's avowals of love, the repeated reexamination of their feelings for each other—dovetail perfectly with overall courtship patterns detected in studies of nineteenth-century couples. The historian Karen Lystra, for example, has described a cycle of "courtship testing," largely orchestrated by women, that served the dual function of assessing the potential mate's depth of commitment and, once the test was passed, deepening that commitment further. "Women . . . took the materials of life at hand and shaped them into obstacles that men had to overcome to prove the emotional depth and sincerity of their love. Illness, debt, family, other men, religious differences, character flaws, and personal inadequacy all formed the plot material of these private cultural dramas." The ultimate "test" frequently occurred just prior to marriage, a final hurdle for men to overcome to prove their worthiness for the altar. This often involved the breaking or the near breaking of the engagement—as Fanny threatened in the January before her wedding to Andrew—followed by an all-out protestation of undying and undiminished love by the suitor and, if all worked out, reconciliation and recommitment to marriage. "This ritual of testing emotional loyalty and commitment," Lystra wrote, made courtship "an intensely dramatic and exciting period of interaction." This emotional drama and excitement helps explain why Fanny preserved these mementoes from that time in her life.[27]

In one remarkable way, however, Fanny and Andrew's romance diverged from the scholarly picture of nineteenth-century courtship. One of the notable features of the ascent of love-based relationships was the consequent decline of family oversight and influence on the decision about whom to marry. If mate choice was governed by the heart, parents could not presume to know more about that emotional inner space than the people involved. The rise of companionate marriage challenged the grounds on which parents were presumed to know best, whether a potential mate would be a good provider, a dutiful father, and an upstanding citizen. Parents and family could judge behavior, but they could not judge depth of feeling and sincerity of mutual affection. Fanny's female relatives did not fit this pattern. They felt themselves quite capable of judging the depth of Andrew's emotional commitment and warning Fanny off. Nor did Charles William Thruston subscribe to the growing cultural sentiment that parents should not interfere in courtship. He interfered in Fanny and Andrew's relationship quite forcefully.[28]

One reason for these deviations from the historical norm might be the Northern and Midwestern biases of these historical studies.

Patterns of courtship in Kentucky, influenced by its Southern origins and connections, may fit less well into these generalizations. Another reason may be the particular family situation of the Thrustons. Charles William Thruston, a recent widower who had earlier lost two young children, may have struggled with giving up his only remaining daughter to marriage. During their courtship, Andrew speculated to Fanny at one point that her father's resistance seemed to stem more from "his opposition to your marrying any one" than from "his objections to me personally."[29]

Another way Fanny and Andrew's relationship diverged from nineteenth-century norms was that they never set up housekeeping separately after they were married. Rather, Andrew moved into the Thruston house on Walnut Street in central Louisville. Perhaps this was a bone thrown to Charles William to reassure him that he would not be losing a daughter (only gaining a son-in-law); perhaps this was Charles William's way of ensuring that his daughter would be looked after if Ballard backslid into his earlier "dissipation." At any rate, given the emphasis placed on the man's role as provider and on the idea of the home as the inevitable and most important consequence of marriage, Fanny and Andrew's move into the Thruston home challenged many nineteenth-century expectations about life after marriage.[30]

The rise of romantic love as the basis for marriage coincided with an increasing emphasis on "the ideology of separate spheres," which accentuated the differences between the cultural roles assigned to men and women. On the family farm of the eighteenth century, women and men both contributed to the labor of the household. In the nineteenth-century commercial city, however, men's proper sphere became increasingly defined by the public realms of politics and business, and women's proper sphere became increasingly restricted to the private realm of the home and the family. Some historians have suggested that the language of romantic love served as a bridge between the two worlds. In other words, the divergence of men's and women's roles was countered by the intense emotional connection in their private lives. Romantic love stressed the common bonds of affection and sympathy that ideally existed between husband and wife—bonds that could bridge the growing gulf between the domestic hearth and the dog-eat-dog economy.[31]

Just as their courtship fit many of the broader patterns found in nineteenth-century relations between the sexes, so did the Ballards' life after marriage fit fairly tidily into the separate spheres schema. Fanny was a wife and mother the rest of her days. When she died more than fifty years later, her obituarist praised her devotion to her family, writing that "it was her greatest pleasure to serve them."[32]

For a slaveholding wife, Fanny's prescribed role meant supervision of the household slaves. In fact, living in her father's house gave Fanny two sets of slaves to boss: her husband's and her father's. According to the 1850 tax list, Andrew Ballard owned two slaves and Charles William Thruston owned four. Since she had been serving as the lead white female in her widowed father's house since 1842, Fanny probably faced less difficulty in exercising authority over the slaves than did many young Southern brides. She was accustomed to the task, although it was by no means an easy one. Many Southern wives complained that the servants turned surly and unmanageable when the master was away, leaving only his wife in command. Rural Southern wives writing letters to absentee husbands often requested advice on how to deal with the servants, and just as many husbands wrote back telling their wives that they trusted their judgment. Coping with disobedience was doubtless a greater problem for a wife trying to run a large plantation than it was for Fanny running her much smaller urban household, but Fanny did still occasionally run into problems.[33]

In late 1849, Andrew traveled to New Orleans to research business opportunities. He received a letter from Fanny reciting some of the problems she was having with Maria and Bob, two slaves. "You make no mention of your intentions in regard to the servants," he wrote back. "I think you had better get rid of both Maria and Bob." Maria he described as "unbearable" and suggested that they either recruit another one of the household slaves, Nancy, to serve as cook or buy "a cook such as will suit us." Bob had been troublesome previously, Ballard wrote, but "I have whipped him so often and to so little purpose that I have not the heart to be continually punishing him." With regard to Bob's ultimate fate, he left that to Fanny's judgment. The records are unclear as to what happened to Bob and Maria. Ballard's papers contain no bill of sale to confirm that they were ever sold off. But this minor little aside in a letter to his wife illustrated a central truth about slavery: physical coercion lay at the base of bondage. Even in an urban and relatively urbane household like the Ballards', even with only very few slaves to manage, even when those slaves had racked up years of service, there inevitably came a time when recalcitrance or resistance by the slave was met with the lash by the master. As people who grew up with slavery, the Ballards accepted this central characteristic of the institution.[34]

Andrew Jackson Ballard does not come across in his papers as a cruel man; indeed, he seems at times overly sentimental. And this letter made it clear that he did not relish the punishment of Bob, but he did it anyway. The letter simply pointed out that the punishments had become pointless; they had ceased to yield the desired results. And so he considered playing the only other card the slave owner had: disposal of the troublesome slave through sale. This was simple pragmatism: Slave Home Economics 101.

The goal of effective household management was, of course, to provide a secure environment in which to raise a family. And within two years of her marriage, Fanny began the second overarching task of nineteenth-century wives—bearing children. She gave birth to four boys and one girl between 1850 and 1858. Their first son, Charles Thruston Ballard, was born in June 1850. A second son, Bland Ballard, was born the next year but died before his first birthday. A daughter, Abigail Churchill Ballard, came next in 1853, followed by Samuel Thruston Ballard in February 1855 and, finally, Rogers Clark Ballard, who was born November 6, 1858. With four children to rear, Fanny's "sphere" must have been quite lively.[35]

If Fanny's sphere was the household, managed with the advice of her husband, Andrew's sphere was the marketplace, in which he sought the occasional advice of his wife. Ballard was a lawyer, but he never appeared to love the practice of law. His legal practice, he told Fanny, subjected him to "many mortifications," which doubtless meant he was not making enough money. He frequently dithered over the choice of profession he had made and told Fanny that if she recommended an alternative plan he would adopt it. His 1849 trip to New Orleans showed that early on in his marriage he thought about abandoning the law, and perhaps getting out from under the Thruston roof. As for what other occupation he might pursue, it is clear that he had no fixed idea. He went to New Orleans to investigate opportunities in the "exchange business," which meant becoming a banker. But he obviously did not relish the thought of entering the banking business, either. "I have been in several of the banking houses of this City," he wrote to Fanny from New Orleans. "I know them all in Louisville and I declare to you that I have never yet seen a man engaged in that business who had a fine, noble, or generous countenance. They all seem, at least from their external appearance to be mean men." This meanness—by which he meant lack of generosity, or tightfistedness—gave him pause. He thought his perception might be due to his own prejudice against "dealing in money," but he also worried that the very nature of the business shaped and distorted the person engaged in it. He was lured by the profitability of banking, but feared its boom-and-bust cycles. Through it all, he regarded Fanny as a partner in the decision. He would not risk investment in the exchange business, he told her, without the "free full and voluntary consent of my beloved wife."[36]

Andrew's letters from New Orleans—written eighteen months into their marriage—are filled with the same notes of loving tenderness that marked the letters from their courtship. Still avidly sentimental, Ballard told her that he had to retire to his room before he broke the seal on one of her letters because he did not want anyone to see him weeping while he read it, overcome by his love for her. He told her that the crowds in the New Orleans streets held no interest for him anymore. "But one thing now my dear Fanny can make me happy and that is your love, your undiminished love." Still, he wished not only to possess her love "but to merit it," a clear reference to his difficulties in earning a living, in mastering his role in the male sphere. "I only want to live comfortably and spend my days with my darling Fanny." These constant avowals of his undying love for her leave the impression of a devoted and loving husband—but perhaps of a less than competent breadwinner.[37]

In truth, the Ballards were not doing all that badly, judging from their tax records. Marriage to Fanny helped Ballard's prospects enormously. In 1847, the year before his marriage, the tax assessor valued his total property at $500. By 1850, two years into his married life, the value of his taxable property had mushroomed to $7,357, largely because he had partnered with Fanny's brother Sam to buy two city lots in Louisville. By 1860, Andrew had expanded his property holdings to include all or part of seven lots throughout Louisville; the total value of all his property stood at $18,235. The Thruston connection was obviously paying off.[38]

The decade of the 1850s thus found Fanny setting up housekeeping and stabilizing her family life. She had reached many of the significant milestones that marked the life of a well-to-do nineteenth-century white woman. She had found a man who loved her and married him. She had set up housekeeping with her husband and given him children. And she was, with the help of a small group of household slaves under her supervision, providing emotional support to her husband and guiding the upbringing of her children.

During this same decade her former slave Cecelia was busily doing many of the same things farther north. But for Cecelia stabilizing her family was made more difficult—indeed, nigh impossible—by the fact of slavery. As she attempted to build her family as a free woman in Canada, she felt compelled to reach out to her former mistress to help her accomplish that task.

Chapter 5

Cecelia: A Family in Freedom

During that fateful spring of 1846, the slave Cecelia emerged on the other side of the Niagara River as the free woman Cecelia Jane Reynolds. How and why she picked those middle and last names is a mystery. Perhaps it was the name of someone significant from her past. Or maybe the name of someone who had helped her reach Canada. Whatever the source, choosing a name of one's own was a matter of great moment for newly free slaves. Taking on a new name symbolized the taking on of a new identity as a free person. It both marked the individual's passage out of bondage and jabbed a metaphorical finger in the eye of the institution that kept Africans enslaved and misnamed.

Many former slaves replaced their first names, which their masters had given them and which often sounded ironic or derogatory. Names like Caesar, Pompey, Cuffee, Charity, Fortune, and others were thrown aside in favor of simple and common American names like Joe, Jim, or Sarah. Cecelia kept her first name—perhaps because her mother, not her master, had given it to her. But like most slaves she had been known in bondage only by that first name. By choosing a surname, Cecelia—like thousands of others—began crafting a new identity for herself in freedom. Many former slaves chose names with obvious significance, such as Freeman or Newman, but more frequently they took familiar Anglo-American surnames.

After the Civil War, this ritual of naming oneself was carried out by millions of former slaves. Some looked to their own personal and family histories, taking as surname that of the earliest master who could be recalled. Others adopted the names of individuals who had played prominent roles in the destruction of slavery, such as Grant, Lincoln, or Stevens. In all cases, they reserved the right to choose their own names—resenting, resisting, and rebuffing white interference. "A new name," wrote the eminent historian of slavery Ira Berlin, "reversed the enslavement process and confirmed the free black's newly won liberty."[1]

When Cecelia crossed the Niagara River, she became part of a stream of African American refugees from slavery that flowed into Canada between the end of the War of 1812 and the passage of the Fugitive Slave Act of 1850 in the United States. That legislation, jeopardizing as it did the freedom of many blacks living in the Northern states, turned a steady stream into a flood, probably more than tripling the number of blacks resident in Canada West (present-day Ontario) during the decade of the 1850s. Robin Winks, widely regarded as an authority on blacks in Canada, estimates that there were thirty thousand fugitives or descendants of fugitives residing in Canada West in 1860. There were probably somewhat fewer than ten thousand when Cecelia made her way from Niagara.[2]

Cecelia hardly fit the typical profile of a runaway slave. A statistical portrait of runaways based on more than two thousand advertisements in Southern newspapers found that the typical runaway slave was usually young and male: eight out of every ten runaway slaves were male, and three quarters of them were in their teens and twenties. Of those relative few who made it to Canada, at least before 1850, the majority also were male. Young males ran more frequently because many of them were unmarried or, if married, childless. They had fewer family attachments and thus felt less constrained by kinship ties.[3]

Cecelia, of course, was unmarried and childless when she decided to make her break, but she did opt to leave behind in Kentucky her mother and her younger brother. Opportunity—in the form of her proximity to the Canadian border—probably played the largest role in Cecelia's decision to flee bondage.

Unlike Cecelia, many fugitives stopped running just after they crossed the border. Most lacked money and could not afford to push on farther. Moreover, Winks wrote, since many of the early runaways had been employed as farmers when slaves, they did not want to go too far into the interior, where they would face unfamiliar planting conditions. Amherstburg, just opposite Detroit, became the most important of these early black farming communities, as former slaves from Kentucky and Virginia pioneered the cultivation of tobacco in Canada during the 1820s.[4]

In addition, as exiles, many fugitives wanted to stay close to the border in anticipation of an eventual return to the United States. Thus small black communities began to grow in a handful of Canadian towns adjacent to the principal fugitive-crossing points in the United States. Aside from Amherstburg, blacks aggregated in Windsor and Colchester, just across from Detroit. Other black communities sprang up in London, Chatham, and Dresden, accessible via Buffalo and Lake Erie. The towns of Niagara, St. Catharines, and Welland, just across the Niagara River near the Falls, would have been likely places for Cecelia to stop.[5]

If she stopped, however, she did not stay long. Having known an urban environment all her life, Cecelia no doubt favored city life, where her chances of employment were greater. So she pushed on to Toronto, probably traveling there by steamer across the tip of Lake Ontario. She arrived sometime prior to November 1846, just over six months after leaving Fanny. At the time of Cecelia's arrival, Toronto's black community numbered fewer than 1,000 in a total population of about 20,000. Six years earlier, a survey had enumerated 528 black inhabitants in Toronto. Benjamin Drew, writing in 1856, estimated the number of blacks in the city to be about 1,000. The black community tended to concentrate in the northwestern section of the city, clustering around sites of employment and Baptist and Methodist churches.[6]

Toronto, and Canada in general, enjoyed a good reputation among American blacks. James G. Birney, a white American, visited the city in 1837 and wrote that any black "of good health and conduct" could succeed in Toronto and Upper Canada. William Howard, a former slave living in Toronto interviewed by Drew, stated that "Canada is the best place that I ever saw. . . . The colored people, taken as a whole, are as industrious as any people you will find.

They have a good deal of ambition to go forward, and take a good stand in the community. I know several who own houses and lands." Drew himself, though not an unbiased observer, wrote of the blacks in Toronto that "their condition is such as to gratify the philanthropist, and to afford encouragement to the friends of emancipation everywhere." To Cecelia and other refugees from the slaveholding United States, Toronto offered freedom, safety, and the chance to prosper.[7]

Cecelia appeared to find her way in Toronto quite rapidly. No doubt she faced hard times initially; if Rogers Clark Thruston's tale is to be believed, she arrived with no money and no clothing. Her employment opportunities fell into a few well-worn "female" categories—nurse for children, general servant, housekeeper, seamstress, and so on. Of course, laboring for one's own benefit—like naming oneself—constituted another milestone in the passage from slavery to freedom. So while the actual work Cecelia did might not have been that different from the tasks she performed as Fanny's slave, as a wageworker she benefited directly from her own labor.[8]

The value put upon free labor came through repeatedly in the interviews Drew conducted with former slaves in Canada. James Sumler, who had been a slave in Virginia, told Drew: "After I got to years of maturity, and saw the white people sitting in the shade, while I worked in the sun, I thought I would like to be my own man." Elijah Jenkins, whose mistress hired him out, stated that "slavery has never looked to me right. It seemed hard when I earned any money to have to carry it to another man, when my wife needed it herself." William Howard also hired himself out in slavery, delivering $7 a month to his mistress. "I thought it honorable to carry to my mistress the money I earned," he told Drew. But as a free man, he thought differently. "It seems to me now that she was not honorable in taking it, if I was in giving it."[9]

In November 1846, Cecelia passed a third great milestone in the life of a former slave: she was legally married. The importance among former slaves of the legal recognition of matrimony should not be underestimated. One of the torments of life under slavery was the instability of the family unit, which existed at the whim of the slaveholder. After the Civil War, for example, thousands of slaves took the step that Cecelia had taken. Even long-married couples, once free, insisted on legal marriage by constituted civil authorities. Like choosing a name, legal marriage reversed the process of enslavement and indicted the institution that had made slave marriages illegitimate. For Cecelia, whose mother was torn from her father and her stepfather by sale, legal marriage no doubt constituted a highly significant step in the process of making her freedom seem real. Cecelia married Benjamin Pollard Holmes in St. James Cathedral in Toronto on November 19, 1846. In lieu of a formal license, their wedding was by "banns"—meaning the proposed marriage was formally proclaimed in the church to give interested parties an opportunity to object. When no one did, Assistant Minister H. J. Grassett formalized their union.[10]

Like Cecelia, Benjamin Holmes was a fairly recent immigrant to Canada from the United States, probably coming to Canada around 1842. Holmes was thirty-three years old in 1846, significantly older than his new bride, who was still in her teens. He had two young sons—James Thomas and Benjamin Alexander—but no wife, so he probably viewed marriage to Cecelia in part as a way to provide care for the boys. Holmes was born in Virginia, but whether he was a slave there cannot be determined. If he was a slave, then most likely the missing wife had either been sold away before he came to Canada or refused to flee when he proposed escaping north. It is also possible that Holmes came north with his wife when she was pregnant with Benjamin, the younger boy. A Canadian census gives the boys' ages as nineteen and eighteen in 1861, and lists the elder son as being born in the United States and the younger son in Canada. This suggests that they emigrated as a family, but that Holmes's first wife likely had died. Perhaps she did not survive childbirth. Different records provide different ages for his sons, however; later U.S. census records show the younger boy born in 1839, and list both sons as having been born in Canada. Given the nature of the historical record, much about Holmes's provenance must remain uncertain.[11]

Job opportunities for black men in Canada did not differ much from those in the Northern United States. They tended toward the

Map of Toronto, 1857. Soon after her escape, Cecelia migrated to Toronto, where she met and married Benjamin Holmes. The couple lived in St. John's Ward on Centre Street. (Toronto Public Library, Toronto.)

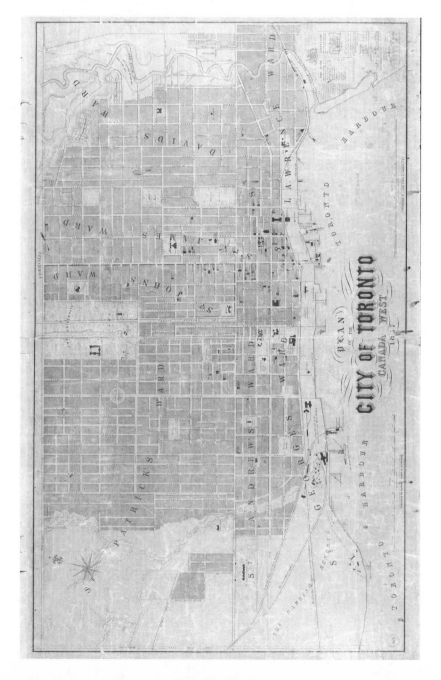

low-wage end of the spectrum, with many working simply as laborers and farmers. Some did become prosperous shop owners and professionals; Wilson Ruffin Abbott made a fortune in real estate and was the leader of Toronto's black elite. Thornton Blackburn, like Cecelia an escaped slave from Kentucky, started the first taxicab business in Upper Canada and also became quite well off. The majority of black wage earners, however, struggled to eke out a living. Benjamin and Cecelia evidently fell into the majority. Holmes worked as a waiter, a fairly common occupation for black men, and one that paid better than work as a common laborer. According to Winks, the job paid about $12 per month. The 1850–1851 city directory for Toronto listed Holmes as a waiter on board the steamer *City of Toronto.*[12]

When Cecelia married Holmes, his oldest boy, James, was somewhere between four and eight years of age, with Benjamin Alexander a year younger. So, like Fanny back in Louisville, Cecelia took on the roles of mother and housekeeper. However, she probably also continued to work outside the home. Given Winks's estimate that lodging cost about $15 a month, there was clearly a gap between Holmes's earnings and the family's needs. Canadian census takers, reflecting the gender ideology of the day, rarely listed women's occupations, but Cecelia may have taken in laundry or sewing or worked as a domestic in someone's house, bringing the boys along with her.[13]

Because so many black women had to work to help make ends meet, the black community never fully embraced the "separate spheres" ideology that governed "proper" gender relations in both Canada and the United States. They were influenced by this ideology, however. The idea of a male breadwinner and a housebound wife colored blacks' ideas of what freedom meant. Indeed, after the Civil War, many emancipated slaves attempted to keep their women out of the fields to avoid any echoes of slavery. But whether in the postemancipation South or in the Canada of the 1840s, economic necessity often made this impossible, as it did for large numbers of poor whites.[14]

The result was that gender roles became blurred, as did the line between the private sphere and the public sphere. The late 1830s and the 1840s were years of community building for black Torontonians. The network of organizations and associations that beat the drum for the abolitionist cause and took care of those blacks who successfully emigrated to Canada, and Toronto in particular, began to form during these years. Black women participated actively in these difficult tasks of community building in Canada, organizing campaigns on behalf of various religious and benevolent institutions. In sum, black women's "sphere" and their notion of social responsibility included active community involvement.[15]

Cecelia doubtless played some role in the wider black community, but only a few scraps of evidence that attest to that role have survived—and these few scraps provide only fodder for speculation, not concrete documentation. For example, Benjamin and Cecelia resided on Centre Street, a principal avenue in black Toronto, so it seems unlikely that they would have isolated themselves completely from the events that played out in the fugitive slave community. In addition, Cecelia had a connection with Charles C. Foote, an abolitionist clergyman and activist living in Detroit in the 1850s. Foote was a graduate of the staunchly abolitionist Oberlin College in Ohio, campaigned for the antislavery Liberty Party in the 1840s, and raised money for the Refugee Home Society—a fugitive relief organization—in Canada. Fanny's first letter to Cecelia was addressed to the care of Foote, so he obviously had some contact with Cecelia. Whether this was just benevolence or whether he had recruited Cecelia to work for the abolitionist cause cannot be known.[16]

In that first letter from Fanny, moreover, she mentions Cecelia's preparations for an imminent trip to Europe "in pursuit of health." It seems unlikely, from the available information on Benjamin and Cecelia, that Cecelia could have afforded a European tour just six years out of slavery. But fugitives from slavery did frequently travel to Europe, particularly England, as part of fund-raising road shows sponsored by abolitionist organizations. Frederick Douglass lectured in England, Ireland, and Scotland in the two years after the initial publication of his life story. Nathaniel Paul—a Baptist preacher and organizer of the black Canadian community of Wilberforce—did likewise for four years in the 1830s. Martin Delany,

Moses Roper, Josiah Henson, and numerous others less well known also carried the antislavery message across the Atlantic. Perhaps Cecelia's trip to Europe was part of her community involvement in the fight against slavery.[17]

In the years after 1840, Afro-Canadian community-building activities took on a greater scope and urgency. As they began to acknowledge the stubbornness of Southern slaveholders, the apathy of Northerners, and the smarminess of electoral politics, many of the black exiles to Canada recognized that they were in for a long residence in Canada before slavery crumbled in the United States. The signs of community mobilization ranged from the religious and charitable to the political and legal. On the religious front, an increasing number of all-black churches—particularly Baptist and Methodist congregations—arose within Toronto. With the black churches came evangelical efforts like the Women's Home Missionary Society and religious education initiatives like the Baptist Sunday School Committee. Benevolent associations sprang up with the aim of assisting the Canadian black community by supporting schools and churches and of providing for the specific needs of fugitive slaves. The Queen Victoria Benevolent Society, organized by the black women of Toronto, and the Toronto Ladies' Aid Association for the Relief of Destitute Colored Fugitives both existed to assist newly arriving refugees from slavery.[18]

Community building on the political and legal spectrum ranged from organizing local vigilance and self-help committees to starting newspapers to campaigning for abolitionist causes. Vigilance committees were needed because the Canadian border did not deter all American slaveholders from sending their agents north to recapture their fugitive bondmen. As in Northern cities in the United States, Toronto's vigilance committees kept an eye out for suspected slave catchers and posted warnings to the community when suspicious characters were seen. The best-known self-help organizations in the black community were probably the True Bands. At least fourteen of these local organizations, usually with strong links to churches, existed as of 1855. Their aim was to foster black independence by raising money for schools, providing poverty relief, and aiding the sick. Some also took on the task of resolving disputes among the membership.[19]

Toronto's black community petitioned government authorities regarding everything from the demeaning nature of touring minstrel shows to the injustice of extraditing former slaves to the United States. They participated actively in the Toronto Anti-slavery Society, founded in 1851. They also helped organize the historic North American Convention of Colored Freedmen in September 1851. The organizers chose Toronto because it was believed to be the safest environment for such a meeting. The convention passed several resolutions aimed at improving black life within Canada, called on American slaves to flee northward rather than to Africa or the West Indies, and formally praised the British government as "the most favourable in the civilized world to the people of colour."[20]

Community building cost money, and black spokespeople and organizations turned to Anglo-American abolitionist organizations for assistance. In addition to the numerous organized black settlements that raised money, churches needed money for buildings, schoolteachers needed subsidies to keep teaching, and missionaries wanted funding for their outreach. The calls varied from pleas for immediate help for destitute fugitives to long-term commitments required to build and support black institutions. Taken together, these requests for money tested the generosity of the Anglo-American charitable and abolitionist community.[21]

The black community was served by two newspapers—the *Voice of the Fugitive*, which began publication on January 1, 1851, and the *Provincial Freeman*, which began weekly publication in early 1854. The *Voice of the Fugitive* came out of Chatham, close to the U.S. border, and it was edited by Henry Bibb, an escaped slave from Kentucky and prominent member of the Canadian black community. The *Voice* responded to the derogatory characterizations of the fugitive slave community that frequently appeared in the white Canadian press and urged a separatist philosophy as the road to independence for Canadian blacks. The *Freeman*, edited by the formidable activist and educator Mary Ann Shadd out of Toronto, took issue with the *Voice*'s separatist leanings. The *Provincial Freeman* stood against anything that smacked of racial isolation. Shadd wanted blacks not to stand outside of Canadian society but to be firmly integrated within it. The *Freeman* upbraided even black-owned institutions if it felt that these institutions impeded the incorporation of blacks into their adopted nation. The *Freeman* encouraged blacks to regard Canada as their home and contribute to the building of a society there, whereas the very name of the *Voice of the Fugitive* implied that Canada was a temporary stop in exile. Finally, the *Freeman* emphasized community self-reliance and financial independence, taking to task any organization that spent its time soliciting funds for support of destitute fugitives.[22]

The issue of fund-raising fueled an intense feud between the rival newspapers and their editors. Shadd criticized Bibb for his support of the Refugee Home Society because it got so much of its money from solicitations. Shadd blasted the fund-raising appeals as painting a picture of blacks as "a class of improvident, thriftless, and imbecile paupers." This feud reflected a cleavage within the overall exile community of which Cecelia and Benjamin Holmes formed a part. Opponents of the almost constant fund-raising derided it as "begging." They highlighted the numerous instances of corruption, which ranged from simple incompetence in the handling of the money to unethically high commissions for certain agents to outright fraud. For opponents, this not only tarnished the effort to raise funds for legitimate causes, but it also raised deeper issues of self-reliance. For black spokespeople to constantly harangue white audiences with woeful tales of destitute fugitives only reinforced the white image of blacks as a dependent and inferior race. It fed the pro-slavery argument that the slaves could not be freed because they could not fend for themselves.[23]

The refugee communities in Canada thus became symbols of the "worthiness" and the work ethic of an entire race. Frederick Douglass invoked the "tremendous responsibility attaching to every colored man, now representing his race in Canada." Partially by virtue of this symbolism, blacks moved to build their own institutions and take control of fugitive relief from organizations dominated by white abolitionists. Organizations like the True Bands came out of this movement. But not all black organizations could follow the example of finding support solely within the black community; white abolitionist societies simply could tap greater resources.[24]

Despite the bitterness and frequent pettiness of the rivalries among black Canadian leaders, all stressed the same goal of an independent, self-reliant, prosperous black community. Most individual blacks kept their eye on the true prize even as the arguments over how to reach that goal roiled the black leadership. Like most white Canadians, black men and women wanted a house and land of their own. Property ownership represented the control of one's own destiny that was denied to those living in bondage. It constituted yet another great landmark on the road from slavery to freedom. Benjamin and Cecelia achieved this goal in March 1854, when they purchased a lot on Centre Street for 100 pounds.[25]

Around this same time, although the exact date is difficult to pin down, Cecelia passed another significant milestone in her life: she became a mother. She gave birth to a daughter in 1853 or 1854 and named her Mamie, a diminutive of Mary, after her mother. Thus in the eight years since she had fled slavery, Cecelia had built a family in freedom: she had taken a name of her own choosing, gotten legally married, purchased property, and seen her own child born free. Still, there was a piece missing—her mother and brother were still in Kentucky. To put slavery fully behind her, Cecelia would need Fanny's help.

So, beginning early in the 1850s, Cecelia—now in her early twenties—began to correspond with her former owner. Only Fanny's side of this correspondence survives in the archives, but as Fanny addresses Cecelia's concerns, it is possible to figure out the gist of Cecelia's letters. One theme runs through all of them—the status of her mother and the possibilities of her freedom. For slaves who escaped but left family behind, such inquiries and communication were precious, albeit tenuous, connections to their kin separated from them by the wall of bondage. For many, according to historian James Oliver Horton, the communication with kin was "almost as precious as freedom itself."[26]

Fanny's first letter is dated March 11, 1852, and is a response to one from Cecelia of a few days earlier. Fanny also refers to "other letters . . . at different times" from Cecelia to Fanny's father, indicating that Cecelia contacted the Thrustons prior to March 1852. Cecelia was evidently cautious about writing to her former owners, and thus used Foote as an intermediary for these first missives. She must have still had fears about revealing her precise location, recognizing that Charles William Thruston did not let slaves slip away from him easily.[27]

Cecelia had good reason to be hesitant. In the years since her escape, the United States had enacted the tough new Fugitive Slave Law. The Fugitive Slave Law of 1850 was part of a larger package of legislation, known as the Compromise of 1850, aimed at patching over the worsening sectional tensions between North and South. Southerners had insisted on a stronger federal Fugitive Slave Law to counter the widespread noncooperation of Northern courts and legislatures when it came to the rendition of fugitive slaves. The new law took the power to adjudicate slaveholders' claims on runaways away from state authorities and vested it in U.S. commissioners. The law prohibited alleged slaves from testifying in their own behalf in order to prove their freedom. It offered no jury trial, no right of habeas corpus, and no appeals. It also obligated every citizen to assist in the return of slaves to their masters and imposed severe penalties on those who aided fugitives or hindered their pursuit.[28]

The law was also startlingly effective. Chances were that if an alleged fugitive was arrested and brought to court, the captive would be returned to slavery. One study of 330 fugitive slave cases brought before federal commissioners between 1850 and 1860 found that the commissioners returned 296 alleged runaways to slavery. Of course, this figure does not count the large number who avoided capture and arrest. The Boston Vigilance Committee, which kept detailed records, helped more than 400 people between 1850 and 1860, many of them bound for Canada, escape the net cast by the slaveholders.[29]

Despite the risks in such an environment, Cecelia reached out to Fanny with "affectionate inquiries" about Mary and Edward. Her mother, Fanny told Cecelia, had been sold to someone else. "After my marriage she desired to be sold," Fanny wrote, but recently Mary had appealed to Fanny to buy her back. "She seems to be so much attached to us and was always so good a servant that I wished to do so, but her present owner was unwilling to part with her." Still, the two had frequent talks, often about Cecelia herself, and Mary "always in tears expresses a hope to see you once more," Fanny wrote. No doubt the news that Mary had been sold discouraged Cecelia's hopes that she could ever get her mother out of bondage.[30]

As for Cecelia's brother, Edward, now sixteen years old, Fanny had discouraging news of a different sort. The boy had suffered since birth with scrofula and had never grown out of it, as had once been hoped. Scrofula was one of many nineteenth-century terms for tubercular disease; it generally referred to tuberculosis of the bones and lymphatic glands, particularly in children. It is thought now that such cases result from drinking unpasteurized milk, and that may be how the bacteria initially infected Edward. Fanny wrote that Edward had grown, although she felt that Cecelia would still recognize him, "for his face has changed very little," but he still required frequent medical attention.[31]

Fanny then proceeded to update Cecelia on the changes in her own life—her marriage to Ballard and the birth of two of her sons. She went on to talk about the marriages and whereabouts of several aunts, uncles, and cousins—people in whom Cecelia probably was not much interested. "I can think of no other news concerning your friends that would interest you," she told Cecelia. Overall, the tone of the letter was light and chatty, as if Fanny were writing to a casual acquaintance. There was no offer of help—no feeling that Fanny herself bore any portion of responsibility to try to reunite Cecelia and her mother. Instead, she consigned it all to God's hands: "If it should be never your lot to meet your parent on earth may God in his mercy and love gather you together in Heaven." In the end, Fanny expressed the benign hope that Cecelia was happy, "much happier than when you were my property." This sentiment strikes the modern reader as almost comic, but given the slaveholders' positive self-image and the prevailing Southern image of slavery as a humane system, Fanny may have genuinely doubted whether freedom was preferable to slavery for Cecelia. The point here is not that Fanny was heartless or cruel, but that living in a slave society put a peculiar set of moral blinders in place when it came to the institution itself.[32]

Cecelia's initial effort to reunite her family thus bore little fruit. Her brother was sickly and her mother was no longer in the Thruston household. Fanny's next letter, dated August 2, 1855, may have given her more hope, however. It was written in response to a letter from Cecelia that dated from January 1855, after Mamie was born. While there had been no real change in the status of Cecelia's mother, the letter did show a change in Fanny's mindset. At the writing of this letter, Fanny had delivered four children, three boys and a girl. The second-oldest son, however, had died, as had Fanny's older brother, Sam, struck by lightning after a fishing trip. These losses may have accounted for the change of heart exhibited in the letter.[33]

Again, Cecelia had inquired about her family, and Fanny told her that Edward was dead. The scrofula "finally settled upon his lungs and he died last Christmas." As for her mother, Fanny reported that Mary's new owner had begun hiring her out. She "was anxious to live with me this year," Fanny wrote, "but we did not succeed in getting her." Her mother was well but looked older, Fanny reported. Mary had become quite attached to one of the Thrustons' slave girls, Alice, the daughter of Vira, who was presumably another Thruston household slave. Mary had raised Alice (Vira must have either died or been sold, although Fanny does not say), and the little girl had taken to calling the older woman Mother. Thus Mary's anxiety to live with Fanny may in fact have been a desire to be close to this adopted daughter.[34]

Fanny's change of heart showed up in the final paragraph of her letter. "I often think of you Cecelia; oftener, since the death of my brother; you were the companion of my childhood, I can never forget you, and far from reproaching you for leaving me, I think and always thought, it is a very natural desire of the slave to be free." She told Cecelia that she need have no fear of reenslavement, that she relinquished all claims to her. (Of course, Cecelia could never be completely free of such fears, since slave catchers and slave traders frequently took free blacks and resold them into slavery in the decade before the Civil War.) "I am and always will be a friend to the slave," wrote Fanny, "and denounce the system of slavery as diabolical, at variance with christianity."[35]

Sometime between 1852 and 1855, something had clearly happened in Fanny's life that made her rethink her previous easy acceptance of slavery. Her brother's freakish accidental death may have contributed to a general mood of introspection. Perhaps having lost her younger siblings, her mother, a young son, and now her only surviving brother, Fanny began to sympathize more with Cecelia's separation from her own family, and realized that she stood as an obstacle to their reunification. Fanny had always been a pious woman, and her altered view of slavery had strongly religious overtones. It is, however, extremely difficult to pinpoint any precise local development that might have triggered a change in Fanny's religious beliefs regarding slavery. Fanny worshiped at staid Christ Church Episcopal, which had never stood out as a bastion of antislavery sentiment.

It is impossible to know precisely what Fanny was hearing from the pulpit of Christ Church during those years. James Craik served as rector of the church, a position he assumed in 1844 and held until his death in 1882. His long tenure raised the profile of the Louisville congregation in the national church, and Craik became an important and influential clergyman. He played an instrumental role in keeping Kentucky in the Union camp during the Civil War. He is also credited with preventing an Episcopal split into Northern and Southern branches, a split that other denominations—notably the Methodists—did not avoid. A gifted orator and writer, Craik wrote numerous books and pamphlets on everything from local and church history to pressing social and political issues to theology. His writings on slavery and the sectional crisis offer some clues as to the point of view that Fanny might have been hearing from her pastor. Craik described slavery as an "evil, great and sore," and Fanny may have taken these words to heart in reaching her conclusion that the institution was "diabolical." But Craik's influence was ambiguous, for he was no friend of emancipation. The evils of slavery redounded mostly to the nation and to the slaveholders, who bore the responsibility of exercising "care and guardianship" over their African American bondservants. For the slaves, Craik argued, bondage was "almost an unmixed blessing." Slavery, Craik said, was a great school in which blacks were slowly being civilized. "A race of barbarians, gradually degraded by many thousand years of ignorance and brutishness to the lowest stage of humanity, has thus been placed in intimate contact, and under the constant and authoritative superintendence and government, of the most enlightened and civilized race upon the globe. . . . The cultivated and master race [are] the friends, protectors, and instructors of the inferior race." Eventually, someday, blacks would be ready for freedom and self-government, but not yet. Raising up an entire race from barbarism took many generations of uplift. As opposed to the benefits reaped by blacks under slavery, emancipation "would be a reassignment of the whole race to their original savage state, aggravated by their newly-acquired vices and capacities for evil." The result would be misery for the freed slaves. The only beneficent alternative was for Southerners to continue holding slaves, to recognize that it was their unique historical burden "to accept the care and guardianship of them," while the black race continued its slow cultural ascent. Abolitionism Craik therefore denounced as a "stupid crime."[36]

While Fanny's changing point of view on slavery may thus have been shaped somewhat by Craik, her apparent sympathy for the "natural desire of the slave to be free" seems unlikely to have been guided by her pastor. Perhaps the increasing intensity of the national debate over slavery, led by the Christian rhetoric of evangelical abolitionists, led Fanny privately to reexamine the relationship between her own spiritual beliefs and slavery. Again, no definite evidence supports this conclusion. Craik had little but undisguised hostility for abolitionism and the theology that supported it, and Fanny remained a dutiful member of Christ Church her entire life.

There was also one great contradiction to the sentiments Fanny expressed in her letter to Cecelia. This was the fact that Andrew and

Fanny Ballard actually increased their slaveholdings during the decade of the 1850s. According to the 1850 county tax list, Andrew Ballard owned two slaves and Fanny's father owned four, meaning there were six in the household. In 1860, the tax assessor counted nine slaves owned by Ballard and three owned by Charles Thruston, for a total of twelve in the household. Fanny may not have played an active part in acquiring more slaves for the family, but her newfound antislavery feelings did not extend to the point of challenging her own husband's acquisitions of human property.[37]

For Cecelia, Fanny's August 2 letter must have offered a mixture of disappointment and hope. The disappointment lay in the brute facts about her family—her brother was dead and her mother was still beyond her reach. The hope came from Fanny's changed outlook. If Fanny sincerely believed that slavery was "diabolical," then maybe she would not be a roadblock to Mary's freedom should Mary ever return to her service. Maybe Fanny would even free her slaves voluntarily, as her relative (through the Clark side of the family) Dr. John Croghan had. It was a lot of maybes, but it was better than nothing.[38]

The next letter from Fanny was dated January 25, 1857, and she wrote it in response to a letter from Cecelia dated January 16. In her letter Fanny made reference to a previous letter that Cecelia evidently never received. "I wrote to you about three months ago by your mother's particular request. . . . I see now that you live in the country three miles out from Toronto, which of course is the reason you did not receive it. Your Mother some time afterwards, told me she heard that you had moved to Chicago in Illinois."[39]

Fanny's references to Cecelia's movements contrast with the archival records regarding the Holmes family. According to the records, Benjamin Holmes lived a remarkably stable life. The land registry and tax assessment records showed that Benjamin and Cecelia owned and resided on their Centre Street property throughout the 1850s. The city directory entries likewise placed the Holmeses on Centre Street. But Fanny's information indicated that Cecelia was not staying still. What do these moves mean? The address "three miles out from Toronto" is the easiest to explain. Cecelia most likely worked as a household servant during her years in Canada, and she may have lived in with her employer for a time. It is impossible to be sure, but the "country address" was probably the residence of her employer. As for the move to Chicago, this may have been merely an unsubstantiated rumor. Or perhaps Cecelia made a brief sojourn to the city as she considered whether to move back to the United States. Or perhaps—to continue a line of speculation begun earlier—she traveled on behalf of the abolitionist cause.[40]

Fanny told Cecelia that it was Mary who had prompted her to write the letter that went awry. And indeed Fanny's letter of January 25 contained an interesting proposal regarding Cecelia's mother. At the end of 1855, Mary's new master had announced his plan to move to New York, and so Mary was put up for sale. "She came to us repeating her desire to live with us," Fanny wrote, "and requested us to buy her." The uncertainties of sale always produced anxieties in the slave population; many feared separation from their families or had heard the horror stories about plantation labor in the Deep South or worried that a new master might be harsh or cruel. Mary doubtless felt these anxieties and moved to counter them. She must have also thought that sale to the Ballards would mean continued contact with Alice and perhaps with Cecelia. If Mary simply vanished in an anonymous sale to some new owner, she and Cecelia would surely lose touch; Fanny was the bridge that connected mother and daughter. Thus Mary approached the Ballards about buying her; she initiated the process. These efforts to structure her own life within the narrow constraints of slavery accord with a great deal of recent scholarship, which has uncovered a vast amount of data on how slaves exercised personal agency even within the confines of bondage.[41]

Mary's initiative and autonomy, of course, were strictly limited by the prerogatives of the master. Her desires did not matter if the Ballards did not have the money or the will to buy her. Fortunately for Mary, the Ballards were willing "to receive her again into our family," Fanny reported. "Mr. Ballard became her purchaser for the sum of six hundred ($600) dollars." Fanny's use of the term "family" was significant; it implied that this was not just an economic transaction. It was an extension of familial bonds to include a new dependent. Scholars who study antebellum Southern family life have found this phrasing repeated over and over, concluding that the concept of family among upper-class whites often meant the entire circle of a man's dependents, including slaves.[42]

But Mary was not merely eager to have Fanny tell Cecelia that once again she had become the Ballards' property. It was the next part of the letter that must have stirred Cecelia's hopes. Andrew Ballard had agreed, upon buying Mary, that he would free her at the end of six years. At the time Fanny was writing, one year had already passed. Mary, Fanny wrote to Cecelia, "is very anxious, very impatient to see you, . . . and requested me to make the following proposition to you—which is—that you will assist her in raising the sum of $500 necessary in securing her immediate freedom." It had been five years since Cecelia initiated contact with Fanny, and the correspondence had yielded dramatic results. By 1857 Fanny had moved from feeling that slavery was perhaps preferable to freedom to pangs of conscience to opening an avenue to freedom for Cecelia's mother.[43]

Purchasing the freedom of one's family members was a common aspiration for blacks who had escaped or avoided slavery. But blacks operated at a notable disadvantage when trying to purchase their own or their family's freedom. Owners controlled the terms of the transaction—the price, the payments, the time limits. Agreements were often informal, stated—as Fanny's was—in a letter or verbally, and thus were subject to different interpretations by slave and master. Since blacks had no legal recourse, the master's interpretation usually carried the day. Still, there are numerous examples of Kentucky blacks who did purchase either their own or their loved ones' freedom, so Cecelia could not have been completely without hope.[44]

However, $500 must have seemed almost an unobtainable amount. The 1859 Toronto tax assessment listed Benjamin Holmes as a waiter with an annual salary of $200 per year and with a house valued at $80. Even if Cecelia brought in an extra $50 worth of income that escaped the tax assessor's notice, the Holmeses would have to save half their income over four years to accumulate $500.

The house and land were assets, but just prior to Fanny's letter, the entire lot had been mortgaged for 100 pounds. Probably the money was used to build a second house on the same lot, which in later years would be rented out. But in 1858, Benjamin and Cecelia mortgaged the lot again, this time for 25 pounds. What they intended to do with the money is impossible to know, but perhaps it was aimed at buying Mary's freedom.[45]

Fanny seemed to appreciate the magnitude of the task Cecelia faced. She reassured her former maid that Mary was "a superior cook & laundress" who would soon be able to repay any amount Cecelia raised by working at a hotel or boardinghouse. In another letter, dated about a month later, when it was clear that Cecelia was having problems raising the money, Fanny told her to "send whatever sum you can afford, and we will credit Mary with it by hastening the time of her freedom."[46]

Fanny made no offer to reduce the price, no gesture toward making it easier for Mary to obtain her freedom. And it is against this economic pragmatism that masters' paternalism and "family feeling" toward their slaves must be weighed. These dependents were also property, and therefore economic assets to be managed shrewdly. "She enjoys good health and is a fine servant," Fanny told Cecelia, almost as if she were trying to persuade Cecelia that Mary was a good investment. "Nothing but her desire to be free, to live with you, would induce me to part with her." Whatever antislavery sentiments Fanny might harbor, she was not about to give Mary away and waste $600.[47]

Fanny's last surviving letter to Cecelia was dated August 11, 1859, two and a half years after her letter putting forward the proposition that Cecelia buy Mary's freedom. The letter was a response to one from Cecelia that Fanny had received "some time ago." Fanny had been ill and had recently given birth to her fifth child—Rogers Clark—so she had not felt up to replying right away. The bulk of this final letter was taken up with short chatty updates about Fanny's various relatives and acquaintances whom Cecelia might have known. In the penultimate paragraph, however, she addressed the issue that must have been paramount in Cecelia's mind. "You inquired . . . if your Mother still lives with us. She does and is very well. You spoke of 'raising money to get her,' let me know in your next how much you think you can raise."[48]

Mary had by then progressed halfway through her promised term of service to the Ballards. The cost to free her had shrunk to just $300, according to the initial terms of the agreement. Yet the long quietus in the correspondence between Fanny and Cecelia indicates that Cecelia must have had trouble finding the money. Significantly, Canada's economy had been rocked by the Panic of 1857, which made the promised land a more difficult place to earn a living. With this letter, Fanny showed that she had gone as far down the antislavery road as she was willing to go. She would free Mary when Cecelia raised the necessary funds to purchase her freedom or when the agreed-upon term of service expired. Compensated emancipation—freedom for the slave once the slaveholder's investment was repaid—was a fairly popular position among many moderate slaveholders of the Upper South in the years immediately preceding the Civil War. Fanny seemed to adhere to this view.[49]

There is no manumission record in the Jefferson County minute books for Mary. By the end of 1861, when her term would have expired, the Civil War was already in full swing. With Union troops occupying the northern part of Kentucky, slavery had begun to disintegrate within the Commonwealth, as hundreds of slaves took advantage of wartime conditions to slip away from their masters. Mary may have been one of these early self-liberators. Alternatively, the pressures of the war may have led the Ballards to postpone or renege on the promise of freedom for Mary, forcing her to wait until the issuance of the Emancipation Proclamation in 1863 or even the end of the war before she could gain her freedom. Ballard family records make no mention of how or when Mary became a free woman.[50]

So Cecelia failed in her bid to reunite her family in freedom. She had achieved much to give concrete meaning to the end of her bondage, but this final act could not be realized. Her failure must have driven home to Cecelia the continued hold that Fanny had on her. The other milestones she had gained largely by dint of her own effort. But to secure Mary's freedom required the cooperation of her old mistress. Fanny had held out the possibility that such cooperation might be forthcoming, but only if Cecelia met Fanny's terms. Despite winning her own freedom, Cecelia still felt the power wielded by the slaveholding class.

Cecelia was certainly not the first former slave to correspond with her former owner. Indeed, it was quite common, and very often concerned the same issues treated by Cecelia—the health and status of loved ones left behind in bondage and the chances for their freedom. One former Kentucky slave, Jackson Whitney, wrote to his former master arguing that as restitution for the harsh treatment Whitney had suffered, the master ought to free Whitney's wife and children and send them up to Canada to rejoin him. Another former Kentucky slave, Horace Hawkins, had a very similar experience to Cecelia's but with happier results. Once settled in Canada, he opened a correspondence with his former master about buying members of his own family and succeeded in liberating several of them. Hawkins then bought his own freedom—allowing him to return safely to the United States—for $200, after dickering his former owner down from $500. Henry Bibb—befitting his role as a newspaper editor—was a prolific correspondent with his former owners. Unlike the largely civil and amicable letters that passed between Fanny and Cecelia, however, Bibb's letters to his former master raged at the destruction of Bibb's family, at the harsh treatment Bibb's mother received, and at the religious hypocrisy of his former master.[51]

The act of letter writing itself raises some interesting questions. It implies that Cecelia was literate, although without access to her actual letters, it is impossible to know with certainty. (Perhaps she dictated them to a literate acquaintance.) If she was literate, did she learn to read and write before she escaped? Did Fanny teach her? House slaves and urban slaves were more likely to achieve literacy than were rural field hands. Alternatively, Cecelia may have taken the opportunities for education that Canada offered. Like former slaves in the United States after emancipation, black exiles in Canada viewed education as critical to securing their freedom and seized hungrily upon educational opportunities they had been denied under slavery. Cecelia's letter writing may have been aimed, in part, at showing her former mistress that she had bettered her condition since fleeing bondage.

Some historians have probed the meaning behind letter writing, which lay at the heart of so much nineteenth-century communication. These scholars have mostly been interested in letters from European immigrants back to their countries of origin, although the late Robert Starobin explored some of these same themes with his groundbreaking collection of African American correspondence. These studies have suggested that letters became critical means for interpersonal communication and thus continuity of personal identity under circumstances of separation. David Gerber wrote that since a sense of personal identity depended partly on the "continuity . . . of personal relationships with our most significant others," letter writing became the vehicle for maintaining those relationships and thus that personal identity. "It is the relationship that is the subject of the personal letter."[52]

These conclusions obviously become more complicated in the context of former slaves and their masters. As Cecelia constructed a new life in freedom, did her sense of personal identity remain constant or did the change in status from slave to free woman fundamentally change her sense of self? Which identity was she affirming by the act of letter writing—the old Cecelia or the new free Cecelia? Most likely, this was not an either-or proposition. Cecelia's letters validated and proved her new identity, yet at the same time affirmed a continuity with her slave past. In some ways, the maintenance of a relationship with her mother required the latter.

The maintenance of that relationship illustrates another complicating factor introduced by slavery. To gain access to her mother, to reaffirm that central mother/daughter relationship and thus her identity as Mary's daughter, Cecelia was required to go through Fanny. There was no direct means of communication, as there was with immigrant letters. To correspond with Mary through Fanny meant, of course, to acknowledge a continuity with Cecelia's past status as a slave, even as it also affirmed her new relationship with Fanny as a free woman. Even though she might be free, Cecelia could never be completely loosed from the bonds of slavery.

Whatever the conscious or unconscious motivations behind her letters to Fanny, Cecelia apparently ceased her correspondence around 1859. Around this time, the promised land did not look quite so promising. First, as mentioned before, a Canadian economic downturn had made it more difficult to make ends meet. Second, the 1850s witnessed a notable change in the attitude of white Canadians toward African American exiles. There had always been isolated instances of racial prejudice and discrimination, but the racial atmosphere grew markedly more hostile during the 1850s. The 1850 Fugitive Slave Law triggered an exodus of African Americans from their no longer safe havens in the Northern states to the safer refuge of Canada. One abolitionist group in Canada estimated an influx of between four thousand and five thousand blacks in the first several months after the law was passed. With the growth of the refugee population, white Canadians, concerned about the influx, became less tolerant. "People may talk about the horrors of slavery as much as they choose," one newspaper wrote, "but fugitive slaves are by no means a desirable class of immigrants for Canada, especially when they come in great numbers."[53]

White hostility was also driven by other factors. The same community-building activities in which blacks took such pride indicated to whites that the refugees might become a permanent minority within Canada. In addition, as cheap Irish labor became more widely available in Canada through European immigration, the economic need for an inflow of cheap black labor lessened. Soon demands for separate black schools and for denying blacks the right to buy property became more common. It should be pointed out, however, that in the eastern part of Canada West, and especially in Toronto, racial prejudice was less marked than further to the west.[54]

As the overall racial environment around her worsened, Cecelia suffered a much more personal setback. Her husband, Benjamin Holmes, died on August 26, 1859, just two weeks after Fanny sent her last letter. Holmes must have known he was fatally ill, for he had dictated his will just one month before. In it, he bequeathed to his two sons the house and lot on Centre Street adjacent to the house and lot in which he resided. His residence and its lot, including all the furnishings, he bequeathed to Cecelia for "her own use and benefit" during the remainder of her lifetime. After her death, the property was to go to the boys.[55]

Judging from the bequests in his will, Benjamin no doubt expected his family to stay in Canada, and the 1861 Canadian census did indeed find Cecelia, Mamie, and the two boys residing in one of the houses on Centre Street, with the adjacent house rented out. But Cecelia again contravened expectations. She packed up her family after the census taker left and moved south, back to the United States, abandoning Canada forever.[56]

Chapter 6

Fanny: The Civil War in Louisville

As Cecelia moved south, Fanny stayed put. She continued to live in her father's house on Walnut Street, devoting herself to her husband and children. In 1860, after Cecelia's husband had died and when Cecelia herself was about to leave Canada, Fanny had four young children in Louisville. Her youngest son—Rogers Clark—was just two years old; Samuel was five; Abby, the only girl, was seven; and her oldest, Charles, was ten. Andrew was practicing law and managing his own—and Charles W. Thruston's—real estate holdings.

In 1860 the nation was about to tear itself in two over the issues of slavery, states' rights, and the indissolubility of the Union. One of the frustrating things in writing about these years in the Ballards' life, however, is that they left very little archival material behind reflecting on the war years. Through official records and other accounts, it is possible to discern the bare outlines of their life during the war, but it is most difficult to determine how they felt about the conflict or the issues that triggered it and followed in its wake. The small cache of archived letters from the family—written by Andrew Ballard to various descendants of the Jesup family, the relatives Fanny had visited before traveling to Niagara—overwhelmingly deal with land prices, rents, and other mundane business matters.

The result is that their story relies heavily on context and logical supposition based on what is known about them rather than on direct documentary evidence. Putting what is known about their living situation together with what Louisville went through during the war allows some educated guesswork about the Ballards' wartime experiences. It is an incomplete and perhaps unsatisfying portrait, but it offers a reasonable depiction of their lives.

As the country hurtled toward sectional conflict and civil war, Fanny and Andrew probably believed that some sort of mutual understanding would be reached between the two sides. Surely the questions swirling around the rights of the Southern states to have chattel slavery could be finessed politically, as had been done in previous compromises. If the Ballards were like most Louisvillians—indeed, most Kentuckians—they wanted to have it both ways: they wanted the Union to be preserved, and they wanted slavery. The hardening positions on both sides that would force a choice between one or the other probably seemed to them irrational and extreme.

Fanny was a churchgoing woman, and her views on the political conflict engulfing the country may have been influenced by the voice she heard from the pulpit of Christ Church Episcopal. The Reverend James Craik did leave behind a record of his views on the political questions of the day. In a well-circulated speech before the Kentucky House in December 1859, Craik lashed out equally at abolitionists' meddling with slavery and at fire-eaters' talk of secession. If abolitionism was a "stupid crime" in his eyes, rebellion against the government was a "more flagrant stupidity." Craik branded abolitionist sentiment a "distempered fanaticism." Abolitionist forces wanted to gain control of the national government in order to regulate "the supposed sins of their fellow-citizens." This was unconstitutional nonsense, Craik insisted. The national government had no power to determine domestic relations in the states and no power to override property rights in the territories. The abolitionist argument for national action against slavery, Craik said, violated the foundational principles of the nation. "Now let us suppose the worst: That a controlling majority of the people become abolitionized," continued Craik, "and determine to use the Federal government as the instrument of perpetrating their folly." Even then, the solution was not to dissolve the Union. The solution was within the Constitution, which provided a remedy for an overreaching federal government. That remedy was the states. It was only within the Union that the balance between state sovereignty and national sovereignty was maintained. That balance was the "foundation of American freedom." Dissolve the Union and there was no restraint on federal power. Preserve the Union and the state sovereignty enshrined in the Constitution could check any threat posed by an ascendant federal government. The states' powers to tax, to arm their people, and to form militias gave force and meaning to political positions based on "reason, and argument, and justice and right." Strong state governments, Craik added, could "control even the most senseless of all senseless things, religious fanaticism." Craik's voice was just one among many that Fanny would have heard, but it expressed the widely held desires of Kentuckians: to preserve the Union and to preserve the states' rights to maintain slavery. It was a viewpoint that seemed increasingly irrelevant as the sectional crisis worsened.[1]

Louisville's—and Kentucky's—desire to have their cake and eat it came from the two great cultural influences that shaped the state. Kentuckians set great store by the Union but harbored strong Southern sympathies at the same time. The Southern roots of many of its citizens, the Southern orientation of its commerce, and its slaveholding all bound Kentucky to the Southern cause. At the same time, as the first western frontier, as a border state that did business with both sections, and as a state whose men had fought and died to preserve the nation in the War of 1812 and to expand it during the Mexican War, Kentucky felt its destiny was ineluctably tied to the Union.[2]

The Ballards no doubt felt these contrasting tugs between their Unionist sympathies and their Southern roots. Some years after Andrew Ballard's death, Rogers Clark characterized his father as "strong for the Union, and anti-Slavery." Certainly in terms of his political commitments there seems little reason to second-guess the first part of that description. Ballard supported the Whig Party before it disintegrated during the 1850s in the heat of the debate over slavery. The Whigs were a nationalist party, pledged to the preservation of the Union. In 1842–1843, Ballard even served a term as state representative for Louisville under the Whig banner. Like many Kentucky lawyers, he staunchly admired Henry Clay, the Lexington-based lawyer turned national icon who dominated the

Whig Party before the war. Clay gained prominence as the "Great Compromiser" who cobbled together agreements acceptable to both North and South. Through complicated and ultimately unworkable arrangements like the Missouri Compromise of 1820 and the Compromise of 1850, Clay regionalized slavery in the South and tried to immunize it from federal interference. The great political bargains engineered by Clay delayed disunion for a generation.[3]

But while they supported the Union, both Andrew and Fanny traced their roots back to Virginia and took pride in that Southern heritage. When Andrew sought new business opportunities shortly after they were married, he looked not to the industrializing cities of the North but to the great Southern entrepôt of New Orleans. And, of course, the Ballards continued to own slaves—a fact that undercuts the second part of Rogers Clark's description of his father. If Andrew Ballard opposed slavery, he did so only in his mind, for he never took any action regarding his own slaves that showed anything but acceptance of the institution of bondage. The county tax rolls for 1860 listed nine slaves belonging to Andrew Ballard and three slaves belonging to Charles William Thruston. The federal slave census in that same year broke down Ballard's slaves by gender and age: four males (aged ten, thirteen, eighteen, and forty) and five females (aged two, eighteen, thirty, fifty, and eighty). The fifty-year-old was probably Mary, if she was still with them.[4]

Thus, despite the repudiation of slavery in her 1855 letter to Cecelia, Fanny was still managing the household slaves as the Civil War loomed. She was doing so, moreover, as the institution itself crumbled around her. During the 1850s, the number of slaves in Louisville declined by some 10 percent, from 5,432 to 4,903, a mere 7.5 percent of the city's total 1860 population. Well over half the remaining slaves were women, as male slaves were sold off to the countryside and the plantations of the Deep South. It seemed that slavery in Louisville was dying naturally under the pressures of urbanism and industrial development. The death throes, however, had not quite reached the Ballard household.[5]

Befitting its caught-in-the-middle status, Louisville tried to finesse the 1860 election by voting neither for Abraham Lincoln, who was too affiliated with the North and the antislavery cause, nor for Kentuckian John Breckenridge, who was too cozy with the uncompromising slaveholders of the South. Only ninety-one voters in the city cast ballots for Lincoln, and while it is impossible to know for certain, Andrew Ballard was probably not among them. Most likely, he went for the candidate favored by other pro-Union, pro-slavery Louisvillians—John Bell of Tennessee. Bell's Constitutional Union Party stood for only one thing—the preservation of the Union— and was significantly silent on the slavery issue. Bell's party drew on a mix of traditional Southern Whigs—like Andrew Ballard—and remnants of the nativist American Party of the 1850s. Bell polled 3,823 votes in Louisville, winning the city. Second place went to the old-line Democratic candidate, Stephen Douglas.[6]

When the shooting finally started in April 1861, Kentucky—and Louisville with it—tried to remain officially neutral. Gung-ho partisans of both sides left the city to enlist in their preferred armies. Five companies of Confederate volunteers departed the city for points south that first April, while Union supporters set up a recruiting station and training camp just across the river in Clarksville, Indiana. The Louisville City Council, meanwhile, appropriated $50,000 to defend the city from attacks by either side. At the state level, the governor declared that Kentucky would not take sides in the conflict.[7]

Over the fall of 1861, however, the state's and the city's neutrality eroded and both began to tilt in favor of the Union. Louisville elected a Unionist slate to the state General Assembly in August. Then in September armies from both sides began to jockey for control of the Mississippi River in the far western part of the state. The Confederates occupied the small town of Columbus, and the Federals occupied Paducah in response, followed soon after by Union occupation of other towns along the Ohio, including Louisville. The Confederates then sent an army into southeastern Kentucky to close off Union advance routes through the mountains. In the end, the state legislators instructed the governor to order only the Confederates out of Kentucky. The state—and the city with it—had joined the Union cause.[8]

Naturally, not all of Louisville's citizens embraced this decision. Some fifty years ago, local historian Robert McDowell titled his book on Louisville's Civil War history *City of Conflict*, not because there were any great battles fought in or over the city itself but because of the stark partisan divide that existed within it. While McDowell noted that the majority of Louisvillians wanted to stay in the Union, "secessionists dominated the upper class. Assertive, opinionated, boisterous, and defiant, they made considerably more noise than their numbers warranted." These Southern partisans drew heavily from the "Main Street wholesale merchant princes," while the pro-Union ranks were filled with industrialists, workers, smaller retailers, and professionals like the Ballards.[9]

The boisterousness of Louisville's Southern partisans did not sit well with the Union troops who flowed in increasing numbers into the city. Having sided with the Union, the city became an important jumping-off spot for troops headed south. By October 1861, Louisville was awash in soldiers from various states north of the Ohio River. By January 1862, some eighty thousand soldiers were in the city. Bored, waiting for orders, and away from home for the first time, many of the soldiers turned drunk and disorderly. Fights between soldiers and locals became common, and Louisville, like Kentucky in general, came to be viewed as largely hostile territory by federal troops and military administrators.[10]

Andrew Ballard planted himself firmly on the Unionist side of the political divide in his city. Early in the war, this opened up new opportunities for him. When Southern-leaning government officials felt they could no longer serve the federal government in good conscience, they abandoned their posts to head south. In filling these newly vacated posts, the Lincoln administration looked for strong Union men. One of Kentucky's resident Southern-leaning officials was the judge of the federal district court, Thomas Monroe. In September 1861, the U.S. district attorney in Kentucky anxiously queried the attorney general as to the whereabouts of Judge Monroe, reporting that he had failed to show up for the most recent term of court held at Covington, Kentucky. It turned out that Monroe had headed south, as had the clerk of the court. In their places,

President Lincoln appointed Andrew Ballard and his brother, Bland. Andrew became clerk of the U.S. district and circuit courts and Bland became district court judge. Given the partisan nature of most political appointments at the time, Lincoln's actions no doubt cemented the Ballards' loyalty to the new Republican Party.[11]

Andrew's position as a federal employee helped stabilize the family's finances at an uncertain time. With the secession of the Southern states, much of Louisville's economic lifeblood drained away. Part of the reason the large Main Street merchants were so avidly pro-Southern was because that was where their customers were located. The influx of soldiers and federal military supplies perked up the economy, but the war-driven boom was less grand than many expected. In August 1861, Andrew—serving as local agent for some of the Jesup family's Louisville landholdings—wrote that "rents have fallen in this city at least one half and it is difficult to collect even that half."[12]

While Andrew's official position provided regular income, the family could not be spared all the vagaries of the war. Fanny and the children would have been subject to the periodic war scares and threats of invasion that rocked the city during the conflict. Once Kentucky cast its lot officially with the Union in the fall of 1861, Confederate armies marched on Louisville. On September 17, they seized Bowling Green and quickly moved north to gain control of the Louisville & Nashville Railroad. Louisville prepared to defend itself, sending out four thousand men to stop the Confederate advance. Many civil and military officials held out little hope that the city could be defended if the Confederates attacked. Fortunately, it did not need to be. The anticipated battle of Louisville never happened. Louisville's soldiers chased off some reconnaissance parties, but the Southern army decided to dig in for the winter at Bowling Green, content for the moment to consolidate its hold on the railroad and on the southern half of the state. Following Union victories in the southeastern mountains, the Confederates abandoned Bowling Green in February 1862.[13]

But they had not quite abandoned the hope of taking Kentucky. In August 1862, Confederate forces moved back into the state with the aim of taking Louisville. Since the first overt threat to the city, Louisville had been transformed into an important logistics center and recruiting depot. Given the city's importance as a gathering point for troops and matériel before they moved south, a successful Confederate takeover could have changed the course of events in the western theater of the war.[14]

The Southern armies came close to taking the city. Confederate forces occupied Lexington and, for a brief period, Frankfort. Louisville braced for an assault, building breastworks and digging trenches. Fresh troops were dispatched to the city, and volunteers were organized for self-defense. By mid-September, Confederate raiding parties were in nearby Shepherdsville. On September 26, five hundred Confederate cavalry captured fifty Union soldiers at Eighteenth and Oak streets in Louisville. The commanding general in Louisville, William "Bull" Nelson, ordered that all women, children, and Southern sympathizers be sent out of Louisville if the Confederates showed that they were going to attack the city.[15]

Louisville's wharf became a mob scene. Fanny may have been in the crowd, attempting to cross the river with her children. "Men, women, and children, in a panic of fright, were fleeing from the city," wrote one observer, "and Louisville was in a howling uproar." All manner of conveyance—from fine carriages to wheelbarrows—waited at the wharf to be ferried across the Ohio. The Confederate general P. G. T. Beauregard promised to build a fortress that would command the Ohio and threatened to destroy the Louisville-Portland canal "so completely that future travelers would hardly know where it was." For his part, General Nelson threatened to burn the city to the ground rather than let the Confederates take it.[16]

The invading Confederate force was being pursued by Union forces under General Don Carlos Buell. The Union army had taken Nashville in February 1862 and now found itself hurriedly marching northward to catch up with the Confederate army headed for Louisville. Unless Buell outflanked the Confederate forces and beat them to Louisville, it seemed likely that the city would be in for a siege.[17]

On September 21, a newspaper reporter scouting out the scene saw a huge cloud of dust coming toward Louisville. The source was the ten-mile-long string of Union troops and supplies under Buell. Outmarching the Confederates, Buell reached Louisville on September 25, refreshed his troops, and pondered the Confederates' next move. Over the next few days, there were small clashes on the outskirts of Louisville, but the great battle for the city was never joined. Instead, Buell marched his forces out of the city and took on the Southern armies at Perryville on October 8. The bloodiest battle of the war in Kentucky, Perryville ended with a Confederate withdrawal, and Louisville was not seriously threatened again for the duration of the war.[18]

With the immediate threat passed and his family safely back home, Andrew may have begun to feel, as a Lincoln appointee, increasingly isolated from his fellow citizens. By September 1862, given the overall poor performance by the Union armies in the war and the growing disillusionment with the administration among moderate Unionists, it could not have been altogether comfortable serving the administration. Several events in the latter part of 1862 contributed to the disenchantment among Louisville's pro-Union, pro-slavery contingent. Many of those who had rallied to the Union cause watched in dismay at what they viewed as the radicalization of the Republican Party. In their view, moderate Unionists were being marginalized within the party in favor of crush-the-South abolitionists. They found support for their perspective with the murder of General Nelson by an aggrieved member of his staff shortly after Buell's forces rescued the city from Confederate invasion.

General Nelson was a Kentuckian who had worked hard to keep the state in the Union but who opposed the abolition of slavery. Nelson had fought in the Mexican War and had been put in charge of organizing Kentucky's volunteers early in the Civil War. He led troops at the battle of Shiloh and the siege of Corinth, Mississippi, in the summer of 1862. Put in charge of Kentucky's defenses against the Confederate invasion, he took a bullet while trying to rally his dispirited troops at the battle of Richmond. He established his headquarters at Louisville's Galt House and began, under Buell's orders, to organize the defense of the city.

Nelson had earned his nickname Bull because of both his size and his temper. While his disciplinary tactics did not endear him to the troops he commanded, he was respected by Kentucky's moderate Unionists as a native son and as a man who represented their interests. In late September 1862, after the immediate threat of a Confederate takeover had been averted but while the potential for an attack on the city still loomed, Nelson quarreled with the ironically named General Jefferson Davis of Indiana. Davis, unable to reach the command assigned him under Buell, had offered Nelson his help in organizing the city's defense. Nelson gave him command of the city militia. The quarrel began when Nelson asked Davis how many men were in his brigade. "About twenty-five hundred," Davis responded. The imprecision of the answer outraged Nelson. "God damn you, don't you know, Sir, you should furnish me with the exact number?" He then suspended Davis from command and threatened to have him arrested.[19]

Davis retreated across the river to Jeffersonville, where he conferred with his army colleagues and shared his complaints about Nelson. He was told to return to Louisville and report directly to Buell. On September 29, Davis showed up at the Galt House to find Buell and almost immediately ran into Nelson. Davis had powerful friends in the Indiana Republican establishment, and he asked the Radical Republican governor of Indiana, Oliver Morton, to serve as a witness to his conversation with Nelson. Davis then accused Nelson of abusing his position as a superior officer. Nelson angrily denied it, and Davis reminded him of his threat to have Davis arrested. Nelson lost his temper. He struck Davis with the back of his hand, shouting, "There, damn you! Take that." Davis left the room, telling Nelson that he had not heard the last of him. Three minutes later, Davis returned, armed with a borrowed pistol. Confronting the unarmed Nelson from a distance of about ten yards, Davis fired. The bullet entered Nelson's heart, and within a half hour he was dead. Davis was not court-martialed or ever put on trial. He was eventually restored to command on the grounds that the shooting was done in self-defense, despite the fact that Nelson had not had a weapon.[20]

While some of Nelson's troops were pleased by the old tyrant's death, many of the moderates in Louisville's Unionist ranks were not. The way they saw it, Nelson had been murdered because he was a Kentuckian, because he opposed abolition, and because he resisted the Radical elements within the Republican Party. His murderer walked scot-free because he was a darling of the Radicals and had friends in high places in the Indiana Republican Party.[21]

A far greater provocation to the loyalties of Louisville's pro-Union, pro-slavery Republicans, however, was in the works. Although in the heat of the invasion scare it passed relatively unnoticed, the issuance of the Emancipation Proclamation on September 22, 1862, changed the objectives of the war. The proclamation declared that as of January 1, 1863, all slaves held in states in rebellion against the United States would be "thenceforward, and forever free." Now the war to preserve the Union would also be a war to destroy slavery. Although it did not technically disturb slavery in Kentucky—since the state was not in rebellion—the Emancipation Proclamation made it clear that the institution would not survive the conflict. It placed the Union army and the national government firmly on the side of abolition.

Kentucky's Republicans, who still clung to the hope that both the Union and slavery might be preserved, were disappointed and outraged. Some Kentucky army officers resigned their commissions to protest the proclamation. One of them was Dr. Henry F. Kalfus, a major in the Fifteenth Kentucky Infantry. "My enlistment was for the purpose of suppressing a rebellion only. Since President Lincoln has seen fit to issue an Emancipation Proclamation, I decline to participate further in a war aimed at freeing the negro." Kalfus's resignation was refused, and the army dismissed him instead. When the former officer arrived in Louisville, however, he was greeted with acclaim. Lincoln's friend Joshua Speed forecast that the proclamation "will do no good; most probably much harm," and he urged Lincoln not to issue it.[22]

Lincoln touched off another storm of protest when he decided in December 1862 to allow the enlistment of blacks into the army. So strong was the outrage in Kentucky that he held off implementing the decision in the state until March 1864. Nonetheless, the offer of freedom for enlistment sparked an exodus of male slaves into other states and into Union army camps. Pro-Union, pro-slavery Republicans fumed that Lincoln was destroying the institution of slavery after promising not to disturb it.

Lincoln's actions no doubt had an impact in the Ballard household. Blacks throughout the city were aware of the policy developments, and they knew slavery was tottering. Fanny's control over the servants probably became attenuated, as both she and the slaves realized that her power was no longer supported by the laws and customs of the society around her. But slaves they remained still. According to the Ballards' property tax returns during the war years, eight slaves remained in the household for the duration of the conflict. Only in 1865—and the years thereafter, of course—are there no slaves listed.[23]

By the spring of 1863, many of Louisville's citizens were openly hostile to the administration. When two Confederate soldiers who had been paroled wore their CSA gray uniforms in the streets of the city and into Christ Church Cathedral, they were warmly received by Louisvillians. People stopped them on the street to shake their hands. A federal officer was taken aback when he visited a ball held at a prominent citizen's home and found that the party was being held to honor the return of several paroled Confederates.[24]

Despite this turn in public sentiment and despite the fact that it was far from clear that his side would ultimately win the conflict, Ballard remained in his position as court clerk. It is difficult to discern how he felt about the distinct antislavery tilt of federal policy. He continued to own slaves, although it is tempting to think that the decline in the number he and Fanny owned—from nine in 1860 to eight the next year—represented the emancipation of Mary, Cecelia's mother. The timing roughly fits with the promise made by Ballard to free her after her six-year term was up. However, as was mentioned before, no hard evidence proves this supposition; to have Mary freed and perhaps reunited with Cecelia is simply wishing for a happy ending. Still, given his reported bargain with Mary over her freedom, it is not impossible to imagine Ballard voluntarily emancipating a family slave.

Indeed, perhaps the Ballards did not resist the drift toward freedom as much as some other slaveholding Louisvillians did. The waning of their commitment to the institution can be seen in Fanny's letter to Cecelia and in Andrew's offer to Mary. In addition, according to Rogers Clark's characterizations of his parents, they were lukewarm on the slavery question. Finally, as a Republican officeholder, Andrew Ballard's views on slavery and emancipation may have migrated in step with his new political party's. Many other Republicans started the war with a favorable or at least neutral view of slavery, only to end up in 1865 with a very different position.

After all, Lincoln himself had begun the war pledging simply to restore the Union and not necessarily to meddle with the institution of slavery. When he was finally persuaded to issue the Emancipation Proclamation and allow the enlistment of black soldiers, he justified both measures as wartime necessities, not as pronouncements on the morality of human bondage. Only by the end of the war was Lincoln publicly proclaiming the evils of slavery and the rightness of the abolitionist cause. The Ballards may have had similarly evolving views.[25]

If so, they were increasingly out of step with their fellow citizens, whose distaste for the Republican administration continued to grow. As Louisville's Unionist sympathies waned, federal officials and military authorities grew increasingly skittish, beginning to see Confederate sympathizers on every street corner. On April 13, 1863, General Ambrose Burnside took command of the Department of the Ohio, which included Kentucky. Burnside issued Order #38, which punished by death the sending or receiving of secret correspondence. People expressing sympathy with the Confederacy were subject to arrest for treason and could be deported south, sent beyond Union lines, or in extreme cases, executed. A downward spiral began, in which army officials, quick to question Louisvillians' loyalties, used heavy-handed efforts to suppress dissent and squelch expressions of support for the Southern cause. These actions, in turn, contributed to the growing disillusionment with the Lincoln administration.[26]

The federal courts were important instruments in the government's war on dissent, disloyalty, and overt Southern sympathies. The federal courts in Kentucky presided over cases involving the confiscation of rebel property, the indictment of Confederate fellow travelers for treason, the seizure of war matériel from steamboats attempting to run supplies down the river, and the enforcement of the new revenue laws. While court clerk was hardly a high-profile job, Ballard would have been intimately involved in the docketing and resolution of these cases. Ballard reported on how busy the courts were in an affidavit from November 1863. The district attorney for Kentucky, Joshua Tevis, was lobbying the attorney general for an assistant and asked Ballard to draw up a report on the business of the court during its current term. Of 360 cases pending in both circuit and district courts, about half were criminal indictments—a goodly portion of which involved allegations of treason. Forty-one were suits brought under the Revenue Act passed July 1, 1862. And eighty-four pertained to the various confiscation acts passed by Congress in 1861 and 1862. Thus at least a third, and probably something more than half, of the criminal cases in this term of court related to the war effort.[27]

In May 1863, a case arose that tested Ballard's loyalties and the loyalties of other moderate Republicans. On May 10, 1863, Ballard wrote to Mary Blair—one of the Jesup daughters—about a plot of land owned on Walnut Street. At the end of the note, Ballard wrote, "I leave this evening for St. Louis to be absent only a few days. Col. S. B. Churchill Fanny's uncle was arrested here yesterday by order of Genl Curtis of St. Louis and both he and Fanny insist that I must go over there." Samuel B. Churchill was Fanny's maternal uncle, the brother of her mother, and an active Confederate sympathizer. Churchill was living in Missouri when rebels fired on Fort Sumter, and he worked with other Southern-leaning Missourians to take the state out of the Union. He was an officer in the Missouri state militia, which, on the orders of the secessionist-minded governor, seized a small federal arsenal in the aftermath of Fort Sumter. The governor then appealed to Confederate president Jefferson Davis for artillery to help seize the much larger arsenal in St. Louis. The threat was quickly squashed by the U.S. Army, which forced the surrender of the secessionist militia without firing a shot (although there were bloody clashes with civilians as the army marched its prisoners back to St. Louis).[28]

Colonel Churchill and the other officers were paroled after signing a pledge "as gentlemen" not to "take up arms or serve in any military capacity against the United States during the present civil war." The officers protested against signing such a demeaning oath. The Missouri militiamen claimed that they had all pledged to uphold the Constitution when they joined the militia, and that was all they had been doing when the army had attacked them without provocation. Nonetheless, they signed the oath and were warned out of St. Louis by the Union commanders. Still, there were repeated reports of spies among the parolees, using the cover of their release to reconnoiter Union positions and report them to Confederate forces. A few months later, in October 1861, Churchill was arrested for aiding and abetting the enemy, but he was discharged from custody three weeks later.[29]

In 1863, as the Union began to crack down more severely on dissent, the military commander in St. Louis ordered Churchill arrested and sent behind Confederate lines. Churchill was visiting Louisville at the time to arrange the affairs of his recently deceased father. His arrest caused a stir among Louisville's elite families who knew the Churchills. Rather than view Churchill as beyond the pale because of his overt secessionist activities, they rallied around one of their own. Thus Fanny asked Andrew to travel to St. Louis to see what he could do about her uncle's situation. And within days, prominent friends of the administration in Louisville were writing President Lincoln asking him to rescind the order regarding Churchill. James Guthrie, a staunch Unionist whom Lincoln once asked to become secretary of war, cabled the president to vouch for Churchill as "a man of intelligence and high character. . . . It will utterly ruin him to have to go South. I respectfully ask that his sentence be commuted." Guthrie stated that Churchill would swear the required loyalty oath to the Union and post a bond to back it up. "I ask this because I know him and rely on his honor, and he is a cousin of my children." Likewise, Joshua and James Speed—probably Lincoln's closest friends in Louisville—wrote the president to ask for leniency for Churchill. Although they approved "of the order sending active rebel sympathizers South, . . . we do not believe that Mr. Churchill is one who should be embraced within the order." They described Churchill as "an old schoolmate and intimate friend." Churchill's father "was a prominent citizen here and a warm Union man." Moreover, the estate of his father needed Churchill's presence to be resolved. "He has indispensable duties to discharge in which many of our and your friends are deeply interested," the Speeds wrote. Finally, the brothers suggested that some private enemy of Churchill's was using the long arm of government to "wreak personal vengeance." Lincoln deferred to his friends' judgment. He wrote to Guthrie that "more than once he [Churchill] has been represented to me as exerting a mischievous influence at St Louis," and so he was unwilling to send him back there against the wishes of his commanders in the field. However, he was willing to let Churchill remain in Louisville, provided that he take the oath of allegiance and that Guthrie pledge himself to Churchill's good behavior. The Speeds, too, had offered their pledge to "inform on him and arrest him should he do anything wrong."[30]

Whether Andrew Ballard accomplished anything on his trip to St. Louis cannot be discovered. What is remarkable about the Churchill incident, however, is that it shows that the familial and social bonds that existed among Louisville's elites could overcome their political differences. During a war that was to pit brother against brother, in this instance the more intimate bonds of familiarity and kinship trumped the bonds of Union or Confederate. Louisville may have been, as McDowell said, a city of conflict, but it could also protect one of its own privileged sons when necessary.

By 1864, the main theater of war was far removed from Kentucky. With Union forces again in control of the whole length of the Mississippi River, the city's southward-flowing commerce began to pick up. Yet this did little to ease the citizens' unease with the Union officials in their midst. The main focus of Louisvillians' hatred was General Stephen Burbridge. Burbridge was named commander of the District of Kentucky in January 1864. On July 16, Burbridge issued Order #59. In order to combat guerrilla activity in Kentucky, the order stated, stringent measures were necessary. Rebel sympathizers living in the vicinity of the location of a guerrilla raid would be sent beyond Union lines and have their property confiscated to repay damages caused by the raid. For each pro-Union citizen killed in the course of a raid, the military authorities would select and execute four guerrillas from among the military prisoners being held. Order #59 was an iron-fisted attempt to solve a classic problem of counterinsurgency. There was Confederate guerrilla activity in the Kentucky countryside. Such an insurgency, to survive and succeed, depended on support among the civilian population. Since it was difficult to get at the guerrilla forces themselves, Order #59 targeted their civilian bases of support. By doing so, of course, it helped create greater reservoirs of sympathy for the insurgent cause.[31]

In its implementation, Order #59 also created new problems. In addition to the guerrilla activity, there was also limited activity by regular Confederate soldiers—diversionary cavalry raids, such as those led by John Hunt Morgan, and surreptitious recruiting trips to persuade sympathetic Kentuckians to sign up for the rebel cause. Finally, there was simple banditry undertaken in the fog of war for personal gain. As it turned out, Burbridge had little inclination to sort through the subtleties when handing out punishments. Two young Confederates, for example, were trotted out for execution after a raid in Henderson, Kentucky, in which a group of bandits had robbed an establishment in Henderson and shot the proprietor. The two soldiers had been part of a company commanded by a commissioned officer in the Confederate army, sent into Kentucky on a recruiting mission. The company had skirmished with some federal soldiers, and the two young men had become separated from the rest of their fellows. They were arrested in July 1864 and taken to the military prison in Louisville. Burbridge, however, did not see the Henderson raid as simple banditry. Where others saw bandits, he saw Confederate guerrillas. He demanded restitution from "rebel sympathizers" in the area, and $18,000 was forcibly collected to pay for the damages. (The store owner refused the money.) And in the two Confederate soldiers, where others saw prisoners of war, Burbridge saw unlawful combatants. Despite pleas to halt the execution, the two young men were killed by firing squad on July 22.

Burbridge's "reign of terror," as one author called it, continued in other ways. Expressions of dissent regarding the administration's war policies could result in arrest and imprisonment. In one notorious incident, twenty-one prominent men in the city—including the chief justice of the state court of appeals—were arrested for treason. By August 1864, the *Louisville Democrat* was commenting on the "large number of political prisoners" being confined in the military prison.[32]

Despite the criticism of his heavy-handed measures, Burbridge did face an actual threat. Guerrilla bands did wage irregular warfare in the Kentucky countryside, disrupting railroads and telegraph communications, killing Unionist officials and prominent pro-Union citizens, and looting and pillaging communities to support their activities. Well-known guerrilla leaders like William Quantrill and Sue Mundy (Jerome Clark)—as well as dozens of lesser lights—were pursued by federal troops, and sometimes by Unionist guerrillas. Many of these men were eventually imprisoned and ultimately hanged by the military in Louisville.

The punching and counterpunching of the guerrilla war made life miserable and dangerous in the countryside during the last years of the war. When Andrew Ballard was asked by the Jesup family to check into some property holdings in outlying counties in August 1864, for example, he wrote back that he was "willing to undertake the business provided you would not expect me to go in person to Todd County. Such is the condition of that part of the country and in fact of almost the entire interior portions of the State that I could not do so with safety." He promised to use his contacts with the lawyers in those counties to transact the business.[33]

War weariness, the forcible suppression of dissent, and the oppressive tactics of the military all contributed to Louisvillians' general distaste for Lincoln's brand of war Republicanism. Added to that was the steady erosion of slavery sped along by the administration's policies. The Emancipation Proclamation had been followed in Kentucky by the enlistment of black soldiers into the Union army in March 1864. By July of that year, authorities estimated that an average of one hundred men per day were enlisting. In March 1865, officials dealt slavery another blow by declaring that families of enlisting soldiers would also be freed. The predictable result was that many wives and children followed their husbands and fathers into the camps. By that time, the government estimated that more than 70 percent of Kentucky's slaves were free.[34]

Given the growing disillusionment with the administration, it is not surprising that the city went strongly for Lincoln's opponent, George McClellan, in the presidential election of 1864. McClellan won almost five thousand votes. Lincoln polled fewer than two thousand, and Andrew Ballard's vote was doubtless counted among them. (Given Lincoln's ninety-one votes four years earlier, some Republicans might have interpreted the 1864 results as at least a moral victory—if not a political one.) The war experience cleaved the city politically, leaving a majority that did not support the administration sharpening its differences with the significant minority that continued to stand behind Lincoln. By this late in the game, the Ballards must have become part of the Republican core that sustained the party in the postwar years.[35]

Nonetheless, telling the story of Fanny's and Andrew's lives during the war leads to something of an unexpected conclusion: the Civil War was not a watershed event for the Ballard family. Their political commitments may have altered, their slaves may have been a little more recalcitrant, but their daily life was little disturbed. The privation and destruction visited upon other Southern cities largely bypassed Louisville, and Andrew Ballard's government post provided him and his family security and a steady income through the uncertain years of war.

Perhaps the biggest single change they faced occurred in November 1865, after the war had ended. Throughout the conflict, Fanny and Andrew had continued to live in the same Thruston family house on Walnut Street, sharing those quarters with Charles

William Thruston. But just seven months after the war ended, on November 25, 1865, Charles William Thruston died. He was just a few days' shy of his seventieth birthday. The local paper's obituary praised the elder Thruston as one of Louisville's "oldest and most honored citizens." The obituarist wrote that "truth, justice, generosity, benevolence, and charity dwelt as angels in his soul. . . . The destitute never appealed to him in vain; they left him with full hands and full hearts. . . . He was ever ready with smiles and words of sincere kindness for all. . . . By Charles W. Thruston's death, a bright link in the golden chain of many lives is broken."[36]

Despite this flowery praise, however, the picture of him that emerges from his own collection of personal papers is different. The archival papers radiate little personal warmth; expressions of emotion and intimacy are few and far between. He comes across exactly as a family patriarch in the Jacksonian age should—practical, worldly, cordial. His family is a frequent topic in his letters, but the issues discussed are mostly ones of either wealth building or estate planning—in other words, the family seen as an economic unit more than an emotional locus. His retirement from active business more than twenty-five years earlier had left him sufficiently wealthy and leisured to pursue any interests he wished. The doing of good works did not figure high on his list. His intention, wrote one relative of Thruston's half brother in St. Louis, was "to devote a part of his time to the noble diversion of fox hunting."[37]

This, of course, does not mean that the obituary's glowing depiction of a loving, generous, and charitable man was inaccurate. It means simply that this aspect of his character is not apparent in his documentary detritus. That detritus can reveal only partial truths; those who knew Thruston personally may have formed quite a different view of him. Given his long years together with Fanny, his death no doubt dealt her a great blow.

Whatever the emotional impact of Charles William's death, it delivered a financial windfall to Andrew Ballard. In his will, Thruston named Ballard one of his executors and devised to him his substantial holdings of investment property around Louisville and various financial instruments. (Fanny got the family house, free and clear of any claim by "any present or future husband.") The effect of Thruston's bequest showed up dramatically in Andrew Ballard's property tax returns. In 1865, Ballard paid state property taxes on assets of $38,450. The next year, following the inheritance, his assets totaled $101,757. Fortunately for the historian, because of the Civil War–era federal income tax, Ballard also left behind tax returns that show how Thruston's demise affected his income. His return for the year 1865 showed a gross income of $7,590. Three thousand dollars of that came from his court clerk's salary and another $3,261 came from rents. The following year, his gross income jumped to more than $17,000. His rental income, thanks to Thruston's properties, more than doubled to $8,551, and his investment income soared from less than $200 the prior year to almost $2,500.[38]

Until 1865, Ballard had been a respectable member of a respectable household, residing under his father-in-law's roof. After 1865, Ballard came into his own as the sole head of that household. Although the loss of her father must have hurt Fanny deeply, at least the Ballard family was spared the financial devastation that the war wreaked on so many other American families.

Chapter 7

Cecelia: A New Life in Rochester

While Fanny weathered the war in her childhood home, the now-widowed Cecelia left Canada in early 1861 with Mamie, Benjamin, and James Thomas in tow. She was again part of a larger stream of African American migration, as she had been when she fled to Canada in the 1840s. With the onset of the Civil War, many black refugees in Canada moved back south to their home country. Even Mary Ann Shadd, the firebrand publisher of the *Provincial Freeman*—the newspaper that had encouraged refugee blacks to integrate into mainstream Canadian society—left Canada at the outbreak of the war to work first as a schoolteacher in Michigan and then as a Union recruiter in Indiana.[1]

Cecelia did not journey so far. She settled in Rochester, New York. Why did she choose Rochester? The city did not have a large African American population. The 1860 census listed only 565 blacks in Rochester—down from the 1850 total by about 20 percent—amid a total city population of 48,000. But Rochester was comfortably close to the Canadian border, so that Cecelia could return should her freedom be threatened. Perhaps even more important, the city had a good reputation as hospitable to blacks.

One of the main factors that set Rochester apart in the eyes of many African Americans was that Frederick Douglass—easily the most prominent black of the antebellum and Civil War eras—had chosen to relocate there in 1847. Douglass had been impressed during an 1842 speaking tour with the city's progressive attitudes toward slavery. Douglass wanted to break from the Boston-centered abolitionists with whom he had gotten his start, but from whom he had become increasingly estranged, and he was looking for a place to publish the *North Star*, his abolitionist newspaper. Local activists Isaac and Amy Post persuaded him to come to Rochester. Like many other reformers, Douglass found Rochester welcoming. "I know of no place in the Union where I could have located at the time with less resistance, or received a larger measure of sympathy and cooperation." In Douglass's description, the city was "the center of a virtuous, intelligent, enterprising, liberal, and growing population." Its people were "not so rich as to be indifferent to the claims of humanity, and not so poor as to be unable to help any good cause which commanded the approval of their judgment." The *North Star* was one of those "good causes" he thought Rochesterians could be persuaded to support.[2]

Rochester attracted reformers of all stripes. Temperance advocates, peace activists, moral reformers, and women's rights campaigners all found a spot in Rochester's reform community. Indeed, many of the same people participated in these different movements for social change. But the reformers who earned the city its credibility with American blacks were the antislavery activists who called the city—or surrounding Monroe County—home. Numerous Rochester citizens, aside from Douglass, played prominent roles in the abolitionist movement and with the Underground Railroad. In 1838, they organized the city's first antislavery society. Activists like E. C. William, Isaac and Amy Post, Jacob Morris, William Falls, Myron Holley, and dozens of others campaigned against slavery, contributed money to the cause, helped shelter fugitive slaves, and guided many toward Canada. When Wilbur Siebert published his pioneering work on the Underground Railroad in 1898, he compiled a list of 3,200 Underground Railroad operators organized by state and county. Monroe County, of which Rochester is the seat, topped the list with thirty-six well-known abolitionist activists.[3]

Rochester's hospitality to reformers grew out of its turbulent religious history, which in turn grew out of the far-reaching socioeconomic changes that accompanied the rise of market capitalism on the New York frontier. The seeds of Rochester's economic future were sown when Myron Holley, construction superintendent on the Erie Canal, ensured that the new waterway passed through the city. Holley, who later became a founder of the antislavery Liberty Party and publisher of an antislavery newspaper, oversaw the canal's route for its final 158 miles to Buffalo. The canal triggered Rochester's rapid growth and rising prosperity in the 1820s and 1830s. In 1823, the small burg of "Rochesterville" had just 2,500 residents. By 1830, after the canal was completed, it had 9,200. By 1840, it had more than 20,000. The canal enabled the city to become a major processing center for agricultural products from the farms of upstate New York. By 1838, it milled more wheat than any other city in the United States, earning it the nickname the Flour City. Small manufactories of all types dotted Rochester's neighborhoods.[4]

The rapid economic changes and the accompanying dislocations in the traditional organization of work helped make Rochester fertile ground for religious revival. In the 1830s, a widespread and fervent religious movement swept many parts of the United States, especially the frontier regions. The route of the Erie Canal became known as the Burned-over District because of the numerous fiery revivalists who urged their followers to lead a higher moral life. Rochester was at the epicenter of this profound religious awakening. In a classic book on religion and social change, historian Paul Johnson called Rochester "the most thoroughly evangelized of American cities." The revivalist preachers stressed moral agency, the freedom of people to shun sin. "God has made man a moral free agent," Charles Grandison Finney preached. If there was evil in the world, it was because people had chosen sin over righteous living. Conversely, the eradication of evil required Christian men and women to make the right choices, the moral choices, the godly choices. This emphasis on the power of individual moral choice to remake the social order ignited the bevy of social reform movements to which Rochester played host.[5]

The revivals thus prepared the theological ground that nurtured abolitionism in Rochester, which attracted activists to the city. Indeed, if Cecelia had been involved at all in antislavery causes in Canada—as was speculated earlier—Rochester must have seemed a natural choice of residence. But even if she were not active in the cause, the community's abolitionist reputation probably made it seem a safe choice for a returning refugee.

Despite the presence of Frederick Douglass and an active cadre of reformers, however, Rochester was hardly free of racial prejudice. The *New York Herald* counseled the citizens of Rochester to throw Douglass's presses into Lake Ontario and banish him to Canada. And while Rochesterians did not take the paper's advice, Douglass wrote, "It was plain that many of them did not well relish my presence amongst them." Douglass felt that eventually the white citizens of Rochester came to tolerate and even enjoy the notoriety he brought to the city, but he bridled at what he called the "vulgar prejudice against color, so common to Americans" that he found among the white population of the city. This "vulgar prejudice" led to a thousand slights—both small and large—by the white community against Rochester's black community. Racial segregation in community institutions was common; even some reform organizations—indeed, even some antislavery groups—were open only to whites. Employment opportunities for blacks were also limited by discriminatory practices. "There were barriers erected against colored people in most places of instruction and amusement in the city," Douglass recalled.[6]

Despite these obstacles, members of Rochester's black community purchased property, built businesses, and founded churches. Austin Steward, one of the most distinguished of Rochester's early black citizens, came to the city in 1816 and opened a meat market in the face of open hostility from the white population. His business grew with the city, and eventually many prominent Rochesterians bought from him. Steward helped establish a local Sunday school for black citizens, where the Reverend Thomas James—later a renowned black activist and preacher—learned to read. The vibrancy of the local black community, which embraced Douglass and the *North Star*, often advertising in its pages, may have been another factor that attracted Douglass to the city. Nonetheless, Douglass was dismayed that many of Rochester's discriminatory practices went unchallenged. The racial barriers "were imposed without any

apparent sense of injustice and wrong, and submitted to in silence."
Douglass would have none of it. Although he was often on the road
promoting the abolitionist cause, he found time to agitate in Rochester when it was needed. School desegregation was a case in point.
He refused to enroll his daughter in the city's schools when he discovered that they were racially segregated. Instead, he sent her to a
local private school, only to find that the teacher there was instruct-
ing his daughter separately and privately "in order not to affront the
parents of some other pupils." Soon after, he sent the child to a
school in Albany and later to Oberlin, Ohio. Douglass did not let
the matter drop, however. He mobilized his friends in Rochester to
campaign for desegregated schools, and the school board finally
designated one school on the east side as an integrated school. Some
of Douglass's younger children attended this school for a time, until
in 1857 the city finally desegregated all its public schools. Thus,
when Cecelia moved to Rochester, the battle had already been won.
If Mamie attended the local schools, she most likely did so alongside
children of both races. "One by one," Douglass wrote, the barriers
against equal black participation "have gradually been removed."[7]

When Cecelia came to Rochester at the beginning of the Civil
War, the city's economy and demographics had shifted from two
decades earlier. The heart of U.S. grain production had moved to
the Midwest by the 1860s, and the milling industry had followed it.
While the city retained a diverse base of manufacturing, its title of
Flour City had morphed to Flower City as dozens of nurseries were
established around the city. And while the rapid growth of the 1820s
and 1830s had brought native-born rural dwellers into the metropo-
lis, by the late 1840s and 1850s, a steady stream of Irish and German
immigrants had arrived to man and manage the city's factories and
shops.[8]

Many of these factory jobs would have been closed to African
Americans, despite Douglass's efforts to overturn discriminatory
employment practices. While the black population contained a
small number of professionals, business owners, and skilled laborers, the majority worked as common laborers, domestics, waiters, or
in other service jobs. According to Cecelia's testimony in her pen-

sion application, she found a job working as a domestic servant for the Craig family in Rochester. This was most likely the family of John Craig, a wealthy landowner from Niagara County who, according to Rochester city directories from the 1860s, served as president of the Rochester Exchange Bank. Cecelia recalled that "D. W. Powers was a son-in-law of the Craig family." Daniel W. Powers was a prosperous young banker who would go on to become one of the best-known financiers and philanthropists in western New York. The Craigs' daughter Helen married Powers in 1856 after the death of his first wife.[9]

The Craig family lived on the corner of East Avenue and Prince Street. This was a fortuitous location for Cecelia because it put her in a position to meet William Larrison, a young man who worked "out at the edge of town on East Avenue" for a "white gentleman." Larrison had come to Rochester only a few years before, traveling from his home in Wilmington, Delaware. Although Delaware allowed slavery, William had evidently never been a slave. "At least," Cecelia recalled, "I never heard him say any thing about having been a slave." In his early twenties, he was younger than Cecelia by about a decade. She described him as "jolly and kind of lively." He was short and rather heavyset, with dark brown skin the color of "ginger cake." His hair was "Madagascar"—meaning straight and black—and he kept it cut short. It is uncertain what kind of work he did. On his army enlistment papers he listed his occupation as "farmer." Perhaps he worked the land for his "gentleman" employer.[10]

Like Cecelia's previous relationship with Benjamin Holmes, almost nothing is known about the courtship between Cecelia and William. Unlike Fanny and Andrew, no cache of "letters of tender interest" exists. All that is known is that the two met, courted, and were married all in about the space of a year. William, Cecelia recalled, "was nothing but a young boy and he had never been married before his marriage to me." The ceremony was informal, held on April 3, 1862, in the parlor of John T. Coit, pastor of St. Peter's Church. Three witnesses—two blacks and one white—were present. As with Cecelia's first marriage, the match had been announced three times in church to give the congregation time to object, but

Cecelia's certificate of marriage, 1862. This certificate was issued by the minister who presided at Cecelia's wedding to William Larrison. It did not serve as official proof of her marriage, but it was a crucial piece of evidence in her pension application. (Larrison Pension File, National Archives, Washington, D.C.)

no one had. No formal license apparently was ever issued, although the pastor did give Cecelia a certificate of marriage.[11]

St. Peter's Church was a relatively new addition to Rochester's collection of churches. It had been built in 1852–1853 as an offshoot of the more established First Presbyterian Church. First Presbyterian, like many other Protestant churches in Rochester, had been galvanized and energized by the revivals of the 1830s, and it had responded with church-planting initiatives in the working-class sections of the city. In part, this was to serve the native-born Protestant workmen who had migrated to the city from the countryside, intermingling with Catholics from Ireland and Germany. In 1849, the city directory listed thirty-five churches in Rochester, seven of which were Presbyterian and four of which were Catholic. The 1861 directory listed about the same number of churches (thirty-seven), but the number of Catholic churches had grown from four to seven. The number of Presbyterian churches had kept pace, growing from seven to twelve. St. Peter's was founded by Levi Ward, a "well-known citizen of Rochester and a member of First Presbyterian." Ward was the city's leading insurance agent before turning to politics in the 1850s, serving as city alderman and eventually as the city's fifteenth mayor. He located St. Peter's at 3 Grove Street because it "was central to a large American population with no place of worship," reported an 1871 ecclesiastical history of Rochester. "His [Ward's] desire was to supply this imperative demand by the organization of a new Presbyterian church."[12]

Coit had been installed as St. Peter's third pastor in June 1860. Educated at Yale and Andover Theological Seminary, Coit had studied for a year and a half in Germany before being called to serve as pastor of the Presbyterian church in Albion, New York. He pastored there for five years before moving to Rochester and St. Peter's. Less than a year after officiating at William and Cecelia's wedding, Coit dropped dead while visiting friends in Albion. His last words, as reported by the Reverend F. DeWitt Ward, were, "Can this be death? Then how beautiful it is to die! I already see the coming glories! This is paradise! Death has no appalling features."[13]

Cecelia recalled that after she and William married, they moved into a house on Tappan Street in Rochester. They rented living space from a "colored" woman, Mrs. Bailey. According to the 1861 city directory, Tappan Street was in Ward 6, on the east side of the Genesee River, which cuts through the middle of Rochester. The federal census of 1860 found only fourteen "colored" residents in Ward 6, yet a search of the manuscript census records did not turn up a Mrs. Bailey. The 1861 city directory, however, lists a seamstress named Delia Bailey living at 31 N. St. Paul Street. Sharing this residence with her was Mary Reynolds, a domestic. Mary Reynolds could be Mamie; Reynolds had been Cecelia's chosen last name after she escaped and before she married Holmes. Mary Reynolds also raises the tantalizing question of Cecelia's mother. If Reynolds was truly a family surname, then Mary Reynolds might very well be her mother. Might she have been freed by the Ballards and then reunited with Cecelia in Rochester? It seems highly unlikely and, more frustrating, is impossible to document with any certainty. It must remain only a wild speculation. A second possibility is listed in the 1864 directory. Maria Bailey, the widow of Stephen Bailey, resided at 86 St. Joseph Street. While there is no listing under Holmes or Larrison or Reynolds at the same address, Cecelia recalled that she and William lived "next door to a German family named Ungling." The 1863 city directory lists a cabinetmaker named "Joseph Unglen," also with an address of 86 St. Joseph. Cecelia remembered that the Unglings lived on St. Joseph Street "near the German Catholic Church."[14]

Both of these Baileys are likely candidates for the Mrs. Bailey to whom Cecelia referred. But the evidence is so limited that precise identification is impossible. The Rochester city directories stopped publishing a separate listing of "colored persons" in 1851, and the later directories do not identify a resident's race. (A step forward in Rochester race relations, perhaps, but a stumbling point for the historian tracking African Americans.) Directory publishers frequently missed less prominent people, especially minorities—so there is simply no way to be sure either Mrs. Bailey is the right one. Moreover, neither Mrs. Bailey is listed in subsequent directories, nor are Mary Reynolds or Mary Holmes, or Cecelia or William Larrison.

It does seem reasonable to conclude from this search for the elusive Mrs. Bailey, however, that Cecelia and William most likely resided east of the Genesee in either the Fifth Ward or the Sixth Ward. Tappan Street and St. Joseph Street were both in the Sixth; St. Paul Street was in the Fifth. Cecelia and William would have been two of only a handful of African American residents in these wards. In 1860, fourteen blacks resided in the Sixth Ward and just nine lived in the Fifth. Similar sprinklings of Rochester's small black population could be found in almost every ward, which showed the city's relative lack of racial discrimination in housing. The presence of Cecelia and William's German neighbors also testified to the relatively open housing market.

Nonetheless, by far the greatest number of Rochester blacks resided in the Third Ward, which lay south of downtown on the west side of the river. According to the 1860 census, there were 565 "colored" residents of Rochester. Of those, 202, or 36 percent, lived in the Third Ward. This area attracted the black domestic workers who labored in the households of Rochester's elite families, who lived in a district known as Corn Hill. The Third Ward also gave these black workers easy access to the downtown area, where many worked in the city's hotels and restaurants. The Third Ward thus became the center of Rochester's small black community, and black-owned businesses and institutions grew up to serve this black enclave. Because Cecelia and William lived and worked on the east side of the river—and William worked "out at the edge of town," according to Cecelia—they were largely cut off from this community.[15]

Very little is known about the twenty months between the wedding and William's enlistment in the army. This period, from April 1862 until December 1863, is one of the many chronological gaps in Cecelia's story. Neither she nor William appears in any city directory listing for the years they lived in Rochester. The only documentary evidence that confirms their continued residence there is Cecelia's own testimony in her pension application. Her affidavit says only that the couple lived on Tappan Street and that William continued to work out on East Avenue. It seems likely that Cecelia also continued to work, even though she does not mention it in her pension brief. Economic necessity most likely demanded that she continue working. If William had been able to keep his new wife out of the labor force, Cecelia would have recalled this dramatic change in her situation. Assuming she did continue to work, it cannot be determined whether she continued to work for the Craigs or for a different family.

William enlisted in the army on December 8, 1863, joining Company H of the Fourteenth New York Heavy Artillery. He was twenty-four years old. William was one of only three or four African Americans in the company, along with George Washington, who worked as the captain's cook, and a man called Big Hank. The black men in the Fourteenth all held noncombat positions: cooks,

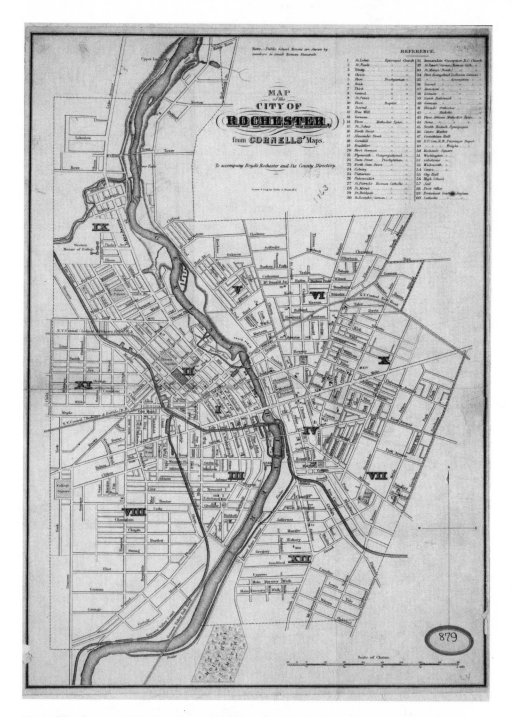

Map of Rochester, 1863. Cecelia and William lived east of the Genesee River in either Ward 5 or Ward 6. Most of Rochester's African Americans, by contrast, lived in the Third Ward, west of the river. ("Rochester Images," from the collection of the Rochester Public Library Local History Division, Rochester, N.Y.)

officers' servants, groomsmen, and so forth. One of William's war-time comrades remembered that each company of the regiment "had a colored man for a cook." William's service records list him as an "under cook," probably serving under a more experienced man. Cecelia remembered that William "enlisted with intention of going as a waiter for the officers." One of the officers of Company H remembered William as "a genial man" who helped take care of the officers' horses. "He was a short stout man, and what we call a light colored Negro."[16]

William thus became one of some 190,000 African Americans who served in the Union forces during the Civil War. Like many thousands of blacks, he served by performing simple logistical and support duties for predominantly white fighting men. In the early phase of the war, this was the only way the country would let black men serve in the armed forces. The army brass thought that by getting the shovels and spatulas into black hands, they could free up white hands to fight the Confederacy. Through 1861 and most of 1862, the government made it clear that it did not envision arming blacks. The idea of putting guns in black hands gave many white Northerners pause, and President Lincoln was extraordinarily careful about offending border-state opinion in those first years. Indeed, when free blacks in the North had tried to join the fight at the outbreak of the war, the army had turned them down. In New York, three regiments of black troops were organized, with arms and equipment supplied by the black population of the state. When they offered their services to the governor of New York in July 1861, however, he would not accept them.[17]

But Frederick Douglass and other abolitionist-minded reformers refused to countenance this waste of black manpower. As Northern armies pushed into the South and as thousands of "contraband" slaves flooded Union lines, Douglass continually raised the issue of turning these men into combat soldiers. He knew that if blacks were allowed to serve in the army, to fight and die for the Union, it would be impossible to return them to slavery after the war and difficult to deny them their full rights as citizens. "Liberty won by white men would lack half its luster," Douglass thundered during one of his many recruitment speeches. "Who would be free themselves must strike the blow."[18]

Some Union officers experimented with black regiments during 1862 in South Carolina, Louisiana, and Missouri. But these efforts usually did not gain official approval. As late as August 1862, President Lincoln declared that he was not ready to accept blacks as combat soldiers, though he would use them as laborers in the army. Over the next several months, however, he changed his mind. The Confiscation Act passed by Congress in July 1862 and the Emancipation Proclamation both authorized the president to raise and arm black regiments. By March 1863, the War Department was taking the initial steps to regularize the recruitment and training of black troops. Unlike white regiments, which were filled out state by state and then mustered into federal service, black combat regiments were federalized from the outset through the Bureau of United States Colored Troops. In April 1863, Lincoln called the black population the "great available and yet unavailed of force for restoring the Union."[19]

Regular army personnel, who were initially hostile to the idea, were partially won over by the numerous avenues for advancement that the new black regiments opened up. Black units were commanded by white officers, and each new regiment required about thirty-five commissioned officers. Widespread recruitment of black troops thus allowed ambitious white officers to ascend the ranks more quickly. The valor of black soldiers also helped win over the skeptics in both the army and the nation. The Confederacy had announced as a matter of policy that black soldiers captured on the field would not be deemed prisoners of war, but rather would be turned over to state authorities, which could sell them into slavery. In the opinion of many observers, this harsh reality led many black units to fight especially ferociously to avoid capture. In addition, the first black unit to be raised among the free blacks of the North—the Fifty-fourth Massachusetts—went into combat alongside white soldiers and displayed such courage and tenacity that this single unit helped sway the argument in favor of using black troops. In July

1863, the Fifty-fourth led the assault on the Confederate stronghold of Fort Wagner in South Carolina. Under withering fire, the unit never broke ranks, despite suffering staggering losses, including the death of its commanding officer, Robert Gould Shaw.[20]

Thus by December 1863, when William Larrison joined up, the argument about whether blacks could join the army as combat soldiers was largely over. Yet the victory had come at a price, as Larrison no doubt felt in Rochester. Public support for the war was eroding. The patriotic bravura that had marked the first months of war had given way to more cynical calculations. In the first years there was broad bipartisan support for the war. At a public meeting held in the city on April 18, 1861, "the people of Rochester" officially proclaimed their "support of the rightfully constituted authorities of the land." The call for volunteers was read, and the names of the first Rochesterians to sign up—thirty-nine in all—were called out for public acclaim. Spirits ran high as public parades of new recruits, flushed with the prospect of adventure, were seen off by cheering crowds. The patriotic ladies of the town appropriated a room in the courthouse to sew shirts, bed ticks, drawers, and other items to send to the soldiers. Flags flew from the city's most prominent buildings, from its liberty pole and from every telegraph pole.[21]

Recruiting was brisk through the middle of 1862. Then, as news of Lincoln's preliminary Emancipation Proclamation spread in September 1862 and as war weariness began to set in, the city's previous unity and strong support began to fade. Moderate opinion began to sour with the expansion of the war's aims from preservation of the Union to the destruction of slavery. Despite the presence of Radical voices like Douglass's, mainstream Republican opinion in Rochester was much more moderate. These moderates favored the war as a means to restore the Union, favored the use of "contraband" slaves within federal lines as laborers to help the Union cause, and favored the Confiscation Acts as a way to punish rebel sympathizers. But the majority did not see the war as a crusade to abolish slavery. The political climate turned decidedly less sympathetic. In two hotly contested races, Rochester voted for a Democratic candidate for governor and a "Copperhead" mayor in 1863. The previous year's unity gave way to political division and partisanship. The town's rival editorial pages again heated up their rhetoric, with Democrats labeled as traitors and Republicans branded as tyrants. In the 1864 presidential election, while Lincoln held Monroe County, his rival George McClellan won the city of Rochester by seventy-four votes.[22]

Recruiting hit a lull, driven more by promises of bonus money and fear of the draft than by pro-Union fervor. There were four Union drafts during the war: one in 1863, two in 1864, and one in 1865. The real point of the drafts was to stimulate volunteer enlistments; by threatening a draft, the federal government pressured districts that were having trouble meeting their quotas of soldiers to redouble their recruitment efforts. To avoid being subject to the draft, districts would raise money to entice volunteers. Volunteer bounties from various government sources could go as high as $1,000 at a time when the annual income for a laborer was around $400. The 1863 draft in Rochester, for instance, furnished the army with only 61 actual soldiers out of 810 who were deemed eligible for military service. The other 749 draftees either paid the commutation fee to opt out of serving or paid a substitute. Nationwide during the two years of conscription, 1 million men enlisted or reenlisted, whereas only 46,000 were formally drafted into the army. (Another 118,000 were drafted but paid a substitute to serve in their stead.) So judging by the numbers alone, this "draft threat" system worked.[23]

Ironically, the apparently unceasing calls for more volunteers, the threat of conscription, and the overall weariness with the war all helped assuage Northern white concerns about black enlistments. "Better them than us" became the philosophy of many white residents. Some white recruiters faced open hostility from their predominantly white audiences, who demanded that black troops be called up first. In 1864, the *Rochester Union* reported that recruiters were "scouring the face of the earth, taking everything white that has a head, trunk, and limbs, and everything black that is a degree above a baboon." The Monroe County Board of Supervisors even considered a proposal to send representatives south to buy up "cheap Negroes" to fill the district's quotas. "It is said that two or three smart agents may be sent down who will buy up and steal all that is required, taking from friend and foe alike."[24]

When William Larrison enlisted in December 1863, therefore, he did so in a markedly different environment than that which had prevailed two years earlier. The question of whether the army should enlist blacks had largely been settled, but increased black enlistment took place amid decreasing popular support for the war. In that context, it is not all that surprising that William took the cautious and noncontroversial—not to mention less dangerous—route of signing up as an officer's servant. Nobody objected to blacks serving in the army as laborers, teamsters, cooks, and servants.

William was recruited by Colonel Elisha G. Marshall, a career military man and a well-known figure in Rochester. Marshall had previously commanded the Thirteenth New York Volunteer Infantry. The Thirteenth had been the first unit recruited mostly from Rochester and the first Rochester unit to see action, but in the spring of 1862, when Marshall took over, morale was low and discipline was lax. Marshall whipped the Thirteenth into shape, inspiring "first fear and then respect" among the soldiers. After leading the Thirteenth in the Peninsular Campaign, the siege of Yorktown, and the battles of Mechanicsville, Second Manassas, and Antietam, Marshall suffered serious wounds at Fredericksburg. When most of the Thirteenth was mustered out, Marshall got the go-ahead in May 1863 to recruit the Fourteenth Heavy Artillery, using the remnants of the Thirteenth as a foundation. According to Cecelia, Marshall knew William well and personally persuaded him to join up.[25]

William left behind no record of his motivations for joining the army. Many soldiers joined for economic reasons, particularly as bonus amounts began to climb in later years. Cecelia remembered that William received enlistment bounty money from the county and from the state, although he never received a $300 federal bounty to which she claimed he was entitled. In addition, although blacks initially received less pay than white soldiers, the prospect of steady earnings may have induced William to join up. Hard times hit Rochester in 1863 and 1864 as war-induced inflation sapped workers' purchasing power. According to one calculation, prices of some consumer goods had doubled since 1860. Maybe the wolf at the door helped Marshall make his case to William.[26]

But there may have been other reasons as well. In his book *A Grand Army of Black Men,* Edwin Redkey compiled and analyzed the writings of black soldiers in the Civil War, including some who, like William, served behind the lines in white regiments as servants and teamsters. He found the dominant motif of these writings to be a desire to aid the fight against slavery and to gain the respect of the nation. "By joining the army, by fighting willingly and dying bravely, African Americans wanted to earn both respect and citizenship," Redkey wrote. So while William Larrison may not have aided the fight for racial equality as dramatically as Frederick Douglass might have wished, by joining a black combat regiment, he may have been moved by similar feelings to offer his own small service to the larger cause.[27]

Nor was serving as a laborer or servant necessarily always a cushy or safe position, especially if you were black. When the Confederate Congress passed legislation denying black soldiers POW status in May 1863, Union general David Hunter wrote the War Department that it was "only a formal announcement of what has for some time been the practice in the Western departments where many colored teamsters, laborers, and servants employed by the army when captured by the enemy have been sold into slavery." In one case from February 1863, for example, two black servants attached to the Forty-second Massachusetts Infantry were captured by Confederate forces in Galveston, Texas. They were denied POW status and sold into slavery by state authorities. So William's position was not without significant risk.[28]

He faced risks in the North, too. The Fourteenth Heavy Artillery's first stop in the war was New York Harbor. Just five months before William's enlistment, antidraft riots had rocked New York City. Mostly Irish immigrants, resistant to conscription in the Union army, attacked the draft office, raided the homes of wealthy Republicans, and lynched at least twelve blacks. It eventually took federal troops, who killed more than a hundred rioters, to restore order to the city. Although the riots were over when the Fourteenth arrived, doubtless there were still racial tensions in the streets.[29]

Cecelia followed William to that first post, traveling with the commanding officer's new wife, the former Miss Erickson. One of the soldiers in the unit recalled Cecelia being there, remembering that William "spoke of her as his wife and seemed to be very fond of her." He also remembered the Larrisons having a "little colored girl with them about 5 years old who was recognized as their child." In fact, Mamie would have been closer to eight or nine years old by this time. The Fourteenth stayed in New York Harbor for about four months. Cecelia spent these months at Fort Richmond on Staten Island, probably in order to be close to her new husband. On April 23, 1864, the unit was ordered to join the Army of the Potomac. They traveled to Washington, and again Cecelia went with them. "The Regt didn't stay but a day at Washington," she recalled later, moving immediately to join the army in the field. At this point, Cecelia turned toward home. William had entrusted some money (perhaps from his enlistment bonus) to one of the unit's officers, who had sent it to his wife in Elizabethtown, New Jersey. Cecelia went there first, spending the night and getting the money, then returned to Rochester, where she remained for the duration of the war.[30]

How Cecelia spent these last eighteen months before the war ended cannot be known with confidence. She does not appear in the city directories of the time, nor is there a trace of her in other sources. Her own recollections say merely that she waited in Rochester for William to return. If she worked, it was probably as a nursemaid or house servant for a white family, the labor that had been her lot since slave times. The war may have created some opportunities for domestic service, as war contracts created new flows of wealth to Rochester merchants and entrepreneurs. Rochester shoe manufacturers, clothing wholesalers, and wool merchants all benefited from military sales and the war's choking-off of traditional supplies from the South and West. Some low-skilled seamstress jobs may have also opened up, as clothing manufacturers adopted new production methods and an intensified division of labor to keep up with military demand. But most war-related manufacturing work would have been closed off to a black woman.[31]

The economic cycle of these last months of the war also inflicted a good deal of hardship on those, like Cecelia, at the lower end of the economic scale. Inflation sapped the buying power of wages, and several local unions banded together in February 1863 to form the Workingmen's Assembly of Monroe County to fight for cheaper coal. William's bonus money and soldier's wages would have been vital supports for Cecelia. While Rochester did have a Volunteer Relief Committee to aid destitute dependents of enlisted soldiers, it was largely ineffective and probably limited to white families. Overwhelmed by requests for aid in the later years of the war, the committee halved the $4 weekly benefits it paid out and limited applications for aid to the dependents of early recruits. It eventually offloaded its responsibilities to Rochester's city government. If Rochester was like most cities in the North, however, such aid was available only to white families.[32]

Meeting her economic challenges might have been made easier by the shrinking of Cecelia's household during these years. It appears that Benjamin Holmes's two sons—now both in their late teens or early twenties—set up housekeeping on their own around this time. James Thomas, the elder brother, appears to have settled close by in Rochester. City directory entries beginning in 1866 show a laborer named James Holmes living at 9 Harrison Street (also in the Sixth Ward). No racial designation or middle initial or any other kind of identifying feature was included in the city directories, so it is impossible to be certain that this man was Cecelia's stepson, but he is at least a likely candidate. In 1873 and 1874, a Mary Holmes is also listed as living at the same address. This may have been his wife, because other documents show that he had two daughters, Emma and Rebecca. These two daughters were both living in Rochester in 1889, and there is an Emma Holmes listed in the 1885 city directory as a domestic, although she lived then at 140 North St. Paul Street. The 1881 directory lists James Holmes as having died on October 6, 1880. Benjamin Alexander Holmes, the younger brother, eventually migrated to Minnesota, although the route he took to get there is more difficult to determine. He may not have left Canada, for example, at the same time as Cecelia. The 1875 Minnesota and 1880 federal censuses both list his two sons as having been born in Canada. The oldest boy, Walter, was born in 1863, and the younger, Eugene, was born in 1869. Thus it seems likely that Benjamin stayed on in Toronto for a few years after the death of his father, wooing his eventual wife, Lucia, and fathering his first son. By 1870, he had established himself in Faribault, Rice County, Minnesota. He worked as a barber for many years and died on September 11, 1896.[33]

While Cecelia struggled to make ends meet, William's wartime service took him to some of the most fiercely fought battles of the eastern theater of the war. The Fourteenth saw action in the battles of the Wilderness, the battle of Cold Harbor, and the siege and occupation of Petersburg, as well as many other less prominent battles. It suffered its highest casualties during the campaign against Petersburg, losing 61 men. Over the course of the war, more than 200 of its soldiers were killed outright or mortally wounded, and another 300 died of disease. At the end of the war, the regiment was moved to duty in Washington, D.C., and was mustered out August 26, 1865. All in all, 527 men of the Fourteenth died during the war.[34]

William actually left the service a little earlier than the rest of his unit. He was discharged on July 8 because of disability (probably a hernia, according to other records). Cecelia remembered that "he was ruptured on his right side very bad. . . . He said he got his rupture by having to walk so much and carry so many heavy things." After his service ended, he returned to Rochester and Cecelia. She had a plan, and William went along with it. In September 1865, shortly after his return, they left Rochester and returned to Louisville.[35]

Chapter 8

Fanny: Postwar Trials

Andrew's post as court clerk and Louisville's deliverance from wartime devastation had enabled the Ballards to pass the war years with their lifestyle relatively intact. Their family house was unscathed; their income was steady and adequate; their sons—too young to join the fight—had been spared the horrors of combat. Indeed, owing to the inheritance from Charles William Thruston, Fanny's father, the Ballard family emerged from the war somewhat better off financially than it had been when the war began.

The Ballards' lives probably changed more in the aftermath of the war. With the Union victory, Louisville and Kentucky both began a process of "readjustment" that changed the city and the state significantly from their antebellum selves. The standard historical term for the period after the Civil War is, of course, Reconstruction. But Kentucky never went through Reconstruction. Since it never seceded from the Union, it was not subject to the Reconstruction Acts passed by Congress to rehabilitate the South. Instead, Kentucky historians refer to a period of "readjustment" after the Civil War, as Kentuckians struggled to reconcile themselves to the end of slavery, the defeat of the Confederacy, and the rise of a new industrial age.[1]

It is difficult to know exactly how Fanny and Andrew viewed the end of slavery. They had gone through much of the war with their own slaveholdings more or less intact. In 1864, according to Andrew's state property tax return, he still owned eight slaves valued at $1,800. It seems likely that they continued to own these slaves through the end of the war and possibly even longer, waiting until the law explicitly forbade slaveholding. The final destruction of slavery within Kentucky and within the nation at large occurred only with the ratification of the Thirteenth Amendment in December 1865. On a practical level, the Ballards no doubt felt emancipation as an inconvenience. They lost ownership of their eight slaves and, from their perspective, $1,800 worth of personal property. This was hardly devastating, not when compared to the fate of some Kentucky plantation owners who, with most of their wealth tied up in black bodies, found themselves transformed into poor men when those bodies were liberated. For the Ballards, emancipation simply meant they would now have to find household servants to replace those slaves who chose to depart.[2]

Not all the former slaves chose to do so. Some older slaves stayed with the family even after emancipation. Rogers Clark recalled the case of his grandfather's personal servant Jack. The old slave and his wife, Susan, cared for the aging Charles Thruston until his death in 1865 and then stayed on with the family. After emancipation, Fanny and Andrew offered the old slave couple a home and cared for them until the servants' own deaths in the 1870s. Likewise, Chloe—a "noted cook and faithful slave" of Julia Churchill, Fanny's maternal aunt—stayed on after emancipation as a Churchill family servant.[3]

Nonetheless, it is clear that the end of slavery meant a change in the composition of the Ballard household. Fanny still had four children at home—the oldest, Charles, was fifteen in 1865 and Rogers Clark was but seven—and doubtless felt that she needed help. Instead of slaves, she needed to hire domestic servants. While black women —most of them former slaves—dominated the ranks of household servants in Louisville during the last third of the nineteenth century, immigrant women, who had never been warmly welcomed before the war, now competed for open slots in the city's well-to-do households. Sure enough, the 1870 census showed two white domestics living in the Ballard house—both of foreign parentage.[4]

On a broader level, the end of slavery forced a rethinking of relations between blacks and whites in all aspects of life. Overall, whites in Kentucky had a very difficult time accepting their former bondmen as their political and economic equals. In many instances, whites used violence, intimidation, and discrimination to maintain their superior social and economic position; in other cases, blacks were simply cast loose to fend for themselves, the cash nexus of the employer/employee relationship replacing the life-encompassing control of the master/slave relationship. When blacks, hobbled by decades of slavery, lack of education, and continuing discrimination, fell into poverty, this was taken as proof of white superiority. Condescension and paternalistic scorn toward blacks characterized the attitude of many well-off whites.[5]

It was not just the end of slavery that made Louisville feel different after the war. The city's population also became more diverse. Freed slaves from rural areas flooded into the city; immigrants came seeking work in the factories that were popping up. And Southern whites—footloose in the wake of the war's devastation—came to Louisville because it was a Southern city that had been spared the ravages of combat. Former Confederates had an influence out of proportion to their numbers. Their undisguised sympathy for the nobility of the Lost Cause fed into Louisville's existing disenchantment with the war and the Republican administration. They stirred the pot of resentment that had already been stewing in their adopted city, and prompted many Louisvillians to forget their wartime Unionism. None of this made it easy to be a Republican officeholder, which Andrew Ballard continued to be after the war. He served as clerk of the federal district court through the rest of the decade.[6]

In the early postwar years, under the regime of presidential Reconstruction as carried out by Andrew Johnson, a fairly lenient policy was followed toward former Confederates. The rich and powerful, excluded from the government's general amnesty, could apply for pardons directly from the president. After some initial stinginess, Johnson soon began dispensing pardons liberally, sometimes hundreds per day. The wholesale pardons complicated the business of the district court of Kentucky, which had dozens of unresolved treason indictments against prominent Kentuckians on its dockets from before the end of the war. In August 1866, the district attorney wrote to the attorney general for advice on how to proceed with the cases. Many of those indicted had been pardoned, but others had not. He did not, he wrote, want to "endanger or embarrass the complete success of the liberal policy of the Executive Department, in its efforts to restore our distracted country to its former unity and prosperity." As a moderate border-state Republican, Ballard probably shared the district attorney's admiration for Johnson's "liberal policy." However, as the D.A. himself admitted, the former Confederates in Kentucky had not exactly warmed up to the idea of Union victory. "It is undeniable that there exists in some of Ky a disposition and determination to persecute Union soldiers and prominent Union citizens and, if possible, to drive them from the State. This feeling is rapidly spreading and increasing." Despite this prevailing sentiment (or perhaps because of it), the attorney general instructed him to drop the treason prosecutions.[7]

The final element of postwar change in Louisville stemmed from the rise of a new industrial economy. Railroads killed Louisville's privileged position as the gateway to the South. A direct railroad line from Cincinnati into Tennessee bypassed Louisville entirely. A city that had built its fortunes on trade and transshipment found itself at risk of being rendered irrelevant. This seismic shift in the city's position forced the big wholesale merchants who had dominated Louisville's political and social life to give ground to a rising corps of industrialists. "Louisville aspires, and hopes to be one of these days a manufacturing town," editorialized one newspaper shortly after the war, "capable of competing with such centers as Cincinnati and St. Louis."[8]

While Louisville never ascended into the first rank of American industrial cities—thanks in part to rearguard actions fought by the city's merchants—industrial employment climbed steadily in the decades after the war. In 1860, census takers counted 7,963 industrial workers in the city. Twenty years later, there were 17,448. Likewise, the number of manufacturing establishments more than doubled, to 1,108, during the same twenty-year period. While the manufacture of steam engines and boilers was the sector that led industrial employment, a wide range of moderate-size factories dotted the Louisville landscape. "The manufactures of the city have

Map of Louisville, 1885. Spared the ravages of the war, Louisville enjoyed a postwar boom that attracted both former Confederates and ex-slaves to the city. (*Atlas of Louisville*, University of Louisville Archives, Louisville, Ky.)

grown and increased in the years since the war to an extent of which few people are aware," wrote one newspaper in 1872. The "mania for manufacturing," as one local historian termed it, was hardly unique to Louisville. The postwar years were the go-go period of America's industrial takeoff, and Louisville was caught up in the same set of transformations that were remaking the national economy. For Andrew Ballard, who had never been able to settle himself adequately in the more individualistic rough-and-tumble economy of antebellum Louisville, the cutthroat corporate capitalism of the new industrial age must have seemed especially alien. His status as a gentleman lawyer—supported by his father-in-law's properties and his government sinecure—must have seemed a haven in an increasingly heartless world.[9]

As the 1860s wore on, however, Ballard found himself in the eye of a bitter political storm. Outraged by Johnson's leniency toward the South and by the unrepentant arrogance of the states and officials of the former Confederacy, Republicans in Congress seized control of postwar policy. Confronted with presidential vetoes of what they considered essential legislation, Republican lawmakers turned against the president, overriding his vetoes, impeaching him, and finally helping to oust him from the White House in the 1868 election. One piece of legislation passed over Johnson's veto was the Civil Rights Act of 1866. This law defined all people born in the United States (except Indians) as national citizens and thus deserving of a basic set of fundamental rights—namely, the right to make a contract, file a lawsuit, and enjoy equal standing in court. The law allowed a federal remedy if state laws violated these rights by authorizing a U.S. district attorney to file suit against violators in federal court.[10]

In a state like Kentucky, where officials sympathized with the former Confederacy's resistance to black civil rights, the civil rights law generated a great deal of business for the federal courts. Like states across the South, Kentucky enacted laws after the war that sharply restricted black rights. African Americans could not vote, serve on juries, or testify in court against whites. When the Civil Rights Act told the state it could not do such things, Kentucky dug in its heels. The legislature refused to alter state law to allow blacks the right to testify against whites, and the state supreme court declared the Civil Rights Act unconstitutional. As a result, when blacks were wronged and could not obtain justice in state courts, they filed suits in federal court under the Civil Rights Act.[11]

Like many moderate Republicans, Ballard probably felt that his party was pushing too hard too fast on the issue of black civil rights. At the same time, however, through legislation like the Civil Rights Act, the federal courts were emerging as primary tools in the national government's effort to remake the South. Caught in the middle, Ballard dutifully attempted to do what the law required of him. In his semiannual reports on the fees and emoluments received by the court, he repeatedly mentioned the fiscal consequences of the Civil Rights Act. For the latter half of 1867, for example, he noted that some $390 in fees due from individuals had not yet been paid. "A very large per centum" of these fees, he explained, "is due from persons of color who have brought suits in this court under the Civil Rights bill. They are paupers and the fees are substantially worthless." He went on to say that another goodly chunk of the unpaid fees came from Union soldiers "harassed by suits in the State Courts" and who "removed such suits to this Court under the Habeas Corpus Act. Such fees are also in the main worthless."[12]

Legal harassment of blacks also spilled over into violence, and the federal courts sometimes had to take up prosecutions to which the state authorities turned a blind eye. In August 1868, for example, two white men—John Blyew and George Kennard—ax-murdered an entire black family. The case found its way to federal court because, according to the indictment, the two men targeted the victims solely on account of their race and the primary witnesses to the crime were black, and thus prohibited from testifying in state court. The two men were convicted and sentenced to death during the fall term of federal court but appealed their conviction on the grounds that the U.S. district court lacked jurisdiction. The Supreme Court agreed, saying that the Civil Rights Act granted crime victims only the right of removal to federal court, and in this case the victims were dead, so they could not institute legal proceedings.[13]

As clerk of court, of course, Andrew Ballard would not have been the focus of white Kentuckians' ire against the intrusions of the federal courts; that would have been reserved for his brother Bland, the sitting federal judge, and for the federal prosecutor. Still, all officeholders in an administration many considered tyrannical and obsessively bent on destroying white Democrats' hold on power must have felt isolated and besieged. Although it is impossible to know for certain, those feelings may have been behind Andrew's decision to resign his position as clerk in 1870.[14]

He moved from being a Republican officeholder to being a Republican mouthpiece. After resigning his position as court clerk, he became the political editor of the *Louisville Daily Commercial*, which had begun life in 1869 as the city's Republican newspaper. In its inaugural issue, the *Commercial* noted that it was swimming against the prevailing political currents. "Prophecies of evil to our undertaking say that the rebel sentiment of Louisville is so bitter, that she is so dependent on Southern trade, and has done so well by being so pronounced in her Southern sympathies, that she won't patronize a Republican newspaper." There was a core of Republican support in the city, however, that kept the newspaper alive until 1902, although it never thrived financially.[15]

Given the political tensions of the post–Civil War period, one wonders how committed Andrew Ballard was to the Republican causes of black civil rights and opportunity for the newly freed slaves. Moderate Republicans generally accepted the idea of equal rights before the law, the need to enforce the new amendments to the Constitution, and the desirability of protecting blacks from violence and blatantly unequal treatment. On the other hand, very few white Republicans in Kentucky endorsed the idea of black political participation. Even after they realized that they needed black votes to compete statewide, they continued to resist the idea of black officeholding and party leadership. Fewer still thought of blacks as the intellectual, moral, or social equals of whites.[16]

One indication of the cautious and conservative views of moderate Louisville Republicans can be found in an 1871 court decision—and the *Commercial*'s reaction to that decision—on racial segregation in the city's streetcars. While Ballard's degree of participation in formulating the *Commercial*'s editorial stance cannot be determined, it is reasonable to assume that he found the newspaper's less than Radical views congenial. While upholding the legal basis of black civil rights, the newspaper tread carefully around the issue of blacks actually claiming or making use of these rights if such actions offended the racial sensibilities of the white community. This ironic position—blacks had legal rights but they should not exercise them—can be seen vividly in the streetcar decision and its aftermath.

Andrew's brother, federal judge Bland Ballard, presided over the case, a landmark in Louisville's civil rights history. Louisville's streetcar lines followed a complicated policy of racial segregation that rubbed raw the sensibilities of Louisville's black community. Black women were generally allowed to ride inside the cars, alongside whites. Black men, with few exceptions, stood on the platform outside the car. In October 1870, Louisville's blacks began a coordinated protest that challenged the discriminatory policies, resulting in the arrest of three men. Tried in state court, the defendants were denied the right to testify against whites, and their legal arguments about discrimination were disregarded. Each was fined $5 for disorderly conduct. One of the men, Robert Fox, then brought suit against the streetcar companies in federal court. At trial, after the testimony was in, Judge Ballard asked the attorney for the companies what issue of legal interpretation the company wished to raise. "None," the lawyer replied. The companies did not contest that under the law they had no right to discriminate against passengers based on race. With nothing to decide as a matter of law, the only question Ballard turned over to the jury was how much in damages the company should pay. On May 11, 1871, the jury awarded Fox $15 in damages.[17]

The *Commercial* put the narrowest construction possible on the decision. "It is a common error that this suit arises out of one of the recent amendments to the Constitution, whereas it is based on the common law which defines duties and liabilities of common carriers, and the Constitution of the United States has nothing to do with it." The *Commercial* took Judge Ballard essentially out of the picture, asserting that "he decided nothing," and that if the case had been brought in the Kentucky Court of Common Pleas, the result would have been the same. The *Commercial*'s careful stance that the decision merely upheld long-established common-law doctrine distanced Louisville's moderate Republicanism from the Reconstructionists in Washington who controlled the national scene.[18]

In the days following the decision, both the Republican *Commercial* and the Democratic *Courier-Journal* advocated precisely the same go-slow approach to the actual application of blacks' equal rights. As blacks began to ride the streetcars, and as episodes of shouting, shoving, and the occasional thrown fist multiplied, both papers appealed for social order. The *Courier-Journal* labeled the black community's actions "aggressive. They have undertaken, in a very turbulent manner, to exercise a right which the prejudices of society and the customs of the country deny them." Nonetheless, the newspaper expected the cooler heads in the African American community to prevail. "There are only a few Negroes who are willing to make themselves obnoxious by entering the cars. The great majority will continue to stand on the platform as has been their custom heretofore."[19]

The *Commercial*, while refraining from blaming black riders for asserting their rights, called on "colored men . . . to abstain from any act liable to provoke a breach of the peace. They should refrain from unnecessarily precipitating this question upon the community; the assumption of their right to ride in the street cars, under the present circumstances, is injudicious, and we hope will not be persisted in." It urged the black community to "use this right as to convince all that they do not seek nor wish to place themselves where they are not welcome, and that they have too much pride and self-respect to force themselves upon those who would prefer to shun them." Again, the moderate stance distanced Louisville's Republicans from the national administration, which was widely perceived to be ramming equal rights down the throat of the South with the point of a bayonet.[20]

The *Commercial* and the *Courier-Journal* also agreed on a potential solution to the disorder: separate cars for blacks and whites. The

Courier-Journal suggested that "the practical solution seems to us to be for the present the complete separation of the two races, giving each its share in the common lot." Likewise, the *Commercial* cited the successful example of other cities where the municipal railway companies set aside every third or fourth car for "the use of the colored people." So, despite some differences in editorial tone from the Democratic organ, the voice of Louisville's moderate Republicans hardly rang with clarion calls for black equality.[21]

As political editor of the *Commercial*, Ballard championed most vigorously the 1871 campaign of John Marshall Harlan—the "gallant Harlan"—for the governorship. "The gallant HARLAN last night closed one of the most magnificent canvasses that has been conducted in this State," ran a *Commercial* column the day before the election. "Let every Republican, every lover of law and order, every friend of our State, every one who would have her what she ought to have been long ago, one of the wealthiest in the whole United States, do his duty by going early to the polls, and casting his vote for Gen. JOHN M. HARLAN and the whole Republican ticket."[22]

Despite Kentucky's obvious Democratic sympathies, in 1871 the Republicans appeared to have a fighting chance. John Marshall Harlan came from a respected Kentucky family, had fought in the war on the Union side, won election during the conflict as Kentucky's attorney general, and practiced law in Louisville after the war was over. A war hero and a capable speaker, Harlan made an attractive gubernatorial candidate. His Democratic opponent, Preston Leslie, had sympathized with the South but opposed secession in the run-up to the war. Politically cautious, Leslie spent much of his political career trying to take positions that would not alienate his allies and thus jeopardize his chances at reelection. Compared with Harlan, Leslie was uninspired and uninspiring; even the Democratic *Courier-Journal* described him as "not a showy orator" and as lacking "personal magnetism."[23]

In addition, Leslie presided over a Democratic Party riven by factionalism. So-called Bourbon Democrats—after the reactionary French royal family—dismissed notions that the war had changed local or national politics. They rejected the Thirteenth, Fourteenth, and Fifteenth amendments to the Constitution—which ended slavery, extended citizenship to blacks, and legalized black voting rights, respectively. They also supported low taxation and offered only limited support for public education and government-sponsored public works. "New Departure" Democrats, on the other hand, urged the acceptance of the amendments, although they criticized many of the laws passed under their authority. They also favored a bigger role for government in the development of the economy and the education of the citizenry. Republicans hoped that quite a few New Departure sympathizers would find they had more in common with them than with members of their own party.[24]

It was not to be, however. Harlan went down to defeat, garnering only about 41 percent of the vote statewide. The *Courier-Journal*, the main organ for the New Departure Democrats, pondered why Harlan had lost so convincingly. Given the magnetism of Harlan and the lackluster appeal of Leslie, given the schism within the Democratic Party itself, and given the strong motivation of Republican voters compared with the apathy shown by many Democrats, why had the Republicans not fared better? "It is an active and live assertion of popular freedom against the insidious workings of the central power," it answered in the classic tones of the defenders of states' rights in the South. "It is a declaration on the part of Kentucky that gives the country to understand that such is our dread of Radicalism that we prefer all else to the bare possibility of a political domination inspired from Washington. . . . It is found that our interior dissensions amount to little when brought face to face with the issue which divides the two contending parties."[25]

Ballard and the *Commercial* put the best possible face on the defeat. It called the loss "a great moral victory," since the margin of Democratic victory was significantly narrower than in earlier statewide contests. Moreover, the newspaper asserted, the Republicans had changed the terms of the debate; going forward, it predicted, one would hear less about "the right of all men to equality before the law" because it would simply become an accepted part of political life. "It must now be admitted that there is a Republican party in Kentucky—an aggressive, fearless, uncompromising party, which boldly accepts the issues of the hour, and, come victory or come defeat, will fight out the battle of freedom, dodging no fair responsibility and shirking no honest cost." Ballard was right. The party had arrived on the political landscape, but it would not win a gubernatorial election for nearly the next thirty years.[26]

Harlan ran and lost again in 1875, but President Rutherford B. Hayes rewarded his service to the party by appointing him to the Supreme Court in 1877. It was on the high court that Harlan earned his lasting reputation. Known as the Great Dissenter, he wrote vigorously in opposition to the Court's judicial dismantling, during the last quarter of the nineteenth century, of the civil rights laws that guaranteed black equality. He protested in vain against the Court's reasoning in the landmark 1896 *Plessy v. Ferguson* decision, which upheld state laws mandating racial segregation. (He was vindicated some sixty years later when the Court overturned *Plessy*'s "separate but equal" reasoning in the 1954 case *Brown v. Board of Education*.) Harlan has been called one of the twelve greatest justices ever to sit on the Court.[27]

In some ways, the lives of Harlan and Andrew Ballard paralleled each other. Although Harlan was eighteen years younger than Ballard, both had been slaveholders before the war, both had been members of the Whig Party, both had been lawyers, both supported the Union during the Civil War and drifted eventually into the Republican Party. There the paths diverged, however. Harlan chose the life of public service, becoming a Supreme Court justice and an eloquent supporter and passionate defender of black civil and political rights. Ballard chose private life, leaving the *Commercial* in 1872 to focus on his property and his family.

An anecdote from Ballard's time as editor raises the question of whether he was sufficiently pugnacious for the no-holds-barred world of post–Civil War political journalism. Serving a brief three-day stint as editor in chief, Ballard continually struck down stories that he took to be too personal or improper. "He had an exceedingly nice sense of propriety," recalled the *Commercial*'s telegraph editor at the time, "and not only disbelieved in every form of personal journalism, but was also of the opinion that no man was justified, under any circumstances, in meddling in another man's business." As admirable as these virtues might have been, they ill suited Ballard to the life of a journalist and editor. "Very little news of any sort went into the *Commercial* during his three days reign."[28]

The tension between Ballard's personal ethics and the conventions of journalism may have played a part in convincing him to leave the *Commercial*, but his daughter Abby's sickness no doubt played a larger role in drawing him away from the public arena and back toward Fanny and the children. Abigail Churchill Ballard— Fanny and Andrew's only daughter—had been born on June 24, 1853. In 1871, Abby had gone east to Vassar College in Poughkeepsie, New York. Vassar, which had been accepting students only since 1865, was considered a bold experiment in female education, a reformist effort aimed at providing a rigorous university education on a par with men's education. Several of the men important to the founding of the school were leading lights in New England's abolitionist and antebellum reform movements, who now devoted part of their energies to the cause of women's rights.[29]

Unfortunately, Abby became ill shortly after her first term began and was fetched home by her older brother Charles in the late winter of 1872. In April, Fanny wrote with relief to Abby's friend Mollie Hill, a fellow Kentuckian at Vassar, that Abby seemed to be on the road to recovery. But just a month later, she wrote that Abby had no doubt been sick for weeks at school and did not seem to be able to shake the illness. In June, Fanny wrote that Abby was very thin and was not eating, but that she was walking a bit every day. She told Mollie that they were taking Abby to Wyoming County, New York, to try the Castile Water Cure.[30]

The "water cure" was a popular remedy for the chronically ill in the nineteenth century. Patients typically took frequent baths in both hot and cold water, drank lots of water, and engaged in vigorous outdoor exercise. The Castile Water Cure, located in upstate New York—ironically, close to Rochester, where Cecelia had resided a few years before—grew rapidly in popularity after the Civil War. Under the administration of Dr. Cordelia Greene—a pioneering woman physician, suffragist, and philanthropist—the sanatorium at Castile became a nationally known haven for the chronically ill. One memoirist credited Castile's good reputation to "Dr. Greene's medical knowledge, her skill in diagnosis, and her original method of treatment by hot and cold water, by electricity, massage, vapor baths, and the system of exercises."[31]

It is not clear how long Abby stayed at Castile; some patients boarded in the town for months. But in November Abby wrote to her college chum Mollie, who had elected not to return to Vassar, that she had caught cold while visiting her brother Sam at Cornell. Sick again, Abby now intended to go south. She told Mollie that while she had not enjoyed college while she was there, she now missed her friends. She wondered if the girls' "particular set" would ever meet again.[32]

This time the Ballards took Abby to Florida, hoping warmth and sunshine would do for her what the waters of Castile did not. They wintered in Saint Augustine, and Abby's condition improved. So concerned and indulgent were her parents that when she developed a fondness for the oranges from a particular grower, Andrew tried to buy the grove outright. By the summer of 1873 the family was back in Kentucky.[33]

Fanny had lost immediate family members to death every decade of her life. In the 1830s, it was her brother and sister. In the 1840s, her mother died. In the 1850s, she lost her second son, and a lightning strike killed her one remaining brother. In the 1860s, she lost her father. And on April 2, 1874, Abby died. She was just a few months shy of her twenty-first birthday.

Abby's death devastated her parents. Five months after her daughter's demise, Fanny sent a final note to Mollie Hill; it was written on black-bordered stationery, a sign of Fanny's continued mourning. They were planning a trip to Europe, she told Mollie, though as yet they had not settled on any concrete destinations. "Our home seems so desolate without our darling Abby that Mr. Ballard is anxious to leave it for one, two, or three years. He would be willing to rent our house to almost anyone who would take care of it, but I am harder to please; few tenants would satisfy me for I cannot bear to think of the slightest desecration to the house my

Abigail Churchill Ballard, ca. 1871. This photo was taken while Abby was a student at Vassar College. Fanny and Andrew's only daughter died of tuberculosis in 1874. (Filson Historical Society, Louisville, Ky.)

daughter so much loved." Years later, Fanny ordered a stained-glass window with the image of an angel as a memorial to Abby, which was placed in Louisville's Christ Church Cathedral.[34]

Abby died of tuberculosis, a disease just beginning to be understood in the 1870s. Unlike the frightful epidemic diseases of the nineteenth century, like yellow fever or cholera, which swept through a community and killed a large number of people in a few weeks, tuberculosis was endemic to the population, killing slowly but steadily. During the 1870s, autopsies revealed that nearly every city dweller had been exposed to tuberculosis, or "consumption," as it was more commonly called. The development of the tuberculin test around the turn of the century confirmed this finding of widespread latent infection. As one commonplace expression put it: "Everyone is sometime or another a little bit consumptive." The bacillus that caused the disease was not isolated until 1882, so in Abby's time diagnosis was based largely on a consumptive "look" or on the telltale coughing up of blood. So common was the disease that the image of the pale, emaciated, tubercular woman "set the standard for white middle-class beauty in the midnineteenth century," according to one medical historian. It gave an ethereal quality to a woman, indicating her delicate nature and superior spirituality, ready to pass over to the next realm at any moment.[35]

The question that agitated medical minds in the 1870s and 1880s was why, if everyone had been exposed, did only some die? They found their answers either in the moral habits of the individual, the characteristics of particular ethnic groups (Jews were thought to contract consumption only rarely, for example), or in the environment. The supposed relationship between climate and disease and between urban life and disease prompted the treks of many well-off consumptives to places like Castile, one of a multitude of rural nineteenth-century springs, spas, and mountain resorts. In searching for a climatological cure for Abby, the Ballards followed prevailing medical advice. Abby's death showed that tuberculosis did not respect class boundaries, despite the medical community's harping on "vicious habits" and poor hygiene as factors in the spread of the disease. It also provided another coincidental link between Fanny's family and Cecelia's, for Cecelia's brother, Edward, had also fallen to tuberculosis.[36]

Abby's death threw Andrew into something of a spiritual crisis. While nothing in Andrew's own hand reveals his torments, other evidence indicates that he was deeply troubled in the years after Abby's death. At first, he sought solace in the church. On February 14, 1875, less than a year after Abby's death, Andrew Ballard was baptized in Christ Church Episcopal. Ballard, who had questioned religion since that long-ago day when Fanny condemned him for playing cards on the Sabbath, now looked to his wife's religion for comfort and hope. He may not have found it, because sometime after Abby's death he backslid on his long-ago promise to Fanny to quit drinking. Rogers Clark, writing a brief biography of his father in 1929 to include with his father's papers, blamed the drinking on "financial reverses," reporting that his father "drank heavily the rest of his days."[37]

The nature of these financial reverses is hard to determine, however, from family financial records. Ballard's property tax returns showed him with fairly substantial landholdings in the city—owning at least a dozen city lots—through the late 1870s until the time of his death. In the last several years of his life, the total value of his properties never fell below $100,000. On the other hand, his state tax returns do show a decline in his assets in the last years of his life, but this bottomed out at around $80,000. What is hard to determine is how much income these properties generated, and the magnitude of Ballard's debts. He did invest with his son Charles in a venture in a Colorado silver mine in the late 1870s that ended badly, but Ballard's financial losses in that incident hardly seem sufficient to drive him to drink.[38]

No doubt, Rogers Clark's statement serves as better evidence of what afflicted Andrew than any historian's speculation. But it is at least worth considering that it was not money but heartbreak that pushed Andrew toward the bottle. The death of Abby may simply have led him to despair, which might in turn have affected his financial savvy. At any rate, there is little reason to doubt Rogers Clark's recollection that something troubled his father in his last years.

The drinking could not have helped his health, and in 1885 Andrew contracted dysentery. On August 11, he wrote to Fanny, who was visiting in North Carolina, that their son had painted a "roseate picture" of Andrew's health to Fanny. Andrew did not gloss over the truth, reporting that he had not been free from diarrhea since July 12. "The attack has been malignant and protracted and I am much reduced in strength," he told her. "In fact I feel as though there was some latent poison lurking in my system." He went on to complain about his doctors, having consulted several during the course of his illness. One wanted him to drink more water. "This I knew would be wrong," Andrew said. Another told him that all he needed was a tonic, so he prescribed a "tincture of iron and recommended a broiled chicken and mutton chop. Now men who talk this way don't understand my case." Happily, however, he reported that his latest doctor seemed to be on the right track. Six days after writing this letter, he was dead.[39]

Dysentery is a particularly awful way to go. It is caused by bacteria that enter the body through the contamination of food or water by fecal material. Depending on the underlying organism causing the infection, prolonged and chronic diarrhea is the result.

Dehydration and malnourishment follow. In the 1880s, there was little a doctor could do except hope the body cleared the infection; Andrew's body did not, and it killed him.

He was seventy years old when he died. He had not been actively involved in business—whether law, journalism, or politics—for at least a decade, his retirement coinciding with Abby's death. The *Commercial* styled Ballard "a most agreeable and instructive talker" who "never sought popularity and has lived of late years a retired life." Likewise, the *Courier-Journal* obituary lauded his sociability more than his accomplishments. "For fifty years the deceased had been a resident of Louisville and always occupied a commanding social position. He was a man of excellent conversational powers, entertaining and instructive, sensible and dignified, and leaves a host of warm friends."[40]

Fanny stayed on in the big house on Walnut Street after Andrew's death. In 1887, her bachelor son Rogers Clark resigned his position with the Kentucky Geological Survey and moved back in with her. This probably suited Fanny fine; one suspects that Rogers Clark was always Fanny's favorite son. Her older boys, Charles and Samuel T., had started the Ballard and Ballard flour mill in Louisville, married, and begun families of their own.

A signal of Rogers Clark's devotion to his mother came in 1884, a year before his father's death. While visiting Rogers Clark at his geologic work in eastern Kentucky, Fanny became very ill. Fearing her death, she asked Rogers Clark to adopt her family's last name as his own, so that the Thruston name would be carried on, and he agreed. He went to the Fayette County Court and had his last name legally changed to Thruston, yielding the rather cumbersome four-surname construction by which he was known for the rest of his days.[41]

Sometime during the late 1880s or early 1890s—it is impossible to know exactly when—Fanny discovered that Cecelia had moved back to Louisville, and the former slave and her mistress reconnected. How and where the reconnection took place are also unknown. However, across the South during this time other former slaves, driven by the limited economic opportunities open to them, sporadically showed up seeking assistance of one kind or another from their former masters. Thus had the old man Adam—Cecelia's might-have-been stepfather—sought out the Thrustons, for example, in 1877. It is interesting to speculate whether Fanny encouraged Cecelia's return to Louisville, whether she facilitated a reunion of Cecelia and Mary, whether Fanny aided Cecelia in her struggle against poverty. Interesting, but ultimately fruitless. Nothing in the archives substantiates the nature of the later relationship between Fanny and Cecelia.

That some kind of renewed contact occurred between the two of them is beyond doubt, however. In an 1895 addendum to her will, Fanny left a bequest for "Cecelia Larison [sic], who was my maid in slave days." The bequest shows that Fanny knew Cecelia was in the vicinity and that she had acquired the married name of Larrison. Fanny's will provided that $100 and a black cashmere shawl go to Cecelia, one of several people for whom Fanny made small bequests as a sign of her affection, including a cousin, a close friend, and her personal servants.[42]

After Fanny's death, Cecelia gratefully acknowledged the tokens. "I am moor than oblige to you for your kindness and all so sympathise with you in the death of your dear mother as we were children together," she wrote to Rogers Clark, who had sent her the money as per Fanny's instructions. "The shawl you speack of in your letter i have not received it. But would be very glade to received it as a rememberance of your mother."[43]

The overall frequency and content of the contact between Cecelia and Fanny exceeded by far the few letters that survive in the family archives. Rogers Clark referred in 1899 to "many letters" passing between Cecelia and Fanny, and of paying Cecelia to bring in as many as she could find. "She brought in a few today and said they were all she could find but as soon as she could find the rest of them she would bring them in also." Apparently, she had no luck, for the five sent from Fanny to Canada are the only ones in Thruston's ample files.[44]

Fanny died April 30, 1896, while visiting Europe. In her will, she left to her older sons the mill property where they conducted their business and the houses in which they lived. The Ballard and Ballard flour mills became quite prominent in Louisville before being bought out by Pillsbury after World War II. Since the elder brothers had benefited from bequests in their father's will and from frequent financial infusions from Fanny, in the interests of "justice" she favored Rogers Clark in her own will.[45]

Fanny's obituary extolled her devotion to her church and to her family. In contrast to the eulogizing of the public life her father led, Fanny was eulogized for her private life. "In her retired life, only the inner circle knew how interesting and clever she was, and how generous and loyal was her friendship. . . . Of her charities it is not well to speak, for she gave them in secret, but there will be many a heart which will ache for her who is gone." Even late in the nineteenth century, when more women were taking on public roles as reformers and advocates, Fanny remained content—at least in the eyes of this obituarist—to plow the fields of domesticity.[46]

Overall, the Ballards negotiated the "readjustment" period after the Civil War with relatively little discomfort. Protected by their wealth, their social position, and their favorable border-state geography, they were spared the trauma of Reconstruction that afflicted other regions of the South. They were able, like many middle-class families of the period, to focus on family, home, and private life, shielding themselves from much of the social disorder that attended the economic dislocation and class and racial friction of the day. They endured private tragedies—the death of Abby, the decline of Andrew—but the road they trod in post–Civil War, postslavery America was much smoother than the road Cecelia traveled.

Chapter 9

Cecelia: Back in Louisville

Cecelia realized few of her postwar hopes. It is nice to think that she returned to Louisville, found her mother, Mary, and began a new life of freedom with her family restored in the Falls City, but no evidence supports this happy ending. Indeed, in the period immediately after the war, the Larrisons disappear from the archival record. Cecelia stated they moved back to Louisville in September 1865, but the first year the Larrisons appeared in the Louisville city directory was 1876. It is quite possible they were in the city but passed over by the annual population surveys done for the city directories and by the 1870 census enumerator. Neither canvass expended a lot of effort counting African Americans.

The best evidence of the Larrisons' presence in Louisville prior to 1876 are Cecelia's own reminiscences of that period, given as part of her pension application. Both she and William worked for the Heite family after their return to Louisville—he as a coachman and she, presumably, as a domestic servant. Cecelia's employment ended with a pregnancy in early 1866. "I got in a condition," she recalled. "I couldn't work—was carrying a child and he [William] got me a room on Main Street near Preston between Floyd and Preston. Dr. Leachman attended me in my confinement in May 1866." She became pregnant again just over three years later. "Dr. Owen deceased attended me in my 2d confinement." These details—William T. Leachman and W. Talbot Owen *were* physicians practicing in Louisville during the 1860s—support the view that the Larrisons were in Louisville in the years before 1876. The fact that they had set their minds on raising a family testified to their faith in the future.

Tragically, however, neither of the new babies survived. The first survived infancy but then died at just five years old; the second lived just four months. In her late thirties during this time, Cecelia was fairly old for childbearing by nineteenth-century standards, and this may have had an impact on the health of the children. The deaths of these children, however, do not appear in the Louisville Death Index for these years, so there is no official documentation of their presence in the Falls City until William's appearance in the 1876 city directory. Their absence probably offers some silent testimony to their economic struggle. Working long hours for low pay at menial jobs was not very conducive to the type of occupational and residential stability that got one noticed by official head counters.[1]

William during these years held a variety of jobs trying to make ends meet. After losing his position with the Heite family, he drove a carriage for Mrs. Wilder, the wife of a local druggist, until the Wilders left town. He worked as a waiter for a time and also as a hack driver for the Louisville Transfer Company, according to Cecelia's recollections. In the 1876 city directory, he is listed simply as a "laborer," not an uncommon designation for black men in Louisville during those years. According to one calculation for 1870, some 41 percent of the black men listed in the city directory were laborers. This reflected a rather unstable and uncertain occupation, marked by frequent periods of unemployment. A laborer might dig ditches, haul boxes, clean streets, sweep floors, work in the sewers, or perform other similar tasks. The common thread was that these jobs were often seasonal—which meant periodic bouts of unemployment—and paid little.[2]

The city directories from later years confirm Cecelia's statements that Larrison moved up the occupational scale. He was listed in 1878 as a waiter at the Willard Hotel and in the 1880s as a coachman. These jobs also were fairly typical for black males. Service occupations in many sectors of the city's economy were held almost exclusively by African Americans. As a coachman, Larrison could expect to bring in maybe $12 per month while working very long hours. As a waiter, a job dominated by black men, Larrison could expect similarly low wages and long hours. Waiting tables also yielded inconsistent pay since a waiter's income stemmed largely from patrons' tips. William and Cecelia's place on Louisville's socioeconomic ladder thus differed little from the wider black population in the city. Like many Southern cities after the Civil War, Louisville saw a great influx of African Americans. In the decade of the 1860s, the city's black population jumped by some 120 percent, and by 1880 blacks numbered more than twenty thousand, nearly 17 percent of the city's total population. The great majority of these people lived in poverty.[3]

This in-migration continued despite the fact that blacks faced overt discrimination from most of the city's white population, who denied them equal access to jobs, public accommodations, and political power. Indeed, given the prevailing opinion among white Louisvillians that African Americans were largely shiftless, immoral, and prone to criminality, city leaders fretted over the swelling black population. As the *Commercial* put it, "The white community looks lightly on the good conduct of the many, while it judges harshly the bad conduct of the few." And yet they came, largely because urban environments in general, and Louisville in particular, offered more opportunities than the countryside for education and employment.[4]

They also came to Louisville seeking safety in numbers. In the years immediately after the war, blacks in rural counties were subject to repeated violent attacks by whites. As overt legal discrimination against blacks came under scrutiny through federal enforcement of the postwar constitutional amendments, white Kentuckians instead directed their wrath directly against black bodies and black aspirations. Some refused to sell land to blacks or extend credit to them. Black children were not allowed into the public schools. Some whites threatened violence, and when blacks made advances anyway, made good on their threats. In rural areas, where protection was weakest, former slaves simply fled. Outrages occurred with frightening regularity. A Freedmen's Bureau report declared that in 1867 20 former slaves had been killed, 18 shot, 11 raped, and 270 mistreated in some other form. A catalog of violence from just one month in 1868 included the destruction of a black school in Monroe

County, the burning of a school and two churches in Bullitt County, and the forcible expulsion of a teacher in a black school in the town of Mayfield. As under slavery, the slightest breach of the unwritten rules of black conduct could bring harsh punishment by whites. When a black woman accidentally brushed against the dress of a county judge's wife on a town street, the judge administered a severe caning to the woman.[5]

The Freedmen's Bureau, the federal agency charged with overseeing the transition of the former slaves to freedom, initially did not extend to Kentucky. But after hearing repeated reports of the treatment given to Kentucky's African Americans, the bureau opened offices in the state in 1866. The bureau provided small amounts of food and clothing, vetted labor contracts, and established a hospital for blacks, but its schools provided its most lasting legacy. By 1869, when the bureau closed down, 250 schools operated across the state, educating 10,360 black citizens. The schools offered just rudimentary learning, but it was the only formal education open to blacks at the time.[6]

Most white Kentuckians hated the bureau. They resented the federal intrusion into Kentucky's internal racial affairs. And they struck back by burning schools, beating teachers, and intimidating students. One historian concluded that Kentucky was "in the forefront in its violent opposition to the activities of the Freedmen's Bureau." The violence came not just from the spontaneous rage of mobs but also from organized and semipermanent bands of "Regulators," including the Ku Klux Klan. These groups targeted blacks predominantly, but whites who sympathized with black aspirations also came under attack. Night-riding, terroristic threatening, and the expulsion of entire black communities reached epidemic proportions in some rural portions of central Kentucky. Lynch law also prevailed—between 1867 and 1871, more than one hundred blacks were lynched across Kentucky. The city offered greater physical safety from such attacks.[7]

In addition to opportunity and security, blacks migrated to the cities seeking information about and possible reconnection with family members from whom they had been separated during the days of slavery. Desperately trying to reverse the cruelty of the auction block, former slaves across the South took to the roadways looking for hints of the whereabouts of children, spouses, and parents who had been sold away in prior years. One former slave in Texas, for example, asked the Freedmen's Bureau's help in locating a long list of his "dearest relatives," none of whom he had seen since being sold away from Virginia twenty-four years earlier. Concluded one agent of the bureau, "In their eyes, the work of emancipation was incomplete until the families which had been dispersed by slavery were reunited."[8]

This quest was what had driven Charles Thruston's former slave Adam to Fanny's doorstep in 1877. Although Fanny recognized Adam as "Cecelia's father," it was not his relationship to Cecelia that Adam sought to rekindle. Sold away from Mary and Cecelia as a young man, he had remarried and raised another family on a plantation in Arkansas. Instead, he had come north hoping to find his mother. Adam's sale to Charles William Thruston by Mary Churchill had torn the boy from his mother, and more than forty years later he had come back to Louisville to see if he could still find her. "It seems absurd," Rogers Clark wrote, "but had he come three years earlier he would have found her still alive." Disappointed in his quest, Adam went to work in a Louisville brickyard to earn his passage back to Arkansas. On the brink of his return, however, he was robbed of all his savings, and so he sought out the Thrustons in the hope that some descendant of his old master would be able to help him. He was not disappointed; Fanny fed him and furnished him with new clothes, a ticket to Memphis, and enough money to get him home.[9]

In coming to Louisville, Cecelia was thus again part of a larger stream of black migration, as she had been when she fled to Canada and as she had been when she returned to the United States. However, in contrast to the many African American migrants to Louisville who were fleeing violence-scarred and poverty-stricken rural areas in Kentucky or other parts of the South, William and Cecelia had spent most of their lives in Northern cities. They could have as easily gone back to Rochester, or to Wilmington, where William hailed from, but they chose Louisville instead. Although no records bear out this assumption, it seems likely that they did so at Cecelia's urging, probably in the hope that she could locate and reconnect with her mother (and perhaps other acquaintances), whom she had left behind some three decades before. Like Adam, Cecelia hoped to reconstruct what slavery had destroyed, what she had been unable to reconstruct so long as slavery existed.

Like Adam, Cecelia was frustrated in her search for her lost family connections, and like the thousands of other African Americans who came to Louisville in the postwar years, William and Cecelia confronted poverty and discrimination in their new home. With William working for low and inconsistent wages, Cecelia augmented the family's meager income by working as a laundress during some of these years. This work, backbreaking in the days before washing machines, was performed almost exclusively by black women. In 1890, according to data compiled by George Wright in his study of black life in Louisville, 84 percent of the city's laundresses were black. Like William, Cecelia worked hard for long hours and low pay.[10]

Whatever their economic struggles may have been, they appeared to have stayed among the "respectable" elements of Louisville's African American community. "The claimant and witnesses are colored people of the better class, honest and reliable and claimant has an excellent reputation," wrote the government's special examiner who scrutinized Cecelia's pension application. This was quite an achievement given the instability in their lives. Cecelia's daughter, Mamie, giving evidence to support her mother's pension application, chronicled that instability by recalling a litany of residential moves. "My stepfather Wm Henry Larrison and my mother were living together from my earliest recollection," she wrote. "They lived together at 1st and Chestnut St and on Centre St near Chestnut and on East Madison bet[ween] Preston and Jackson and on Walnut bet[ween] Preston and Jackson and Brook St bet[ween] Market and Jefferson and . . . on College St bet[ween] 1 and 2d." In contrast, Fanny Ballard resided at the same address all her life. Mapping these address changes shows that, like most Louisville blacks, the Larrisons stayed fairly close to the downtown core. None of their residences, however, seemed to have been inside the black neighborhoods that were developing to the east and west of this core. Rather, the family probably lived along the alleys in white areas, where shotgun cottages for those blacks who served whites proliferated.[11]

Louisville during this time was not yet a legally segregated town. George Wright argued that Louisville's whites practiced a form of "polite racism" during these last decades of the nineteenth century, content to employ blacks, live in close proximity to blacks, even ride streetcars with them, so long as blacks remained docile, loyal, and "in their place." Their place, of course, was at the bottom of the social and occupational scale. As a legal matter, segregation during these years was inconsistent and often unevenly applied. The policies of Louisville's streetcar companies, for instance, demonstrated this. One allowed them to ride, but only in the back. Another allowed black women to ride inside the cars, but not black men. And a third banned black men (but not women) entirely. It was these practices that blacks had challenged in federal court before Judge Ballard. And despite their ostensible legal victory in that case, blacks continued to face discrimination on the streetcars. By the 1880s, they were often being forced to sit in the back of the cars. In housing, there was no law requiring racially separate housing on the books until 1914, and even that was soon overturned in the courts. Informal residential segregation did exist, however. The large influx of blacks resulted in the growth of predominantly black neighborhoods. Even on racially mixed blocks, Wright found certain patterns (for example, whites on one side, blacks on the other) that betrayed hints of discrimination.[12]

It is undeniable, however, that blacks made notable progress in Louisville and across Kentucky during these years. By the mid-1870s, some of the racial violence had quieted. With the federal amendments in place, Kentucky had to adjust to postwar reality. In 1872, the state legislature finally passed a bill giving blacks the same rights as whites in the state's courts. While some localities had fought the implications of the Fifteenth Amendment (which gave blacks the right to vote) with lengthy residence requirements for voters or gerrymandered voting districts, eventually most blacks in Kentucky were allowed to vote. White Kentuckians came to realize that since blacks made up only about one-sixth of the total population, their political participation constituted little threat to white control.[13]

Blacks made other gains as well. By 1876 they sat on federal juries. By 1882 they sat on state juries. The state government ordered the creation of black public schools. Louisville had a black newspaper. Black lawyers had gained entrance to the bar. African Americans even held minor political offices in some towns. Racially integrated churches, workplaces, and neighborhoods existed in different locales all across the state.

Many of these gains resulted from black protest and pressure. Protest meetings were held as early as 1866 in Louisville, and by March of that year a statewide black convention was organized and held in Lexington. Local committees drafted petitions and protested the treatment of African Americans to local, state, and federal officials, and similar statewide conventions were held through the 1870s, 1880s, and 1890s. Each significant anniversary in the long march toward freedom from slavery also called forth large celebrations and protests by black citizens across Kentucky. January 1 was Jubilee or Emancipation Day and was usually celebrated with parades, music, and political speeches by black leaders. As the home of the largest black community in the state, Louisville saw the largest and often most overtly political of these public gatherings. Other occasions that called forth large black demonstrations were July 4 and, in 1870 at least, the passage of the Fifteenth Amendment. More than ten thousand blacks converged on the streets of Louisville to celebrate the passage of the amendment, marching to Courthouse Square, where once slaves had been auctioned, and listening to speeches extolling the ballot as the blacks' ultimate weapon against discrimination.

Were Cecelia and William part of these protest movements? No hard evidence exists to answer that question. As a Union veteran, William may have been swept up in the cause; after all, many black soldiers felt that equal rights should be the logical result of their military service to the nation. Even if the Larrisons did not take an active part, the conversations and debates within the black community over the issues of equality and civil rights were part of the social fabric in which they found themselves. Whatever the case, William and Cecelia's problems in the 1870s stemmed less from legalized racism and more from pervasive racial discrimination, which kept them living precariously. Personal grief over losing their two young children could only have added to their troubles.

It was not until 1880 that the Larrisons finally achieved a measure of stability. William found relatively steady employment as a driver with the Louisville Transfer Company, and the family was able to move to a residence at 126 College Street and stay there through the rest of the decade. Sometime in the period from 1883 to 1885, however, this newfound stability was seriously threatened when William again found himself unemployed. The imprecision of the date reflects the imprecision of the sources. In May 1898, Cecelia stated in her pension claim that William "got out of a job here and said he was going away to look for work. That was 15 or 16 years ago last Jan'y." Cecelia's memory thus put the event in 1882 or 1883. Further on, however, she recalled that William's unemployment occurred after they had been at the College Street address about five years. According to the city directories, the Larrisons first moved to College Street in 1880, which would put William's job loss around the year 1885. This dating fits better with the other evidence from the city directories, which list Cecelia—but not William—residing at 126 College Street in 1886.[14]

Cecelia was alone because William was out tramping, looking for work. When work was scarce in Louisville, working-class men—both white and black—often left town to find work, either out in the countryside doing farm labor or on the steamboats that plied the Ohio. Cecelia herself did not view William's departure as anything out of the ordinary. "He some times would go to the country and stay a week or 2 and come back and bring in something," she remembered, "and some times he would get a job [on] the boats as cabin boy." This time, however, it was different. William did not return after a week or two. Months passed with no word from him, and Cecelia had no idea where he was. In her pension claim, Cecelia and other witnesses testified that she was not overly concerned at first, but she began to get restless as the wait for William became longer. She wrote to the chief of police in Wilmington, Delaware, to see if William might have drifted back to his previous home. She got no reply. Her daughter, Mamie, said that Cecelia sought information about William from every conceivable source but, again, with no result.[15]

She never heard from him again. "I never have seen or heard of my husband . . . since he left here 15 or 16 years ago," she recalled, "and I have written and tried every way to find out about him." Cecelia eventually came to accept that he was dead—from some unknown cause in some unknown locale surrounded by people unknown to him. In the 1888 city directory, she is listed for the first time as the widow of William.[16]

In the 1890s, when she applied for her widow's pension, she also had to convince the government's examiner that William was dead. "I believe he is dead or I would have heard from him or he would have been home," she stated. "Nothing in the world would have ever kept him away." Other witnesses backed her up. Mamie spoke of the couple's apparent contentment with each other and stated that William had never shown attentions to any other woman. Another witness said, "I certainly do believe honest to God that Larrison is dead or he would have come back to his family if he had to walk in [the] Canal. He was just that kind of a man."[17]

William's disappearance undercut the family's tenuous economic stability. Cecelia continued to work as a laundress and no doubt Mamie went to work as well, though there is no record of her economic activities. William's disappearance also forced Cecelia to liquidate her last remaining asset, her stake in the house that she and Benjamin Holmes had purchased in Toronto. Holmes had divided the property in his will and left half to Cecelia and half to his sons. In November 1887, roughly two years after William vanished, Cecelia sold the lot for $250. It may also be around this time that Cecelia made contact with Fanny again, perhaps to ask for help as she and Mamie struggled to make ends meet.[18]

In fact, though, it was Mamie who engineered their salvation. On April 17, 1888, she married Alexander Reels, a secondhand furniture dealer who had emigrated to Louisville from Louisiana with two children, James and Eulalie, sometime during the 1870s. Reels said that he first met the Larrisons around 1879 or 1880, probably shortly after his arrival in town. Reels, like William, had served in the army (in Reels's case Company A of the Third Louisiana Colored Infantry), and he and William swapped tales about the war.[19]

Reels liked his economic independence. He was more entrepreneurially minded than William, and he became part of the small but growing class of black businessmen in Louisville who operated their own retail businesses. According to one count, the number of black businesses listed in the Louisville city directories grew from just seventeen in 1865 to ninety ten years later. According to the 1880 census, Reels made a living as a coal dealer, but the city directories through the 1880s listed him as a dealer in secondhand furniture. Furniture stores—even those dealing in used furniture—could often be some of the most lucrative retail businesses for black entrepreneurs. Reels's income and position no doubt helped stabilize Cecelia's and Mamie's economic fortunes following William's disappearance.[20]

Reels was significantly older than Mamie, although their exact ages are difficult to determine. According to birth dates from various records, Reels was born sometime between 1836 and 1844. Mamie was born sometime between 1855 (most likely) and 1868 (highly unlikely); that makes Reels anywhere from eleven to more than thirty years her senior. In his affidavit, Reels judged William Larrison to be a couple of years younger than he was.[21]

Reels moved Cecelia and Mamie out of their longtime residence on College Street and into his home, which also served as his place of business, on Preston Street. Once again, regular moves became part of the family's life. In 1890 and 1891, Reels had a store on Floyd Street; by 1894 he was back on Preston; in 1897 he spent a year on

Jefferson Street, returning to Preston Street for the next three years. Mamie was listed once apart from her husband; in 1896 she worked as a laundress out of her husband's store. Cecelia, too, appeared sporadically in the directories through the 1890s. In 1891, she was reported to have a business at the same site as Reels's store. Although the directory did not specify, she probably took in washing, as her daughter would do a few years later. In 1894, Cecelia was listed in the directory as a nursemaid residing at 212 West Oak Street. In 1897, the listing reported her as a domestic servant living on Jefferson Street. And in 1899, she was back where she started the decade, running an unspecified business out of her son-in-law's store. Obviously, Cecelia ventured regularly into the work world, frequently "living in" as a caregiver for children or as a servant, but falling back on the Reels's home/business as a refuge during her periodic bouts of unemployment. Just as obviously, even with Reels's business income, it required the regular—if sporadic—efforts of all three members of the family to make ends meet.[22]

Compared to the large cache of intimacies between Andrew and Fanny Ballard that survives in the archives, there is nothing on the emotional relationship of Mamie and Alexander Reels. Their affidavits in support of Cecelia's pension application and an official marriage record provide the only surviving documentation of their relationship.

Their marriage record also showed, coincidentally, the tightening web of Jim Crow legislation in Louisville. After the few fitful movements toward racial equality in the 1870s, racial lines in Louisville and across Kentucky began to harden anew during the last two decades of the nineteenth century. As it did across the South, racial segregation crept in piecemeal, locality by locality, law by law. Restaurants, hotels, theaters, and other public accommodations that had never opened their doors to blacks felt less pressure to do so as segregation became official state policy. As for Mamie and Alexander's marriage record, it was listed in a separate register reserved for black couples. The city apparently wanted to prevent race mixing even at the level of bureaucratic recordkeeping.[23]

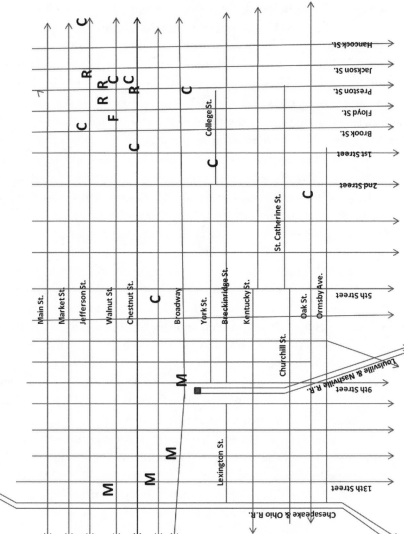

Map of the Louisville residences of Cecelia and Fanny, ca. 1870–1909. This map charts the different addresses where Cecelia (indicated by C), Mamie (M), and Alexander Reels (R) resided in the last years of the nineteenth century. Note that in some years Cecelia resided just blocks from the house where Fanny (F) lived her whole life. (Derived from Louisville city directories, University of Louisville Archives, Louisville, Ky., and Larrison Pension File, National Archives, Washington, D.C. Not all streets are shown.)

In some ways, the establishment of separate public institutions for blacks constituted political victories for the African American community. Orphanages, schools for the blind and deaf, asylums for the mentally ill, and other public institutions all set up separate departments for blacks. Although inadequately funded by the state, segregated public institutions were viewed as preferable to no public institutions at all, which had often been the case for Kentucky's black residents a decade before. "Through sheer determination and while occupying the bottom rung of the economic ladder," historian Marion Lucas concluded, "by 1891 they had acquired expanded political and legal rights, a system of public schools, and inclusion in most state social service programs, though always on a segregated basis." While many black leaders were hopeful that these political and institutional victories would result in full equality for blacks in the near future, the white community moved in the opposite direction, steadily increasing the degree of racial separation and putting a legal imprimatur on existing inequalities.[24]

While Mamie's marriage to Reels helped both daughter and mother survive the economic and emotional impact of William Larrison's disappearance, they were far from secure. As mentioned previously, Cecelia had probably already renewed contact with Fanny by the time of Mamie's marriage, perhaps to seek aid following William's presumed death. Her need for such aid increased toward the end of the century. Over the winter of 1898–1899, she had to rely on public charity, receiving half a load of coal from the mayor's office. And she found herself turning again to the Ballard family to help her. "I thought i would send you this few lines to aske you if you would pleas assist me a little with a littel money," she wrote on Valentine's Day in 1899. "I fell doun about 2 weeks ago on the ice and hurt my self very bad and i am not abel to do any thing[.] I have not got my pension yet but i will pay you back as soon as i get it if you will oblige me. . . . I am very much in need."[25]

With Fanny dead, the burden of the rekindled relationship between Cecelia and the Ballards fell on Rogers Clark's shoulders. He was decidedly less sympathetic than his mother. Cecelia was the "last of the old negroe slaves to return to her old mistress for aid and support in her declining years and, my parents being dead, I suppose it will fall to my lot to render her such aid as she may require during the remainder of her life," he wrote grudgingly. "Cecelia ran off when she was only 20 years old, and that over fifty years ago. I fail to see any legal or moral claim that she can have on the family for support."[26]

Rogers Clark's grumpy paternalism fits well into the overall pattern of relations between former masters and former slaves. Many former masters remained skeptical of blacks' abilities to care for themselves in freedom. Rogers Clark expressed his absolute confidence that "she will call for more money." Despite her long years living in freedom by her earnings from her own labor, he described her as "practically a pensioner on the children of her former mistress." His account of meeting Cecelia betrayed little sympathetic understanding that her poverty rested in good measure on her limited opportunities for education and employment, coupled with her growing decrepitude as she got older. For Rogers Clark, it was just the unfortunate lot of former masters to have to take care of former slaves.[27]

Cecelia's letter asking for aid showed she had a different view of the transaction than Rogers Clark. In Rogers Clark's eyes, Cecelia was begging. Cecelia's letter, however, clearly asks for a loan, not a handout—thus the promise to pay the money back when she received her pension. Her pension claim had not gone smoothly, however. The guardians of the public treasury had several reasons for viewing it suspiciously. The lack of formality that had attended her marriage to Larrison—no formal license had ever been issued, although Cecelia did have a certificate of marriage signed by a pastor—made them want more proof that she was actually Larrison's wife. Another issue that had bedeviled her claim was the name under which Larrison had enlisted. In her initial claim, Cecelia had written that she was "claiming pension as the widow of Wm. H. Larrison who served under name Wm. H. Harrison." The enrolling clerk had apparently opted to give William the more easily recognizable name of a past president, and this eponymous error snarled the paperwork behind Cecelia's claim. A third issue also raised the suspicions of the pension commissioners: William's missing corpse. In the absence of a body or a death certificate, they needed to verify somehow Cecelia's claim that he was not coming back.[28]

For all these reasons, Cecelia's initial claim was routed to a special examiner, who took the next two years—from 1896 to 1898—to document Cecelia's claims. He forwarded his report to the commissioner of pensions in Washington, D.C., on June 23, 1898. The examiner was convinced, first off, that Cecelia was an actual widow. "It is not uncommon," he wrote, "for a man to be lost overboard from one of these river steamboats and all that is ever heard of it is of an unknown man being drowned and it is possible this is the case with claimant's husband." If Larrison had been alive, the examiner added, he would in all likelihood have already applied for a pension himself. The examiner suggested checking in Rochester and Wilmington to see if William had showed up in his "old haunts." If not, "I believe the presumption of his death would be strong enough to warrant favorable adjudication of the claim." As to William's identity, the examiner admitted the evidence was not as strong. He had interviewed several of William's comrades from the Fourteenth Heavy Artillery, who confirmed that Cecelia was his wife, although they had trouble remembering exactly who William was. One remembered a "Billy Harrison" who was known in the company by both surnames, but this witness recalled the man dying during the siege of Petersburg, Virginia, in March 1865. Nonetheless, the examiner believed that a quick check with the surviving officers of the Fourteenth New York Heavy Artillery or their widows would probably support Cecelia's claim.[29]

His argument failed to convince the pension bureaucracy, however. On April 28, 1899, the commissioner of pensions rejected Cecelia's pension claim, for the reason that "the evidence on file after special examination of the claim fails to prove identity of claimant's husband Larrison with the soldier William H. Harrison." After hearing about Cecelia's pension claim, Rogers Clark wrote that he did not know whether she was entitled to the money or not, but knowing that her case had "been put off from time to time," he pronounced it likely that she would "leave her claim to her daughter as her only legacy."[30]

Things went from bad to worse for Cecelia over the summer of 1899. In May of that year, her son-in-law, Alexander Reels, had some sort of accident. With Reels bedridden, it fell to Cecelia to nurse him, while Mamie worked to support the family. But Cecelia could still do something to boost their finances. In June, she approached Rogers Clark again, this time revealing that she had "many letters" from Fanny. Rogers Clark offered to pay Cecelia $5 for the lot. A few days later, she brought over the five letters that currently reside in the archives and got her payment. "Suppose I shall have to buy the others later," Rogers Clark sighed. Unfortunately, Reels never recovered from his fall; he died on September 13, 1899. "Paralysis" is listed as the cause of death on his death record. Facing destitution, Cecelia turned again to Rogers Clark. "i am going to aske you a favor again as i am in distress on acont of the Death of my son in law this morning at 2 Oclock," she wrote. "Will you pleas let me have a few dollors to help me at this present time of distress as i would like to get me a littel something to Norrish me[.]" There is no record of Rogers Clark's response.[31]

Reels's death threw Mamie and Cecelia back on their own resources. Instability again ruled their lives; in the next ten years, the two women were listed at seven different addresses in the city directory. Cecelia also was going blind, which limited the amount of money she could bring in. She was listed only sporadically in the directories after 1899, and most often her occupational designation was laundress. On one pension affidavit testifying to her disabilities, the affiant wrote that Cecelia was entirely blind in one eye and rapidly losing sight in the other. She also stated that Cecelia was nearly lame from "running a needle in her foot over a year ago." Cecelia was "entirely unable to do any thing toward earning a living." Thus Mamie shouldered the wage-earning burden, working as a nursemaid and domestic to support her mother.[32]

With her earning potential limited, Cecelia again turned to the pension system. Two weeks after Reels's death, she took action. She did what most pensioners whose claims were denied or delayed did— she wrote to her congressman, in this case Kentucky senator William Lindsay. She asked for his help in reopening her case. She told him that the variation in her husband's name was "slight, but sufficient to reject a poor colored woman's claim." She also asked Rogers Clark to write a letter in her favor to the commissioner of the Pension Bureau. "I thought if you would pleas send me a few lines to Washington to Clay Evans it may do me some good," she pleaded.[33]

By making her individual petition to Senator Lindsay, Cecelia did exactly what the pension system wanted her to do. By the 1890s, pension money had become a principal means by which politicians and parties—particularly Republicans—maintained and strengthened their political power. The pension laws were complex enough and the pension bureaucracy inefficient enough that timely intervention by one's legislator could shake money free, leaving the pensioner beholden to the man in power, and likely to remember the favor on Election Day. The pension system went through various mutations in the years after the war, steadily expanding the number of people to whom it paid money. By the 1890s, it had morphed into America's first welfare system—"an open-ended system of disability, old-age, and survivors' benefits for anyone who could claim minimal service time on the northern side of the Civil War," according to Theda Skocpol, a Harvard historical sociologist who studied the pension system. At first, pension claims reached an apparent peak in the early 1870s, when payments were tied to death or injuries suffered during the war. But several pieces of congressional legislation expanded both the benefits of pensions and the number of eligible pensioners. The Dependent Pension Act of 1890, under which Cecelia claimed benefits, finally threw open the floodgates by discarding the need to prove a service-related injury. Now any disability, no matter when suffered, qualified veterans—or their dependent survivors—for a pension. The system became financial fuel for congressional favors to constituents—"patronage democracy," to use Skocpol's term.[34]

Claims were encouraged by a specialized army of pension attorneys, whose agents scoured the country advertising for potential claimants. Cecelia probably learned about her eligibility through such a system of advertising and laid her case in the hands of John Raum, a Washington, D.C.–based pension lawyer who shepherded her application through the pension bureaucracy. Limited by law to a $10 fee for each application, attorneys like Raum had a vested interest in a high volume of applications. For Cecelia, the system worked. With Senator Lindsay applying pressure on the pension board and attorney Raum digging up new testimony from some of William's wartime comrades, Cecelia's case was reopened on August 21, 1899. On October 11, her claim was accepted, and she began receiving regular monthly payments of $12 from the federal government.[35]

The monthly pension, while welcomed, hardly guaranteed Mamie and Cecelia's solvency. Still, it was a dependable source of income, augmented by Mamie's work as a laundress and nursemaid. In 1906, however, Cecelia's overworked body broke down. Unable to care for herself, she became totally dependent on Mamie, who eventually had to give up her job as a nursemaid to care for her mother. Now the government stipend became Cecelia's last lifeline. Dr. T. H. Hayes, Cecelia's physician during this period, noted that Mamie "gave up her employment at a great sacrifice and tenderly and lovingly nursed her blind and invalid mother." Over the next two years, Mamie stayed by Cecelia—trying to preserve her mother's frail health. But it was a losing battle. Cecelia developed an acute nephritis—a kidney ailment—that killed her on June 4, 1909. Dr. Hayes, marveling at Mamie's compassion for her dying mother, wrote, "I have yet to meet any child who was so attentive to parents as Mamie A. Reels was to her mother. . . . She supplied her every want." On June 7, Cecelia was buried in Louisville Cemetery, which had opened in 1886 as a burying ground for blacks, in a plot collectively owned by the Sons and Daughters of Bethel, a black mutual-aid society.[36]

Even her death was not unattended by bureaucratic controversy. Mamie applied for reimbursement from the Bureau of Pensions for a portion of the burial expenses but was denied because the physician's affidavit listed the date of death as June 4, while the death certificate filled out by the undertaker listed it as June 5. Only after the undertaker submitted a sworn statement that the discrepancy had been the result of an oversight did Mamie receive the $12.40 she was due from the government.[37]

For Cecelia, the end of slavery yielded little in terms of opportunity, social mobility, education, or quality of life. She had, of course, freedom, but she had been free for almost two decades before slavery was abolished. Indeed, in some ways, Cecelia seemed less free after 1865 than before it. Her return to Louisville brought her into the boiling pot of Southern resentment about the war, emancipation, and the campaign for black civil rights. It subjected her to legal discrimination, contempt, and condescension from the white community, and a persistent threat of violence. One wonders if she and William would not have been better off staying in Rochester, or moving to Wilmington or even Toronto—although the North hardly embraced blacks' newly won freedom with enthusiasm.

But to ask only what was in it for her probably misstates Cecelia's own motivations. She did not come back to Louisville to pursue individual betterment or an easier life. She came back to try to rebuild what slavery had taken from her: an extended family, an intimate connection with her mother, a chance, perhaps, to call Louisville home in a way that had been impossible when she had been Thruston property. What the Thirteenth Amendment did for her was to remove any lingering fears of reenslavement and thus throw open the entire country—including most especially the former lands of bondage—to her quest. What the end of slavery did was to give her hope—ultimately, and sadly, frustrated and unrealized—but hope nonetheless.

Conclusion
The Bonds of Slavery

According to the official record of her death, Cecelia was born in 1846, the same year she claimed her freedom from slavery at Niagara Falls. Perhaps, as Lincoln said of the nation at Gettysburg, Cecelia experienced a "new birth" when she shed her slave status, or perhaps Mamie—who was doubtless the source of this information—perceived things that way.[1]

Mamie's perception may have had something to do with the steady tightening of racial segregation in Louisville and in Kentucky during the first decades of the twentieth century. The process that had begun in the 1880s and 1890s only became more pronounced after the turn of the century. In addition to those public accommodations from which blacks had been traditionally excluded, other establishments that had previously admitted blacks began to exclude them during these years. Kentucky also passed its notorious Day Law in 1904, prohibiting racial integration in the state's colleges and universities.[2]

In Louisville proper, the year of Cecelia's death saw a blatantly racist mayoral campaign waged by the Democratic nominee. Residential segregation had become more pronounced as well; the neighborhoods of California and Smoketown in Louisville, for example, developed into all-black communities by 1900. In addition, the downtown housing stock had begun to deteriorate, leaving many blacks mired in slumlike conditions and many wealthier whites fleeing the urban core to newer suburbs. Rogers Clark Ballard Thruston, for example, began living at his brother's estate, Lansdowne, in Louisville's "first suburb," Glenview. In 1914, the city passed an ordinance legalizing residential segregation, though the law was later overturned by the Supreme Court, showing that Louisville's black community was still fighting back. Nonetheless, as she witnessed the worsening social and economic conditions for blacks in those years, Mamie may have invested personal significance in her mother's decision to escape slavery.[3]

Mamie herself soon left Louisville behind her. She appeared in the 1910 census as a nursemaid working in a private home and in the 1911 city directory. Then she disappeared. Her name is found neither in the city directories nor in the 1920 census. She did not go back to Rochester; her name is not listed in that city's directories for these years, either. She may have struck out for some other city in the North like Chicago or Dayton or Indianapolis, a small part of the Great Migration of blacks from the South to the North during the early decades of the twentieth century. Whatever she did, she left behind nothing in available archival records that allows her to be traced.[4]

As for Rogers Clark, the descendant of the other main figure in this story, he went on to devote his life to the study of his family's and the nation's history. In the 1880s and 1890s, Rogers Clark had worked as a geologist first for the state and then for a land company financed by himself and his brothers. He worked extensively in the mountains of eastern Kentucky and provided much of the raw material for the literary depiction of this region and its people by two prominent Kentucky authors, James Lane Allen and John Fox Jr. Using the knowledge obtained in his geologic work, Rogers Clark bought large sections of mountain property rich in coal and timber, then made his fortune by selling them.[5]

By the time of Cecelia's death, he had scaled back his business activities and ratcheted up his historical research. He resuscitated and modernized Louisville's Filson Historical Society (then known as the Filson Club) with his own money and the donation of his large collections of letters and papers from members of his family. Having lost untold numbers of documents in a 1906 fire at Lansdowne, he insisted that the Filson obtain a fireproof repository for its holdings. "His vision broadened the horizon of The Filson Club from a socially restricted historical society and collection to the formation of a solid nucleus of an ever-growing body of original historical material," proclaimed Thomas Clark, the dean of Kentucky historians, in 1984. Rogers Clark became president of the club in 1923, continuing his in-depth researches into his family's past and the nation's past at the club's downtown headquarters. For the modern-day researcher, looking through the collections that Thruston himself helped organize, nothing conveys the meticulousness of the man so much as the short summary notes attached to almost every document, detailing the date, identifying the subjects, and providing helpful context in understanding the relations of the people involved.[6]

Without Rogers Clark's efforts, Cecelia's story—and hence an important piece of Fanny's story—would have been lost. And yet, he seemed peculiarly incurious about Cecelia. Thruston was an early fan of photography, for example—the Filson has thousands of Kodak prints that he took on various journeys. He took pictures of his vacations, his silverware, and even his toenails, but there is no picture of Cecelia or any of the other former slaves he came across in his life. Similarly, he was an astute observer and a valuable font of information about mountain people: their customs, manners, and modes of speech. But he never made any similar effort to learn about the days of slavery or the lives of African Americans, even when people like Adam and Cecelia showed up on his doorstep.

Perhaps he felt he already knew the subject from his own family's papers and reminiscences. It is obvious from the collections that he was not uninterested in slavery and that he appreciated its historical importance. He separated documents dealing with slaves, for example, from his grandfather's other business papers, and he paid Cecelia to deliver the letters written to her by Fanny, then transcribed them and wrote an explanatory introduction. But he never sought Cecelia's point of view, did not collect her letters to Fanny (if they existed), did not ask her many questions about her life. It is not that he was a snob. By all accounts an unpretentious man, he had mingled easily with the humble folk of the Kentucky mountains. It is not that he was incurious about history for, indeed, it was his passion. Rather, it seems that for Thruston, like for so many white Kentuckians of his day, race remained a peculiar blind spot. He died in 1946.

Ballard and Thruston descendants remained prominent in Louisville through the rest of the twentieth century. The families produced business leaders, community benefactors, and one United States senator (Thruston Ballard Morton), leaving behind at least two parks and one prominent local high school bearing the Ballard name.

By contrast, with Mamie's departure, the Holmes/Larrison/Reels story more or less dead-ends. James Reels—Alexander's son and Mamie's stepson—evidently lived on in Louisville. He appears regularly in city directories through the 1920s and 1930s as a laborer for the Ewald Iron Company in Louisville. But he is the only trace that remains.

There is no grand gesture of reconciliation or repentance or forgiveness that ends the story of Cecelia and Fanny. These two women were bound together by the most intimate of oppressions, mistress and maid. They grew up in the same household, corresponded sporadically during Cecelia's sojourn in Canada, and renewed personal contact late in the century, but theirs is not a story that ends tidily. The social categories of race and class and gender that helped to define their lives and divide them as individuals were not superseded or overturned.

Even in death, race and class structured the relationship between Fanny and Cecelia. Fanny was laid to rest in Cave Hill Cemetery, a quintessential Louisville institution, with beautiful parklike grounds and many memorials to prominent Louisvillians, most of them white. Cecelia's grave in a group plot in the Louisville Cemetery—in section B, lot 39—today cannot be located with precision. No stone marks the spot, no marker records her name.

Their story is also full of gaps that reflect the all-too-common emptiness of the archival record when it comes to the lives of ordinary people, especially women and minorities. Their story has to be reproduced and reimagined from the fragments that remain. The picture produced from those fragments showed Fanny to be a reluc-

Rogers Clark Ballard Thruston montage. These photos show Rogers Clark as a fifteen-year-old young gentleman in 1873, an established scion of a prominent family (undated) later in the nineteenth century, and as an older man pursuing his research interests at the Filson Historical Society. (Filson Historical Society, Louisville, Ky.)

tant slaveholder and Cecelia a reluctant slave. Yet the power of the institution of slavery was so strong that it forged a bond between them that persisted even into freedom. Slavery was not simply a relationship between master and slave but a network of relationships between entire families. While still in her mother's arms, Cecelia passed into Charles William Thruston's hands. He then gave her to Fanny, whose father continued to hold Cecelia's mother and brother as slaves even after Cecelia fled. It was to Fanny and then to Fanny's son to whom Cecelia turned when in financial trouble. And it was through her son that Fanny bequeathed her tokens of affection to Cecelia. Slavery entailed a web of personal connections that extended beyond a single generation.

Ironically, it was slavery's power to break up families—to sever mother from child, in Cecelia's case—that strengthened the hold of that web on Fanny and Cecelia. Had Mary not been enslaved, Cecelia would have had no need to write Fanny from Canada to bargain for her mother's freedom. Had slavery not prevailed until 1865 in Kentucky, Cecelia might have had no need to journey back to Louisville to seek Mary. Because slavery was not just about the master and the slave but about the master's family and the slave's family, the chains of bondage always consisted of more than just a single strand.

It was Mamie—born free and living her entire life in freedom—who seemed to feel the hold of that web most lightly. Mamie may also be the key to appreciating what freedom meant for Cecelia. Cecelia's life was never easy; it consisted mostly of hard work for limited material rewards under circumstances very often prejudiced against her success. But freedom gave her the chance to marry, to build a life with her husband and daughter through their own labor, and to ensure that her child never bore the burdens of slavery. Some vision of that future must have beckoned Cecelia on that night when, as a fifteen-year-old girl, she left her mistress behind and stepped into a boat that took her across the Niagara River into freedom.

Acknowledgments

A book is always a collective project. My collective has included the ever-helpful archivists at the repositories I consulted. The staff at the Filson Historical Society in Louisville, Kentucky, where I first became interested in the stories of Cecelia and Fanny, was unfailingly helpful and knowledgeable. I also thank the Filson for permission to publish the portraits and photographs of the members of the Ballard and Thruston families. The archivists at the Earl K. Long Library at the University of New Orleans, the Huntington Library in San Marino, California, the National Archives in Washington, D.C., and the University of Louisville also helped me locate important sources—either in person or through e-mail exchanges—that helped fill in some of the gaps in these two women's lives. I would also like to thank Janice Nickerson, who did vital research in Canada on my behalf, tracking down the traces Cecelia left behind in Toronto. The Toronto Public Library, the Rochester Public Library in New York, the New York State Library, and Niagara University also helped me by obtaining and scanning the illustrations used in the book.

The manuscript benefited from the careful review given it by the readers and editors of the University Press of Kentucky. I would also like to thank my wife, Sue, and my brother, Curt, for reading the entire manuscript and suggesting improvements before it was submitted to the press. Portions of the manuscript were also read by David Hudacek and Andrew Deiss, both of whom deserve my gratitude. Finally, my family gave this project endless encouragement and unflagging support; without their love, I would not have completed it.

Notes

Preface

1. Bingham, *Mordecai* relied on an extraordinary collection of family correspondence; Ulrich, *Midwife's Tale* used the extensive run of Martha Ballard's diaries; Demos, *Unredeemed Captive* utilized the Reverend John Williams's sermons to describe the plight of his kidnapped daughter, Eunice. For interesting reflections on these books and more conventional biographies, see Lepore, "Historians Who Love Too Much."

1. Eight Minutes from Freedom

1. Rogers Clark Ballard Thruston, June 5, 1899, in a short explanatory note attached to his mother's papers, Ballard Family Papers (hereafter cited as BFP). On Niagara's place in the transit of fugitive slaves to freedom, see Sennett, *North Star Country*, 185–92. Harriet Tubman led many slaves to freedom across the Niagara. On local Niagara landmarks significant to Harriet Tubman's story, see Blockson, *Hippocrene Guide*, 64, 76. A description of the eight-minute ferry journey is found in Barham, *Descriptions*, 12, 19.

2. According to Franklin and Schweninger, "Networks to return . . . slaves were well established. In southern Ohio, Indiana, and Illinois, many residents sympathized with the South." *Runaway Slaves*, 27, 149–60.

3. Franklin, *Southern Odyssey*, 130–39.

4. Kieffer, *Maligned General*, xi, 96–97, 242, 250.

5. "Two Days at Niagara," 729; Franklin, *Southern Odyssey*, 115.

6. Barham, *Descriptions*, 127.

7. Ibid., 158–59; "Two Days at Niagara," 728. On Niagara's development, see Dubinsky, *Second Greatest Disappointment*; Sears, *Sacred Places*, 12–30; John F. Sears, "Niagara Falls," in Boyer, *Oxford Companion*, 554.

8. Barham, *Descriptions*, 106.

9. Ibid., 70, 9; Southern traveler quoted in Franklin, *Southern Odyssey*, 115.

10. Barham, *Descriptions*, 20, 107.

11. Ibid., 20, 27, 29, 65; Franklin, *Southern Odyssey*, 115.

12. "Two Days at Niagara," 730; Barham, *Descriptions*, 12, 33, 65, 169. Similar overuse of the "sublime" showed up in soldiers' accounts of the Mexican War, according to David Johannsen. See *To the Halls of the Montezumas*, 84.

13. Franklin, *Southern Odyssey*, 134–36; Middleton, "Law and Ideology," 357–58; Hardy and Robinson, "Freedom and Domicile Jurisprudence," 306–16.

14. See Finkelman, *Imperfect Union*, 75.

15. Franklin, *Southern Odyssey*, 137; Finkelman, *Imperfect Union*, 112–25; *Commonwealth v. Aves*, 18 Pickering 193.

16. Finkelman, *Imperfect Union*, 131; on the religious revival in New York state and its relation to the antislavery cause, see Sennett, *North Star Country*.

17. Franklin, *Southern Odyssey*, 138–39; Finkelman, *Imperfect Union*, 296–302.

18. Quoted in Franklin, *Southern Odyssey*, 132.

19. Barham, *Descriptions*, 19; Sennett, *North Star Country*, 148, 281; Butler, "Starting Anew," 77; Winks, *Blacks in Canada*, 146.

20. On the changing historiography of the Underground Railroad, see John Michael Vlach, "Above Ground on the Underground Railroad: Places of Flight and Refuge," and David W. Blight, "Why the Underground Railroad and Why Now? A Long View," in Blight, *Passages to Freedom*, 97, 243. The book that first argued for a revisionist view of the romantic image of the Underground Railroad was Gara, *Liberty Line*.

21. *True Wesleyan*, August 14, 1847, available at www.wesleyan.org/doc/true_wesleyan.

22. *Buffalo Republic*, July 12, 1847; *Buffalo Commercial Advertiser*, July 12, 1847; *Albany Evening Journal*, July 14, 1847 (reprinting the article from the *Buffalo Express*).

23. *Albany Evening Journal*, July 14, 1847; *Buffalo Republic*, July 12, 1847; *True Wesleyan*, August 14, 1847. On Southerners' views of the increasing intensity of abolitionist feeling in the North, see Franklin, *Southern Odyssey*, 165–66.

24. *True Wesleyan*, August 14, 1847; *Pennsylvania Freeman*, July 13, 1847, July 22, 1847.

25. Rogers Clark Ballard Thruston, June 5, 1899, BFP.

26. Wade, *Slavery in the Cities*, 223; James Oliver Horton, "A Crusade for Freedom: William Still and the Real Underground Railroad," in Blight, *Passages to Freedom*, 186–87; Franklin, *Southern Odyssey*, 138; Franklin and Schweninger, *Runaway Slaves*, 250–51, 275–79.

27. Rogers Clark Ballard Thruston, June 5, 1899, BFP.

28. The historical literature on slave agency and resistance before, during, and after the Civil War is vast. For two early and groundbreaking works in this mold, see Genovese, *Roll, Jordan, Roll* and Gutman, *Black Family*. The degree to which this view has become accepted by historians can be seen in the matter-of-fact summaries given to this vast literature in recent works of synthesis. See, for example, Foner, *Reconstruction*, 3–4; Franklin and Schweninger, *Runaway Slaves*, xiii–xv. The author of one monograph on slavery stated that he did not separately focus on slave resistance because resistance ran through the entire topic of slavery. See Morgan, *Slave Counterpoint*, xxi–xxiii. For a summary statement on slave resistance in Kentucky, see the standard work on Kentucky history, Harrison and Klotter, *New History of Kentucky*, 170–73.

29. On the various motivations of slaves who ran away, see Franklin and Schweninger, *Runaway Slaves*, 19–48; Vlach, "Above Ground," 97–98. On relations between maids and their mistresses, see Fox-Genovese, *Within the Plantation Household*, 152, 162–63.

30. Quoted in David W. Blight, "Introduction: The Underground Railroad in History and Memory," in Blight, *Passages to Freedom*, 2.

2. Fanny: Learning to Be a Slave Owner

1. Rogers Clark Ballard Thruston, June 5, 1899, BFP. John Hope Franklin has written that slaveholders' own self-image as "kind, God-fearing, humane masters" obscured their understanding of slaves' motivations for running away. Franklin and Schweninger, *Runaway Slaves*, 248. On masters' self-perception within Kentucky, see Aron, *How the West Was Lost*, 144.

2. Rogers Clark Ballard Thruston, June 5, 1899, BFP.

3. Fox-Genovese, *Within the Plantation Household*, 112, 115; Johnson, *Soul by Soul*, 101; Frost, *I've Got a Home in Glory Land*, 97–98.

4. Rogers Clark Ballard Thruston, June 5, 1899, BFP. For white Kentuckians' attitudes toward slavery more generally, see Hudson, "Slavery in Early Louisville," 262, 282–83.

5. Frances Fitzhugh to John O'Fallon, July 26, 1824, Thruston Family Files (hereafter TFF).

6. Yater, *Two Hundred Years*, 34.

7. Ibid., 37.

8. Charles William Thruston to John O'Fallon, October 15, 1825, Charles William Thruston Papers (hereafter CWT Papers), box 1, folder 6. On the expansion of slavery, see Henretta et al., *America's History*, 246–47; Hopkins, *History of the Hemp Industry*, ix–x, 4, 85–86.

9. Lucas, *History of Blacks in Kentucky*, 4–5; Harrison and Klotter, *New History of Kentucky*, 135; Hopkins, *History of the Hemp Industry*, 4, 24–30, 196. The numbers for Fayette County come from Aron, *How the West Was Lost*, 133. Louisville figures are from *Louisville Directory of 1832*, 132.

10. Hopkins, *History of the Hemp Industry*, xi, 132–33.

11. Lucas, *History of Blacks in Kentucky*, 8, 11. On Thruston's slave purchases, see Charles William Thruston Miscellaneous Papers (hereafter CWT Misc.); on the sale of the ropewalk, see Charles William Thruston to John O'Fallon, January 26, 1837, CWT Papers, box 1, folder 6.

12. *Louisville Public Advertiser*, April 30, 1828, August 23, 1828.

13. Examples of hiring contracts can be found in CWT Misc. On slave hiring more generally, see Lucas, *History of Blacks in Kentucky*, 101–7; Yater, *Two Hundred Years*, 42–43; Mary Lawrence Bickett O'Brien, "Slavery in Louisville, 1820–1860," in Kleber, *Encyclopedia of Louisville*, 826; Wade, *Slavery in the Cities*, 38.

14. Charles William Thruston to John O'Fallon, September 28, 1829, CWT Papers, box 1, folder 6; bill of sale, November 1, 1846, CWT Misc.; Tax Assessment Records, 1830.

15. Charles William Thruston to John O'Fallon, December 8, 1827, CWT Papers, box 1, folder 6. For a general discussion of why slaves ran away, see Franklin and Schweninger, *Runaway Slaves*, 17–48; Lucas, *History of Blacks in Kentucky*, 57, 62–64.

16. *Daily Louisville Public Advertiser*, December 16, 1830.

17. Frost, *I've Got a Home in Glory Land*, 9; Lucas, *History of Blacks in Kentucky*, 61.

18. Power of attorney, January 4, 1831, CWT Misc.

19. Franklin and Schweninger, *Runaway Slaves*, 156–57; Lucas, *History of Blacks in Kentucky*, 61.

20. "Papers concerning Baldwin Jones a Colored Man," [1829–30?], CWT Misc. Unfortunately, there is nothing on the final outcome of this case in Thruston's papers.

21. Bill for services rendered in 1832 by Hays & Scott, CWT Papers, box 4, folder 25, "Ropewalk Business Papers"; bill from Thomas Jefferson for services rendered during 1834, CWT Misc.

22. Wade, *Slavery in the Cities*, 94–95; receipt of Charles William Thruston, July 20, 1836, CWT Misc.

23. For the various transactions involving Wesley, see bill of sale, Julius Bohannan to Charles William Thruston and Alfred Thruston, January 20, 1832; bill of sale, Alfred Thruston to Charles William Thruston, December 4, 1833, CWT Misc.

24. Hanes Maclellan to Charles William Thruston, October 30, 1837, CWT Misc.

25. Bill of sale, Charles William Thruston to T. and J. Arterburn, September 17, 1846, CWT Misc.

26. On the interstate slave trade in Kentucky, see Harrison and Klotter, *New History of Kentucky*, 167–68; Lucas, *History of Blacks in Kentucky*, 84–100; O'Brien, "Slavery in Louisville," 826; Yater, *Two Hundred Years*, 81.

27. The conclusions of this paragraph derive largely from Gudmestad, *Troublesome Commerce*, 4, 200–201.

28. Charles William Thruston to John O'Fallon, January 26, 1837, CWT Papers, box 1, folder 6.

29. Charles William Thruston to John O'Fallon, April 25, 1836, CWT Papers, box 1, folder 6. On the Panic of 1837, see Watson, *Liberty and Power*, 205–6; Henretta et al., *America's History*, 337–38. On its impact in Kentucky, see Harrison and Klotter, *New History of Kentucky*, 127, 131.

30. Charles William Thruston to John O'Fallon, January 26, 1837, CWT Papers, box 1, folder 6; Tax Assessment Records, 1836 and 1840.

31. Rogers Clark Ballard Thruston, June 5, 1899, BFP.

32. Virginia Hale to Rogers Clark Ballard Thruston, February 21, 1932, TFF, "Thruston Family" folder.

33. This account from a Virginia county history can be found in TFF, "Thruston Family" folder.

34. Ibid.

35. Harrison and Klotter, *New History of Kentucky*, 18–19, 48.

36. Rogers Clark Ballard Thruston to Mrs. Alfred Penn, June 20, 1932, TFF, "Charles Mynn" folder; deed, October 12, 1787, CWT Papers, box 1, folder 1.

37. For population figures, see Harrison and Klotter, *New History of Kentucky*, 48–49. For Thruston family information, see Rogers Clark Ballard Thruston to Joseph Thruston Farrar, December 17, 1943; Rogers Clark Ballard Thruston to Mrs. Alfred Penn, June 20, 1932, TFF, "Charles Mynn" folder; Thruston family tree, undated, TFF, "Thruston Family" folder.

38. James J. Holmberg, "Clark, George Rogers," in Kleber, *Encyclopedia*

of Louisville, 197–98; Rogers Clark Ballard Thruston to Lucy Brown Beale, June 6, 1941, Rogers Clark Ballard Thruston Papers (hereafter RCBT Papers), box 1, folder 4.

39. Rogers Clark Ballard Thruston to Joseph Thruston Farrar, December 17, 1943, TFF, "Charles Mynn" folder.

40. Ibid.

41. Abraham Hite to General Jonathan Clark, December 13, 1800. A copy of the letter is contained in Rogers Clark Ballard Thruston to Miss Marguerite German, October 4, 1940, TFF, "Wills, etc." folder.

42. Rogers Clark Ballard Thruston to Joseph Thruston Farrar, December 17, 1943, TFF, "Charles Mynn" folder.

43. Franklin and Schweninger, *Runaway Slaves,* 100.

44. Ibid., 103–9; Lucas, *History of Blacks in Kentucky,* 57.

45. Rogers Clark Ballard Thruston to Joseph Thruston Farrar, December 17, 1943, TFF, "Charles Mynn" folder; Rogers Clark Ballard Thruston to Sara Banta, August 27, 1932; Banta to Thruston, August 31, 1932, TFF; Franklin and Schweninger, *Runaway Slaves,* 122.

46. Franklin and Schweninger, *Runaway Slaves,* 78, 84–85; Lucas, *History of Blacks in Kentucky,* 58.

47. Rogers Clark Ballard Thruston to Joseph Thruston Farrar, December 17, 1943, TFF, "Charles Mynn" folder.

48. Ibid.

49. Frances Ballard to Cecelia Holmes, August 2, 1855, BFP.

3. Cecelia: Learning about Being a Slave

1. Bill of sale, William Cotton to Charles W. Thruston, October 4, 1831, CWT Misc.

2. Johnson, *Soul by Soul,* 5.

3. *Coot v. Cotton* (1831), case #2410, Supreme Court of Louisiana Historical Archives, box 111; Johnson, *Soul by Soul,* 48.

4. For Cecelia's birthplace, see Death Books, microfilm reel #6; records of the U.S. Bureau of the Census, 1900, microfilm T-623, roll 531. On forced-sale breakups of Kentucky slave families, see Lucas, *History of Blacks in Kentucky,* 24–26; on the lack of legal status for slave marriage, see Henretta et al., *America's History,* 249; Harrison and Klotter, *New History of Kentucky,* 173. On reasons for running away, see Franklin and Schweninger, *Runaway Slaves,* 49–67.

5. Rogers Clark Ballard Thruston, June 5, 1899, BFP.

6. Bill of sale, Mary J. Churchill to Charles William Thruston, Janu-

ary 4, 1831, CWT Misc. In this scenario, Mary would have been about twenty-two years old when Edward was born.

7. Wade, *Slavery in the Cities*, 56–59; Lucas, *History of Blacks in Kentucky*, 14; Yater, *Two Hundred Years*, 42; O'Brien, "Slavery in Louisville," 825.

8. Wade, *Slavery in the Cities*, 64, 70–71.

9. Yater, *Two Hundred Years*, 42; O'Brien, "Slavery in Louisville," 25. See generally Genovese, *Roll, Jordan, Roll*; Henretta et al., *America's History*, 249–51; Faust, "Culture, Conflict and Community."

10. Wade, *Slavery in the Cities*, 19–27, 330. Wade's figures show a female-to-male ratio among slaves in Louisville of 1.08:1 in 1820, 1.11:1 in 1830, 1.48:1 in 1840, 1.25:1 in 1850, and 1.49:1 in 1860.

11. See generally ibid., esp. 38, 84–91, 143–44; also 61.

12. Frances Ballard to Cecelia Holmes, January 25, 1857, BFP; Lucas, *History of Blacks in Kentucky*, 102, 107; Wade, *Slavery in the Cities*, 48–51.

13. Wade, *Slavery in the Cities*, 144, 149, 173–78.

14. Ibid., 28–29; Deborah Gray White, "Simple Truths: Antebellum Slavery in Black and White," in Blight, *Passages to Freedom*, 35.

15. Lucas, *History of Blacks in Kentucky*, 14; Grady Clay, "Alleys," in Kleber, *Encyclopedia of Louisville*, 25.

16. Bill of sale, Algernon Thruston to Charles William Thruston, March 23, 1823; bill of sale, Mary J. Churchill to Charles William Thruston, January 4, 1831, CWT Misc.; Wade, *Slavery in the Cities*, 30–32; Lucas, *History of Blacks in Kentucky*, 10. See also Fox-Genovese, *Within the Plantation Household*, 152–53.

17. Schwartz, *Born in Bondage*, 110, 114.

18. Henry Bibb's experience is cited by Lucas, *History of Blacks in Kentucky*, 7.

19. Fox-Genovese, *Within the Plantation Household*, 112, 115; Wade, *Slavery in the Cities*, 28–30; Johnson, *Soul by Soul*, 92.

20. Schwartz, *Born in Bondage*, 118; Johnson, *Soul by Soul*, 92.

21. Papers dated December 9, 1832, and May 22, 1835, CWT Papers, box 1, folder 6.

22. Lucas, *History of Blacks in Kentucky*, 6; Schwartz, *Born in Bondage*, 110.

23. Frances Ballard to Cecelia Holmes, August 2, 1855, BFP.

24. Rogers Clark Ballard Thruston, June 5, 1899, BFP.

25. On corporal punishment as "education," see Schwartz, *Born in Bondage*, 109.

26. Fox-Genovese, *Within the Plantation Household*, 152, 162–63; Schwartz, *Born in Bondage*, 186.

27. Fox-Genovese, *Within the Plantation Household*, 112, 115.

28. For the duties of household slaves in Kentucky, see Lucas, *History of Blacks in Kentucky*, 6–7.

29. *Louisville Daily Journal*, February 10, 1842.

30. On the creation of these diverse social networks, see Wade, *Slavery in the Cities*, 144; on the limitations placed on house servants' participation in these networks, including opportunities for courtship, see Schwartz, *Born in Bondage*, 186.

31. On the operation of the Underground Railroad in Kentucky, see Lucas, *History of Blacks in Kentucky*, 66–73; Hudson, "Crossing the 'Dark Line.'"

4. Fanny: A Woman's Place

1. Tax Assessment Records, 1847.

2. Edmonia [surname unknown] to Matilda January, March 27, 1832, TFF, "Thruston Family" folder.

3. T. Lewiuske to Frances Thruston, April 13, 1840, BFP. Rogers Clark's quote is from a notation attached to his mother's papers.

4. Yater, *Two Hundred Years*, 58, 61; Webster, "Louisville in the Eighteen Fifties," 132.

5. *Louisville Daily Courier*, June 12, 1855; Yater, *Two Hundred Years*, 58, 61–65.

6. Yater, *Two Hundred Years*, 65–70; George Yater, "Bloody Monday," in Kleber, *Encyclopedia of Louisville*, 97.

7. Webster, "Louisville in the Eighteen Fifties," 133; Yater, *Two Hundred Years*, 65; Harrison and Klotter, *New History of Kentucky*, 102.

8. Rothman, *Hands and Hearts*, 163.

9. Ballard's reminiscences of the courtship can be found in a chronicle entitled "Souvenirs," dated February 9, 1848, in Andrew Jackson Ballard Papers (hereafter AJB Papers), box 1, folder 1.

10. Ibid.

11. Christ Church Cathedral register, 1829–66, reel 1, pp. 82, 84.

12. "Souvenirs," February 9, 1848, AJB Papers, box 1, folder 1; Mary Lou (Smith) Madigan, "Ballard, Bland W.," in Kleber, *Encyclopedia of Louisville*, 58; *Biographical Encyclopedia*, 431.

13. Ballard Family Files (hereafter BFF), "Ballard Family Special" folder. James's whereabouts during the Indian attack on his family were surmised by Rogers Clark Ballard Thruston. See BFF, "Ballard Notes" folder.

14. *Biographical Encyclopedia*, 431; Tax Assessment Records, 1838 and 1847.

15. "Souvenirs," February 9, 1848, AJB Papers, box 1, folder 1.

16. Ibid.

17. Ibid.; Ott, *Fevered Lives*, 13–14; Rothman, *Hands and Hearts*, 92; Lystra, *Searching the Heart*, 122–23.

18. "Souvenirs," February 9, 1848, AJB Papers, box 1, folder 1.

19. Ibid.; Andrew Jackson Ballard to Frances Thruston, December 11, 1847, AJB Papers, box 1, folder 1.

20. Andrew Jackson Ballard to Frances Thruston, December 29, 1847, AJB Papers, box 1, folder 1.

21. Andrew Jackson Ballard to Frances Thruston, January 1, 1848, AJB Papers, box 1, folder 1.

22. Andrew Jackson Ballard to Frances Thruston, January 8, 1848, AJB Papers, box 1, folder 1.

23. Andrew Jackson Ballard to Frances Thruston, January 10, 1848; Rogers Clark Ballard Thruston notation, 1929, AJB Papers, box 1, folder 1.

24. Andrew Jackson Ballard to Frances Thruston, February 15, 1849, AJB Papers, box 1, folder 1.

25. Fanny's notation appears on the outside of the envelope containing the packet of letters from Andrew, AJB Papers, box 1, folder 1.

26. Rothman, *Hands and Hearts*, 9, 11–12, 103, 104–6; Lystra, *Searching the Heart*, 13, 28, 31; Christopher Wells, "Courtship and Dating," in Boyer, *Oxford Companion*, 164–65.

27. Lystra, *Searching the Heart*, 157–58, 166–83, 190.

28. Ibid., 158; Rothman, *Hands and Hearts*, 119–22.

29. Andrew Jackson Ballard to Frances Thruston, December 11, 1847, AJB Papers, box 1, folder 1. See also Rothman, *Hands and Hearts*, 117, on fathers' reluctance to see their daughters marry.

30. Rothman, *Hands and Hearts*, 148.

31. Ibid., 107; Wells, "Courtship and Dating," 164.

32. Obituary, n.d., newspaper not identified, in BFF, "Ballard Family Newspaper Clippings" folder.

33. Fox-Genovese, *Within the Plantation Household*, 140; Tax Assessment Records, 1850.

34. Andrew Jackson Ballard to Frances Ballard, December 22, 1849, AJB Papers, box 1, folder 1. See Lucas, *History of Blacks in Kentucky*, 43–46; Harrison and Klotter, *New History of Kentucky*, 169–70; Franklin and Schweninger, *Runaway Slaves*, 241; Davidson et al., *Nation of Nations*, 339; Morgan, *American Slavery*, 310–13.

35. Ballard family information from genealogical chart in TFF.

36. Andrew Jackson Ballard to Frances Ballard, December 22, 1849;

Andrew Jackson Ballard to Frances Ballard, December 19, 1849, AJB Papers, box 1, folder 1.

37. Andrew Jackson Ballard to Frances Ballard, December 15, 1849; Andrew Jackson Ballard to Frances Ballard, December 19, 1849, AJB Papers, box 1, folder 1.

38. Tax Assessment Records, 1847, 1850, and 1860.

5. Cecelia: A Family in Freedom

1. Ira Berlin, "Before Cotton: African and African American Slavery in Mainland North America during the Seventeenth and Eighteenth Centuries," in Blight, *Passages to Freedom*, 26–27; Davidson et al., *Nation of Nations*, 625.

2. Winks, *Blacks in Canada*, 240.

3. Franklin and Schweninger, *Runaway Slaves*, 25–27, 210; Yee, "Gender Ideology," 56. For a conflicting interpretation on the gender of fugitive slaves, see Griffler, "Beyond the Quest," 6–7.

4. Winks, *Blacks in Canada*, 144–45; Vlach, "Above Ground," 113.

5. Winks, *Blacks in Canada*, 144–46; Vlach, "Above Ground," 113–14; Butler, "Starting Anew."

6. Drew, *North-Side View*, 94; Hill, "Blacks in Toronto," 80, 84.

7. Hill, "Blacks in Toronto," 76, 80; Drew, *North-Side View*, 94, 112. See also Frost, *I've Got a Home in Glory Land*, 254–62.

8. Yee, "Gender Ideology," 58; Frost, *I've Got a Home in Glory Land*, 267–68.

9. Drew, *North-Side View*, 98, 112–14.

10. Davidson et al., *Nation of Nations*, 625; Berlin, "Before Cotton," 29; Lucas, *History of Blacks in Kentucky*, 17; Robertson, *Landmarks of Toronto* (viewable online at http://homepages.rootsweb.com/~maryc/old5.htm).

11. Census of Canada, 1861, Toronto, St. John's Ward; state census of Minnesota, 1875, Rice County (Faribault); U.S. federal census, 1880, Faribault, Rice County, Minnesota, from www.Ancestry.com (online database).

12. Frost, *I've Got a Home in Glory Land*, 267–71. Profiles of some prominent black citizens can be found on the City of Toronto's Web site, www.city.toronto.on.ca/blackhistory. Winks, *Blacks in Canada*, 246; Armstrong, *Rowsell's City of Toronto*; Yee, "Gender Ideology," 58.

13. Winks, *Blacks in Canada*, 246; Yee, "Gender Ideology," 58.

14. Davidson et al., *Nation of Nations*, 625.

15. Yee, "Gender Ideology," 60–73; Frost, *I've Got a Home in Glory Land*, 272.

16. Hembree, "Question of 'Begging,'" 316; Frances Ballard to Cecelia Holmes, March 11, 1852, BFP. On Charles C. Foote, see Hayden, *Early History*, 337–38; *Proceedings of the Convention of Radical Political Abolitionists*, 57; *Proceedings of the National Liberty Convention*. These documents and others are available online as part of the Samuel J. May Anti-slavery Collection at Cornell University, dlxs.library.cornell.edu/m/mayantislavery/index.htm. Foote studied under famed revivalist Charles Grandison Finney at Oberlin and was one of several clergymen and former students who gave addresses at Finney's funeral in July 1876. See the Web site www.gospeltruth.net/reminiscenses/remin02.htm.

17. Hembree, "Question of 'Begging,'" 316; Frances Ballard to Cecelia Holmes, March 11, 1852, BFP; Winks, *Blacks in Canada*, 160–61, 168; Baker, introduction, 23.

18. Winks, *Blacks in Canada*, 143; Yee, "Gender Ideology," 63–64, 71–72; Hill, "Blacks in Toronto," 78–81, 84.

19. Hill, "Blacks in Toronto," 85; Yee, "Gender Ideology," 71.

20. Hill, "Blacks in Toronto," 85–87; Silverman, "'We Shall Be Heard,'" 61.

21. Hembree, "Question of 'Begging,'" 316–17.

22. Silverman, "'We Shall Be Heard,'" 59–64; Hembree, "Question of 'Begging,'" 324–25; Yee, "Gender Ideology," 70–71.

23. Silverman, "'We Shall Be Heard,'" 64; Hembree, "Question of 'Begging,'" 324; Winks, *Blacks in Canada*, 261.

24. Hembree, "Question of 'Begging,'" 318–23.

25. Instrument #53113, York County Land Registry Records; Winks, *Blacks in Canada*, 247.

26. James Oliver Horton, "A Crusade for Freedom: William Still and the Real Underground Railroad," in Blight, *Passages to Freedom*, 177.

27. Frances Ballard to Cecelia Holmes, March 11, 1852, BFP.

28. James Brewer Stewart, "From Moral Suasion to Political Confrontation: American Abolitionists and the Problem of Resistance, 1831–1861," in Blight, *Passages to Freedom*, 88.

29. These numbers are cited in Lois E. Horton, "Kidnapping and Resistance: Antislavery Direct Action in the 1850s," in Blight, *Passages to Freedom*, 166.

30. Frances Ballard to Cecelia Holmes, March 11, 1852, BFP.

31. Ibid.

32. Ibid. See also the discussion of morality and Southern guilt in McLaurin, *Celia*, 142–43, 165n.

33. Frances Ballard to Cecelia Holmes, August 2, 1855, BFP.

34. Ibid.

35. Ibid. On the kidnapping of free blacks, see Franklin and Schweninger, *Runaway Slaves*, 182–89; Lucas, *History of Blacks in Kentucky*, 115.

36. Craik, *Slavery in the South*, 7–15 (available online at www.library .umass.edu/spcoll/digital/antislavery/288.pdf); Kenneth Dennis, "Craik, James," and Olivia Frederick, "Christ Church Cathedral," in Kleber, *Encyclopedia of Louisville*, 178, 229.

37. Tax Assessment Records, 1850 and 1860.

38. Fanny mentions the actions of Dr. Croghan in Frances Ballard to Cecelia Holmes, August 2, 1855, BFP. See also J. Blaine Hudson, "Bishop, Stephen," in Kleber, *Encyclopedia of Louisville*, 94; Hudson, "In Pursuit of Freedom," 306.

39. Frances Ballard to Cecelia Holmes, January 25, 1857, BFP.

40. *Brown's Toronto General Directory, 1856; Caverhill's Toronto City Directory for 1859–60;* instrument #53113, March 12, 1854; instrument #63844, September 12, 1856; instrument #71754, March 9, 1858, York County Land Registry Records.

41. Frances Ballard to Cecelia Holmes, January 25, 1857, BFP. The volume that helped establish this interpretation of slave culture is Genovese, *Roll, Jordan, Roll*. See also Faust, "Culture, Conflict and Community," 83–98; Henretta et al., *America's History*, 249–51. For Kentucky examples, see Lucas, *History of Blacks in Kentucky*, 101–7; Barnett, "Virginians Moving West," 221–23, 240–42. For a critique of the overemphasis on personal agency, see McLaurin, *Celia*, 137–38.

42. Frances Ballard to Cecelia Holmes, January 25, 1857, BFP. On antebellum Southern notions of family, see Fox-Genovese, *Within the Plantation Household*, 24–25, 133; Franklin and Schweninger, *Runaway Slaves*, 248–49; Aron, *How the West Was Lost*, 144; Henretta et al., *America's History*, 251.

43. Frances Ballard to Cecelia Holmes, January 25, 1857, BFP.

44. Lucas, *History of Blacks in Kentucky*, 52–57; Hudson, "In Pursuit of Freedom," 319–24; Hudson, "Crossing the 'Dark Line,'" 42–43.

45. 1959 Toronto tax assessment roll, St. John's Ward; instrument #63844, September 12, 1856; instrument #71754, March 9, 1858, York County Land Registry Records. At this time in Canada, both pounds and dollars were in use and accepted as legal tender. See Powell, *History of the Canadian Dollar*, 23.

46. Frances Ballard to Cecelia Holmes, February 23, 1857, BFP.

47. Frances Ballard to Cecelia Holmes, January 25, 1857, BFP.

48. Frances Ballard to Cecelia Holmes, August 11, 1859, BFP.

49. Compensated emancipation was usually coupled with the idea of the colonization of former slaves; that is, the freed slaves would be expected to emigrate to Liberia. See Harrison and Klotter, *New History of Kentucky*, 176; Henretta et al., *America's History*, 384–85; William H. Brackney, "Antislavery," in Boyer, *Oxford Companion*, 43.

50. On the Jefferson County manumission records, see Hudson, "In Pursuit of Freedom," 294–98. On the war-driven disintegration of slavery in Louisville, see Yater, *Two Hundred Years*, 91–92.

51. Lucas, *History of Blacks in Kentucky*, 80–81.

52. Gerber, "What Is It We Seek to Find in First-Person Documents?" 313. For slaves' letters, see Starobin, *Blacks in Bondage*; Horton, "A Crusade for Freedom," 177.

53. *British Colonist*, June 17, 1852, quoted in Hill, "Blacks in Toronto," 87; Horton, "Kidnapping and Resistance," 161; Yee, "Gender Ideology," 56–57.

54. Winks, *Blacks in Canada*, 248–51; Hembree, "Question of 'Begging,'" 325.

55. Instrument #3844, City of Toronto Deeds, Volume F, York County Land Registry Records.

56. Census of Canada, 1861, Toronto, St. John's Ward; Toronto tax assessment roll, St. John's Ward.

6. Fanny: The Civil War in Louisville

1. Craik, *The Union*, 24–26; Craik, *Slavery in the South*, 15.

2. Yater, *Two Hundred Years*, 82; Harrison and Klotter, *New History of Kentucky*, 181–82.

3. Rogers Clark Ballard Thruston, biographical sketch of Andrew Jackson Ballard, n.d., BFF, "Correspondence" folder; *Biographical Encyclopedia*, 431. Harrison and Klotter, *New History of Kentucky*, 98, 112; Daniel Walker Howe, "Clay, Henry," in Boyer, *Oxford Companion*, 134.

4. Tax Assessment Records, 1860; U.S. federal census, 1860, slave schedules, Louisville, Jefferson County, Ky.

5. Yater, *Two Hundred Years*, 80–81; Bush, *Louisville and the Civil War*, 26.

6. Yater, *Two Hundred Years*, 82–83; Bush, *Louisville and the Civil War*, 26–27; Harrison and Klotter, *New History of Kentucky*, 184–85.

7. Yater, *Two Hundred Years*, 83; Harrison and Klotter, *New History of Kentucky*, 188–89.

8. Harrison and Klotter, *New History of Kentucky*, 189–92; Yater, *Two Hundred Years*, 84–85.

9. McDowell, *City of Conflict*, 17, 22, 44; Yater, *Two Hundred Years*, 83.

10. McDowell, *City of Conflict*, 44, 56, 64–70, 74–75; Yater, *Two Hundred Years*, 93; Bush, *Louisville and the Civil War*, 45–48.

11. Rogers Clark Ballard Thruston, biographical sketch of Andrew Jackson Ballard, n.d., BFF, "Correspondence" folder; James Harlan to Edward Bates, September 17, 1861, U.S. Department of Justice, Records of the Attorney General's Office, General Records, Letters Received (hereafter AGLR), 1809–70, box 1: Kentucky, 1832–70; http://ajr.fjc.gov/servlet.

12. Andrew Ballard to Mary Blair, August 14, 1861, in A. J. Ballard, "Correspondence, 1855–1879," Janin Family Papers (hereafter JFP), box 1; McDowell, *City of Conflict*, 153.

13. Yater, *Two Hundred Years*, 85–86, Harrison and Klotter, *New History of Kentucky*, 196–97; McDowell, *City of Conflict*, 47–50.

14. Yater, *Two Hundred Years*, 82, 86–87; McDowell, *City of Conflict*, 62.

15. Yater, *Two Hundred Years*, 88–89; Harrison and Klotter, *New History of Kentucky*, 199.

16. McDowell, *City of Conflict*, 86–87; Yater, *Two Hundred Years*, 88.

17. Yater, *Two Hundred Years*, 88; Harrison and Klotter, *New History of Kentucky*, 200; McDowell, *City of Conflict*, 89.

18. Yater, *Two Hundred Years*, 89–91; Harrison and Klotter, *New History of Kentucky*, 201; McDowell, *City of Conflict*, 75–80.

19. Bush, *Louisville and the Civil War*, 66–67.

20. *Harper's Weekly*, October 18, 1862, quoted in Yater, *Two Hundred Years*, 86; Bush, *Louisville and the Civil War*, 66–67; McDowell, *City of Conflict*, 91–105.

21. McDowell, *City of Conflict*, 105; Bush, *Louisville and the Civil War*, 68–69.

22. Harrison, *Antislavery Movement in Kentucky*, 102–4; Bush, *Louisville and the Civil War*, 76; Yater, *Two Hundred Years*, 91; Harrison and Klotter, *New History of Kentucky*, 179; McDowell, *City of Conflict*, 135–36.

23. "State Property Taxes: Receipts and Returns," AJB Papers, box 1, folder 13.

24. Bush, *Louisville and the Civil War*, 76; McDowell, *City of Conflict*, 136.

25. Harrison and Klotter, *New History of Kentucky*, 179; McPherson, *Battle Cry of Freedom*, 312, 498, 502–4, 557–58, 562–63.

26. Bush, *Louisville and the Civil War*, 77; Yater, *Two Hundred Years*, 93.

27. Affidavit by Andrew Jackson Ballard, November 12, 1863, AGLR.

28. Andrew Ballard to Mary K. Blair, May 10, 1863, JFP; McPherson, *Battle Cry of Freedom*, 290–92.

29. U.S. War Department, *War of the Rebellion*, series 2, vol. 1:111–14, 553; series 2, vol. 2:250.

30. Ibid., series 2, vol. 5:627, 631.

31. For information on Stephen Burbridge's activities I have consulted Bush, *Louisville and the Civil War*, 79–85; Yater, *Two Hundred Years*, 93.

32. Bush, *Louisville and the Civil War*, 81; *Louisville Democrat*, August 10, 1864.

33. Andrew Ballard to Major Aug. Stubalson, August 2, 1864, JFP; Yater, *Two Hundred Years*, 93–94; Harrison and Klotter, *New History of Kentucky*, 204–5.

34. Yater, *Two Hundred Years*, 91–92; Harrison and Klotter, *New History of Kentucky*, 179–80; McDowell, *City of Conflict*, 157–58.

35. Yater, *Two Hundred Years*, 94.

36. *Louisville Daily Journal*, November 26, 1865.

37. Clark Fitzhugh to John O'Fallon, January 22, 1837, Dennis Fitzhugh Papers, folder 4.

38. Will of Charles W. Thruston, October 22, 1853, CWT Papers, box 1, folder 6; income taxes, AJB Papers, box 1, folder 6; "State Property Taxes: Receipts and Returns," AJB Papers, box 1, folder 13.

7. Cecelia: A New Life in Rochester

1. Winks, *Blacks in Canada*, 237; Hembree, "Question of 'Begging,'" 327; Silverman, "'We Shall Be Heard,'" 68.

2. Du Bois, *City of Frederick Douglass*, 6, 12–13; Sennett, *North Star Country*, 181; Schmitt, "Rochester's Frederick Douglass," 13.

3. Siebert, *Underground Railroad*, 414–15; Sennett, *North Star Country*, 179.

4. Sennett, *North Star Country*, 179–85; Donovan Shilling, "The Rebel of Rose Ridge: Myron Holley's Days in Rochester," *Crooked Lake Review* (Fall 2005), www.crookedlakereview.com/articles/136_137/137fall2005 /137shilling.html; Schmitt, "Rochester's Frederick Douglass," 13.

5. Johnson, *Shopkeeper's Millennium*, 3–4, 14.

6. Douglass quotations from Schmitt, "Rochester's Frederick Douglass," 14, 18.

7. McKelvey, "Lights and Shadows," 6; Schmitt, "Rochester's Frederick Douglass," 14, 18; Du Bois, *City of Frederick Douglass*, 11.

8. McKelvey, "Germans of Rochester," 7–13; McKelvey, "Rochester in Retrospect and Prospect," 11–13; Rosenberg-Naparsteck, "Two Centuries of Industry."

9. Affidavit of Cecelia Larrison, May 6, 1898, Larrison Pension File (hereafter LPF); Peck, *History of Rochester*, 512; Schmitt, "Rochester's Frederick Douglass," 14.

10. Affidavit of Cecelia Larrison, May 6, 1898, LPF.

11. Ibid.

12. *Daily American Directory of the City of Rochester for 1840–50*, 13; *Rochester Daily Union City Directory for 1861*, 37–39; Ward, *Churches of Rochester*, 55; Johnson, *Shopkeeper's Millennium*, 116–17; McKelvey, "Rochester Mayors," 13–14.

13. Ward, *Churches of Rochester*, 61–62.

14. Affidavit of Cecelia Larrison, June 18, 1898, LPF; *Rochester Daily Union City Directory for 1861*, 45, 58, 278; *Boyd's Rochester and Brockport Directories, 1864–65*, 78; *Boyd's Rochester Directory, 1863–64*, 269; U.S. federal census, 1860, ward 6, Rochester, Monroe County, N.Y.

15. Du Bois, *City of Frederick Douglass*, 17–18; affidavit of Cecelia Larrison, June 18, 1898, LPF.

16. Affidavit of Chauncey Webster, July 7, 1899; affidavit of Cecelia Larrison, June 18, 1898; affidavit of Stanley Shippy, September 6, 1898; affidavit of Joseph P. Cleary, July 22, 1898, LPF.

17. Rosenberg-Naparsteck, "Growing Agitation," 27.

18. Ibid., 28; McPherson, *Battle Cry of Freedom*, 564.

19. Cornish, *Sable Arm*, 94; McPherson, *Battle Cry of Freedom*, 500; Redkey, *Grand Army*, 4–6; McPherson, *Marching toward Freedom*, 60.

20. On the Fifty-fourth Massachusetts and the acceptance of black combat troops, see McPherson, *Marching toward Freedom*, 70–80; Redkey, *Grand Army*, 7; Cornish, *Sable Arm*, 106, 118, 152–55, 163; McPherson, *Battle Cry of Freedom*, 564–66, 686–87.

21. Fisher, "Civil War Draft, Part One," 7–9; McKelvey, "Rochester's Part in the Civil War," 6.

22. McKelvey, "Rochester's Part in the Civil War," 18–20; Marsh, "History of Rochester's Part in the Civil War," 5–10, 17–23, 33–37, 47.

23. Fisher, "Civil War Draft, Part One," 4–11, 24.

24. Fisher, "Civil War Draft, Part Two," 13; Rosenberg-Naparsteck, "Growing Agitation," 28–29.

25. Affidavit of Cecelia Larrison, June 18, 1898, LPF; Marsh, "History of Rochester's Part in the Civil War," 28; Elisha G. Marshall obituary, *New York Times*, August 4, 1883.

26. Affidavit of Cecelia Larrison, June 18, 1898, LPF; Marsh, "History of Rochester's Part in the Civil War," 50–51.

27. Redkey, *Grand Army*, 2.

28. Cornish, *Sable Arm*, 163.

29. Bernstein, *New York City Draft Riots;* Henretta et al., *America's History*, 463–64; Jonathan M. Berkey, "Draft Riots, Civil War," in Boyer, *Oxford Companion*, 193.

30. Affidavit of Chauncey Webster, August 8, 1899; affidavit of Cecelia Larrison, May 6, 1898, LPF.

31. McKelvey, "Rochester's Part in the Civil War," 10–11.

32. Ibid., 12–13; Cornish, *Sable Arm*, 188.

33. Family information on Cecelia is from U.S. federal census, 1880, Faribault, Rice County, Minnesota; state census of Minnesota, 1875; Minnesota cemetery inscription index, on Ancestry.com; transactions 19749 and 19750, book B, June 29, 1876; transaction 6679, book O, September 18, 1889, York County Land Registry Records; *Boyd's Rochester Directory, 1866–67*, 138; *Rochester Directory, 1873*, 150; *Rochester Directory, 1874*, 158; *Rochester Directory, 1881*, 206; *Rochester Directory, 1885*, 241.

34. Phisterer, *New York in the War of the Rebellion*, 1477.

35. William H. Harrison, New York Military Service Record, #1780; affidavit of Cecelia Larrison, May 6, 1898, LPF.

8. Fanny: Postwar Trials

1. Harrison and Klotter, *New History of Kentucky*, 234.

2. Andrew Ballard's tax information is in "State Property Taxes: Receipts and Returns," AJB Papers, box 1, folder 13.

3. See Rogers Clark's annotations on Jack on the slave's original bill of sale, November 1, 1846, CWT Misc. Chloe is mentioned in Emily Zane to Frances Thruston Ballard, March 15, 1896, RCBT Papers, box 1, folder 1.

4. U.S. federal census, 1870, Louisville, Jefferson County, Ky.

5. Harrison and Klotter, *New History of Kentucky*, 234–36; Lucas, *History of Blacks in Kentucky*, 187–88.

6. Yater, *Two Hundred Years*, 95–96.

7. Foner, *Reconstruction*, 190–91; Benjamin Bristow to Henry Stansberry, August 1, 1866, AGLR.

8. Yater, *Two Hundred Years*, 95, 98.

9. Ibid., 98–103.

10. Foner, *Reconstruction*, 243–45; Henretta et al., *America's History*, 485–88.

11. Lucas, *History of Blacks in Kentucky*, 292–95; Harrison and Klotter, *New History of Kentucky*, 244.

12. "Return of Fees and Emoluments for July 1, 1867 to December 31, 1867," AJB Papers, box 1, folder 6.

13. *Blyew v. United States*, 80 U.S. 501 (1872); "Kentucky (Federal Courts), June 13, 1854–July 16, 1869," AGLR; Waxman, "'Presenting the Case of the United States as It Should Be,'" available online at www.usdoj .gov/osg/aboutosg/sgarticle.html. (Blyew and Kennard were eventually convicted in state court in 1890 and 1876, respectively, but both served fewer than ten years before being pardoned.)

14. Rogers Clark Ballard Thruston, biographical sketch of Andrew Jackson Ballard, n.d., BFF, "Correspondence" folder; *Biographical Encyclopedia*, 431.

15. Yater, *Two Hundred Years*, 96; Donald B. Towles, "Newspapers," in Kleber, *Encyclopedia of Louisville*, 655.

16. Lucas, *History of Blacks in Kentucky*, 302–5.

17. Ibid., 296–97; *Louisville Daily Commercial*, May 14, 1871.

18. *Louisville Daily Commercial*, May 14, 1871.

19. *Louisville Daily Courier-Journal*, May 13, 1871, May 14, 1871.

20. *Louisville Daily Commercial*, May 13, 1871, May 14, 1871.

21. *Louisville Daily Courier-Journal*, May 15, 1871; *Louisville Daily Commercial*, May 13, 1871.

22. *Louisville Daily Commercial*, August 6, 1871.

23. *Louisville Daily Courier-Journal*, August 9, 1871; Harrison and Klotter, *New History of Kentucky*, 245–46.

24. Harrison and Klotter, *New History of Kentucky*, 242–46.

25. *Louisville Daily Courier-Journal*, August 9, 1871.

26. *Louisville Daily Commercial*, August 8, 1871.

27. Charles Thompson, "Harlan, John Marshall," in Kleber, *Encyclopedia of Louisville*, 368; Harrison and Klotter, *New History of Kentucky*, 246.

28. *Louisville Daily Courier-Journal*, August 18, 1885.

29. For a brief history of Vassar, see http://faculty.vassar.edu/daniels/ index.html.

30. Frances Ballard to Mollie Hill, April 19, 1872; Ballard to Hill, May 26, 1872; Ballard to Hill, June 17, 1872, AJB Papers, box 1, folder 3.

31. On the water cure, see Greene, "Recollections of Early Days at the Water Cure," 87; Atwater and Kohn, "Rochester and the Water-Cure," 5–6.

32. Abby C. Ballard to Mollie Hill, November 10, 1872, AJB Papers, box 1, folder 3.

33. W. Hardee to Andrew Jackson Ballard, May 6, 1873, AJB Papers, box 1, folder 3.

34. Frances Ballard to Mollie Hill, September 25, 1874, AJB Papers, box 1, folder 3; Pringle Mitchell (Tiffany Glass Co.) to Frances Ballard, June 6, 1895, AJB Papers, box 1, folder 4; *Louisville Courier-Journal*, July 5, 1896.

35. Ott, *Fevered Lives*, 6–7, 13, 24–25, 30–31.

36. Ibid., 35–44; Starr, *Social Transformation*, 191; Frances Ballard to Cecelia Holmes, August 2, 1855, BFP.

37. Christ Church Cathedral register, 1864–81, reel 1, p. 212; Rogers Clark Ballard Thruston, biographical sketch of Andrew Ballard, 1929, AJB Papers, box 1, folder 1.

38. On the Ballards' finances, see generally AJB Papers, box 3, folders 13, 15, 16; for the Colorado venture, see box 6.

39. Andrew Jackson Ballard to Frances Ballard, August 11, 1885, RCBT Papers, box 1, folder 1.

40. *Louisville Daily Commercial*, August 18, 1885; *Louisville Daily Courier-Journal*, August 18, 1885.

41. Hambleton Tapp, "Rogers Clark Ballard Thruston: A Good Kentuckian," article from unidentified magazine, n.d., TFF, "Thruston Family" folder; Clark, "Rogers Clark Ballard Thruston," 410.

42. A copy of the will is in Frances Ballard to Rogers Clark Ballard Thruston, March 4, 1895, BFF, "Ballard Family Special" folder.

43. Cecelia Larrison to Rogers Clark Ballard Thruston, June 25, 1896, BFP.

44. Rogers Clark Ballard Thruston, June 5, 1899, BFP.

45. Frances Ballard to Rogers Clark Ballard Thruston, March 4, 1895, BFF, "Ballard Family Special" folder; Yater, *Two Hundred Years*, 221.

46. Obituary, n.d., newspaper not identified, in BFF, "Ballard Family Newspaper Clippings" folder.

9. Cecelia: Back in Louisville

1. Affidavit of Cecelia Larrison, May 6, 1898, LPF.

2. Ibid.; *Caron's Directory of the City of Louisville, 1876*; Ferguson, "'Living by Means Unknown,'" 362; Wright, *Life behind a Veil*, 84.

3. *Caron's Directory of the City of Louisville, 1878*; *Caron's Directory of the City of Louisville, 1883*; Wright, *Life behind a Veil*, 80–84; Yater, *Two Hundred Years*, 108–9; Ferguson, "'Living by Means Unknown,'" 360–64; Foner, *Reconstruction*, 81–82.

4. Yater, *Two Hundred Years*, 109.

5. Lucas, *History of Blacks in Kentucky*, 187–95; Harrison and Klotter, *New History of Kentucky*, 237–38.

6. Lucas, *History of Blacks in Kentucky*, 185–87; Harrison and Klotter, *New History of Kentucky*, 238.

7. Lucas, *History of Blacks in Kentucky*, 185–95; Harrison and Klotter, *New History of Kentucky*, 237–39.

8. Foner, *Reconstruction*, 82.

9. Rogers Clark Ballard Thruston, June 5, 1899, BFP.

10. Wright, *Life behind a Veil*, 84.

11. Special examiner to Commissioner of Pensions H. Clay Evans, June 23, 1898; affidavit of Mamie Reels, May 6, 1898, LPF; Yater, *Two Hundred Years*, 109–10; Lucas, *History of Blacks in Kentucky*, 275–76; Ferguson, "'Living by Means Unknown,'" 363–69.

12. Wright, *Life behind a Veil*, 4–5, 52–54, 103–7; Lucas, *History of Blacks in Kentucky*, 296–98; "Segregation," in Kleber, *Encyclopedia of Louisville*, 798–99; Yater, *Two Hundred Years*, 152–53.

13. The discussion here and below of the progress achieved by blacks during this period draws on Lucas, *History of Blacks in Kentucky*, 298–301.

14. Affidavit of Cecelia Larrison, May 6, 1898, LPF; *Caron's Directory of the City of Louisville, 1880*.

15. Affidavit of Cecelia Larrison, May 6, 1898, LPF; affidavit of Mamie Reels, May 6, 1898, LPF.

16. Affidavit of Cecelia Larrison, May 6, 1898, LPF; *Caron's Directory of the City of Louisville, 1888*.

17. Affidavit of Cecelia Larrison, May 6, 1898; affidavit of Mamie Reels, May 6, 1898; affidavit of Anthony Bland, June 10, 1898, LPF.

18. Instrument #1694, November 1, 1887, book E, York County Land Registry Records.

19. Affidavit of A. L. Reels, May 10, 1898, LPF.

20. U.S. federal census, 1880, Louisville, Jefferson County, Ky.; Wright, *Life behind a Veil*, 93; Lucas, *History of Blacks in Kentucky*, 279–80.

21. Affidavit of A. L. Reels, May 10, 1898, LPF; U.S. federal census, 1880, Louisville, Jefferson County, Ky.; William H. Harrison, New York Military Service Record, #1780; affidavit of Mamie Reels, May 6, 1898; affidavit of Chauncey Webster, August 8, 1899, LPF; Frances Ballard to Cecelia Holmes, August 11, 1859, BFP.

22. Affidavit of A. L. Reels, May 10, 1898, LPF; *Caron's Directory of the City of Louisville, 1890*; *Caron's Directory of the City of Louisville, 1891*; *Caron's Directory of the City of Louisville, 1894*; *Caron's Directory of the City of Louisville, 1897*; *Caron's Directory of the City of Louisville, 1899*.

23. Jefferson County Marriage Book 3C ["Colored"], 340.

24. Lucas, *History of Blacks in Kentucky*, 313–15, 327; Wright, *Life behind a Veil*, 124–28; "Segregation," in Kleber, *Encyclopedia of Louisville*, 798–99; Yater, *Two Hundred Years*, 151.

25. Cecelia Larrison to Rogers Clark Ballard Thruston, February 14, 1899, BFP.

26. Rogers Clark Ballard Thruston, June 5, 1899, BFP.

27. Ibid.

28. Affidavit of Cecelia Larrison, May 6, 1898, LPF.

29. Special examiner to Evans, June 23, 1898; affidavit of Stanley E. Shippey, September 6, 1898; affidavit of Henry H. Clark, September 26, 1898; affidavit of Chauncey Webster, August 8, 1899, LPF.

30. Summary page, LPF; Rogers Clark Ballard Thruston, June 5, 1899, BFP.

31. Rogers Clark Ballard Thruston, June 5, 1899; Cecelia Larrison to Rogers Clark Ballard Thruston, September 13, 1899, BFP; Louisville Mortuary Record Book 10, 227.

32. Affidavit of Sophia Alexander, February 21, 1899, LPF.

33. Cecelia Larrison to Hon. William Lindsay, September 28, 1899, LPF; Cecelia Larrison to Rogers Clark Ballard Thruston, September 27, 1899, BFP.

34. Skocpol, *Protecting Soldiers and Mothers*, 102, 120–30.

35. Claimant's brief for reopening, n.d.; widow's pension approval, October 11, 1899, LPF.

36. Statement of attending physician, October 5, 1909, LPF.

37. Acting commissioner, Bureau of Pensions, to Mamie A. Reels, November 2, 1909; affidavit of T. H. Hankins, November 5, 1909, LPF.

Conclusion: The Bonds of Slavery

1. Louisville Mortuary Record Book 14, 245.

2. Wright, *History of Blacks in Kentucky*, 43, 54–58; Harrison and Klotter, *New History of Kentucky*, 348, 381–82.

3. Yater, *Two Hundred Years*, 150–53.

4. U.S. federal census, 1910, Louisville, Jefferson County, Ky.; *Caron's Directory of the City of Louisville, 1911*; Wright, *History of Blacks in Kentucky*, 26–27; Phyllis Hurd, "Glenview," orig.courier-journal.com/reweb /community/placetime/eastcounty_glenview.html.

5. Tapp, "Rogers Clark Ballard Thruston," TFF, "Thruston Family" folder.

6. Ibid.; Clark, "Rogers Clark Ballard Thruston," 411–35.

Bibliography

Published Sources

Armstrong, J., ed. *Rowsell's City of Toronto and County of York Directory, for 1850–1851.* Toronto: Henry Rowsell, 1850.

Aron, Stephen. *How the West Was Lost: The Transformation of Kentucky from Daniel Boone to Henry Clay.* Baltimore, Md.: Johns Hopkins University Press, 1996.

Atwater, Edward, and Lawrence Kohn. "Rochester and the Water-Cure, 1844–1854." *Rochester History* 32 (1970): 1–28.

Baker, Houston A. Introduction to *Narrative of the Life of Frederick Douglass, an American Slave,* by Frederick Douglass, 7–27. New York: Penguin, 1982.

Barham, John. *Descriptions of Niagara: Selected from Various Travellers; with Original Additions.* Gravesend, England: William Barham, 1846.

Barnett, Todd. "Virginians Moving West: The Early Evolution of Slavery in the Bluegrass." *Filson Club History Quarterly* 73 (1999): 221–48.

Bernstein, Iver. *The New York City Draft Riots: Their Significance for American Society and Politics in the Age of the Civil War.* Oxford: Oxford University Press, 1990.

Bingham, Emily. *Mordecai: An Early American Family.* New York: Hill and Wang, 2003.

The Biographical Encyclopedia of Kentucky of the Dead and Living Men of the Nineteenth Century. Cincinnati: J. M. Armstrong, 1878.

Blight, David, ed. *Passages to Freedom: The Underground Railroad in History and Memory.* Washington, D.C.: Smithsonian Books, 2004.

Blockson, Charles L. *Hippocrene Guide to the Underground Railroad.* New York: Hippocrene, 1994.

Boyd's Rochester and Brockport Directories, 1864–65. Rochester, N.Y.: Andrew Boyd, 1864.

Boyd's Rochester Directory, 1863–64. Rochester, N.Y.: Andrew Boyd, 1863.

Boyd's Rochester Directory, 1866–67. Rochester, N.Y.: Andrew Boyd, 1866.

Boyer, Paul, ed. *The Oxford Companion to United States History.* New York: Oxford University Press, 2001.

Brown's Toronto General Directory, 1856. Toronto: W. R. Brown, 1856.

Bush, Bryan S. *Louisville and the Civil War: A History and Guide.* Charleston, S.C.: History Press, 2008.

Butler, Nancy. "Starting Anew: The Black Community of Early Niagara." In *Slavery and Freedom in Niagara,* edited by Michael Power and Nancy Butler, 41–76. Niagara-on-the-Lake, Ontario: Niagara Historical Society, 1993.

Caron's Directory of the City of Louisville, 1876. Louisville, Ky.: Caron Directory, 1876.

Caron's Directory of the City of Louisville, 1878. Louisville, Ky.: Caron Directory, 1878.

Caron's Directory of the City of Louisville, 1880. Louisville, Ky.: Caron Directory, 1880.

Caron's Directory of the City of Louisville, 1883. Louisville, Ky.: Caron Directory, 1883.

Caron's Directory of the City of Louisville, 1888. Louisville, Ky.: Caron Directory, 1888.

Caron's Directory of the City of Louisville, 1890. Louisville, Ky.: Caron Directory, 1890.

Caron's Directory of the City of Louisville, 1891. Louisville, Ky.: Caron Directory, 1891.

Caron's Directory of the City of Louisville, 1894. Louisville, Ky.: Caron Directory, 1894.

Caron's Directory of the City of Louisville, 1897. Louisville, Ky.: Caron Directory, 1897.

Caron's Directory of the City of Louisville, 1899. Louisville, Ky.: Caron Directory, 1899.

Caron's Directory of the City of Louisville, 1911. Louisville, Ky.: Caron Directory, 1911.

Caverhill's Toronto City Directory for 1859–60. Toronto: W. C. F. Caverhill, 1859.

Clark, Thomas. "Rogers Clark Ballard Thruston: Engineer, Historian, and Benevolent Kentuckian." *Filson Club History Quarterly* 58 (1984): 408–35.

Cornish, Dudley Taylor. *The Sable Arm: Black Troops in the Union Army, 1861–1865.* 1956. Reprint, Lawrence: University Press of Kansas, 1987.

Craik, James. *Slavery in the South; or, What Is Our Present Duty to the Slaves?* Boston: Prentiss and Deland, 1862.

———. *The Union: National and State Sovereignty Alike Essential to American Liberty.* Louisville, Ky.: Morton and Griswold, 1860.

Daily American Directory of the City of Rochester for 1849–50. Rochester, N.Y.: Jerome and Brother, 1849.

Davidson, James West, et al. *Nation of Nations: A Narrative History of the American Republic.* Vol. 2. 2nd ed. New York: McGraw-Hill, 1994.

Demos, John. *The Unredeemed Captive: A Family Story from Early America.* New York: Vintage, 1994.

Drew, Benjamin. *A North-Side View of Slavery: The Refugee; or, The Narratives of Fugitive Slaves in Canada.* Boston: John P. Jewett, 1856.

Dubinsky, Karen. *The Second Greatest Disappointment: Honeymooning and Tourism at Niagara Falls.* New Brunswick, N.J.: Rutgers University Press, 1999.

Du Bois, Eugene E. *The City of Frederick Douglass: Rochester's African-American People and Places.* Rochester: Landmark Society of Western New York, 1994.

Faust, Drew Gilpin. "Culture, Conflict and Community: The Meaning of Power on an Antebellum Plantation." *Journal of Social History* 14 (1980): 83–97.

Ferguson, Dean. "'Living by Means Unknown to Their Neighbors': The Informal Economy of Louisville's Blacks, 1865–1880." *Filson Club Historical Quarterly* 72 (1998): 357–77.

Finkelman, Paul. *An Imperfect Union: Slavery, Federalism, and Comity.* Chapel Hill: University of North Carolina Press, 1981.

Fisher, Donald. "The Civil War Draft in Rochester, Part One." *Rochester History* 53 (1991): 1–24.

———. "The Civil War Draft in Rochester, Part Two." *Rochester History* 53 (1991): 1–30.

Foner, Eric. *Reconstruction: America's Unfinished Revolution.* New York: Harper and Row, 1988.

Fox-Genovese, Elizabeth. *Within the Plantation Household: Black and White Women of the Old South.* Chapel Hill: University of North Carolina Press, 1988.

Franklin, John Hope. *A Southern Odyssey: Travelers in the Antebellum North.* Baton Rouge: Louisiana State University Press, 1976.

Franklin, John Hope, and Loren Schweninger. *Runaway Slaves: Rebels on the Plantation.* New York: Oxford University Press, 1999.

Frost, Karolyn Smardz. *I've Got a Home in Glory Land: A Lost Tale of the Underground Railroad.* Toronto: Thomas Allen, 2007.

Gara, Larry. *The Liberty Line: The Legend of the Underground Railroad.* Lexington: University Press of Kentucky, 1961.

Genovese, Eugene. *Roll, Jordan, Roll: The World the Slaves Made.* New York: Pantheon, 1974.

Gerber, David A. "What Is It We Seek to Find in First-Person Documents? Documenting Society and Cultural Practices in Irish Immigrant Writings." *Reviews in American History* 32 (2004): 305–16.

Greene, Edward. "Recollections of Early Days at the Water Cure with Dr. Cordelia Greene." *Historical Wyoming* (April 1958): 87–92.

Griffler, Keith. "Beyond the Quest for the 'Real Eliza Harris': Fugitive Slave Women in the Ohio Valley." *Ohio Valley History* 3 (2003): 3–16.

Gudmestad, Robert. *A Troublesome Commerce: The Transformation of the Interstate Slave Trade.* Baton Rouge: Louisiana State University Press, 2003.

Gutman, Herbert. *The Black Family in Slavery and Freedom, 1750–1925.* New York: Pantheon, 1976.

Hardy, James D., Jr., and Robert B. Robinson. "Freedom and Domicile Jurisprudence in Louisiana: *Lunsford v. Coquillon.*" *Louisiana History* 39 (1998): 293–317.

Harrison, Lowell. *The Antislavery Movement in Kentucky.* Lexington: University Press of Kentucky, 2004.

Harrison, Lowell, and James Klotter. *A New History of Kentucky.* Lexington: University Press of Kentucky, 1997.

Hayden, Amos S. *Early History of the Disciples in the Western Reserve, Ohio.* Cincinnati: Chase and Hall, 1875.

Hembree, Michael F. "The Question of 'Begging': Fugitive Slave Relief in Canada, 1830–1865." *Civil War History* 37 (1991): 314–27.

Henretta, James, et al. *America's History.* Chicago: Dorsey, 1987.

Hill, Dan. "The Blacks in Toronto." In *Gathering Place: Peoples and Neighbourhoods of Toronto, 1834–1945*, edited by Robert F. Harney, 75–105. Toronto: Multicultural History Society of Ontario, 1985.

Hopkins, James. *A History of the Hemp Industry in Kentucky.* Lexington: University Press of Kentucky, 1951.

Hudson, J. Blaine. "Crossing the 'Dark Line': Fugitive Slaves and the Underground Railroad in Louisville and North-Central Kentucky." *Filson History Quarterly* 75 (2001): 33–84.

———. "In Pursuit of Freedom: Slave Law and Emancipation in Louisville and Jefferson County, Kentucky." *Filson History Quarterly* 76 (2002): 287–326.

————. "Slavery in Early Louisville and Jefferson County, Kentucky, 1780–1812." *Filson Club Historical Quarterly* 73 (July 1999): 249–83.

Johannsen, David. *To the Halls of the Montezumas: The Mexican War in the American Imagination.* New York: Oxford University Press, 1985.

Johnson, Paul. *A Shopkeeper's Millennium: Society and Revivals in New York, 1815–1837.* New York: Hill and Wang, 1978.

Johnson, Walter. *Soul by Soul: Life inside the Antebellum Slave Market.* Cambridge, Mass.: Harvard University Press, 1999.

Kieffer, Chester. *Maligned General: The Biography of Thomas Sidney Jesup.* San Rafael, Calif.: Presidio, 1979.

Kleber, John, ed. *The Encyclopedia of Louisville.* Lexington: University Press of Kentucky, 2001.

Lepore, Jill. "Historians Who Love Too Much: Reflections on Microhistory and Biography." *Journal of American History* 88 (June 2001): 129–44.

Louisville Directory of 1832. Louisville, Ky.: Richard W. Otis, 1832. Reprint, Louisville, Ky.: G. R. Clark, 1970.

Lucas, Marion. *A History of Blacks in Kentucky.* Vol. 1, *From Slavery to Segregation, 1760–1891.* Frankfort: Kentucky Historical Society, 1992.

Lystra, Karen. *Searching the Heart: Women, Men, and Romantic Love in Nineteenth-Century America.* Oxford: Oxford University Press, 1989.

Marsh, Ruth. "A History of Rochester's Part in the Civil War." In *Rochester in the Civil War,* edited by Blake McKelvey, 4–76. Rochester, N.Y.: Rochester Historical Society, 1944.

McDowell, Robert. *City of Conflict: Louisville in the Civil War.* Louisville, Ky.: Civil War Roundtable, 1962.

McKelvey, Blake. "The Germans of Rochester: Their Traditions and Contributions." *Rochester History* 20 (1958): 1–28.

————. "Lights and Shadows in Local Negro History." *Rochester History* 21 (1959): 1–27.

————. "Rochester in Retrospect and Prospect." *Rochester History* 23 (1961): 1–28.

————. "Rochester Mayors before the Civil War." *Rochester History* 26 (1964): 1–20.

————. "Rochester's Part in the Civil War." *Rochester History* 23 (1961): 1–24.

McLaurin, Melton. *Celia: A Slave.* New York: Avon, 1993.

McPherson, James. *Battle Cry of Freedom: The Civil War Era.* Oxford: Oxford University Press, 1988.

————. *Marching toward Freedom: Blacks in the Civil War, 1861–1865.* New York: Facts on File, 1991.

Middleton, Stephen. "Law and Ideology in Ohio and Kentucky: The Kidnapping of Jerry Phinney." *Filson Club History Quarterly* 67 (1993): 347–72.

Morgan, Edmund. *American Slavery, American Freedom: The Ordeal of Colonial Virginia*. New York: Norton, 1975.

Morgan, Philip. *Slave Counterpoint: Black Culture in the Eighteenth Century Chesapeake and Low Country*. Chapel Hill: University of North Carolina Press, 1998.

Ott, Katherine. *Fevered Lives: Tuberculosis and American Culture since 1870*. Cambridge, Mass.: Harvard University Press, 1996.

Peck, William F. *History of Rochester and Monroe County, New York, from the Earliest Historic Times to the Beginning of 1907*. Vol. 1. New York: Pioneer, 1908.

Phisterer, Frederick, comp. *New York in the War of the Rebellion, 1861–1865*. Albany: J. B. Lyon, 1912.

Powell, James. *History of the Canadian Dollar*. Ottawa: Bank of Canada, 2005.

Proceedings of the Convention of Radical Political Abolitionists . . . 1855. New York: Central Abolition Board, 1855.

Proceedings of the National Liberty Convention . . . 1848. Utica, N.Y.: S. W. Green, 1848.

Redkey, Edwin, ed. *A Grand Army of Black Men: Letters from African-American Soldiers in the Union Army, 1861–1865*. Cambridge: Cambridge University Press, 1992.

Robertson, John Ross. *Landmarks of Toronto*. Vol. 3. Toronto: J. Ross Robertson, 1898.

Rochester Daily Union City Directory for 1861. Rochester, N.Y.: Curtis, Butts, 1861.

Rochester Directory, 1873. Rochester, N.Y.: Drew, Allis, 1873.

Rochester Directory, 1874. Rochester, N.Y.: Drew, Allis, 1874.

Rochester Directory, 1881. Rochester, N.Y.: Drew, Allis, 1881.

Rochester Directory, 1885. Rochester, N.Y.: Drew, Allis, 1885.

Rosenberg-Naparsteck, Ruth. "A Growing Agitation: Rochester before, during, and after the Civil War." *Rochester History* 46 (1984): 1–40.

———. "Two Centuries of Industry and Trade in Rochester." *Rochester History* 51 (1989): 1–20.

Rothman, Ellen K. *Hands and Hearts: A History of Courtship in America*. New York: Basic Books, 1984.

Schmitt, Victoria Sandwick. "Rochester's Frederick Douglass, Part One." *Rochester History* 67 (2005): 1–28.

Schwartz, Marie Jenkins. *Born in Bondage: Growing up Enslaved in the Antebellum South*. Cambridge, Mass.: Harvard University Press, 2000.

Bibliography

Sears, John F. *Sacred Places: American Tourist Attractions in the Nineteenth Century.* New York: Oxford University Press, 1989.

Sennett, Milton. *North Star Country: Upstate New York and the Crusade for African American Freedom.* Syracuse, N.Y.: Syracuse University Press, 2002.

Siebert, Wilbur. *The Underground Railroad: From Slavery to Freedom.* New York: Macmillan, 1898.

Silverman, Jason. "'We Shall Be Heard': The Development of the Fugitive Slave Press in Canada." *Canadian Historical Review* 65 (1984): 54–69.

Skocpol, Theda. *Protecting Soldiers and Mothers: The Political Origins of Social Policy in the United States.* Cambridge, Mass.: Harvard University Press, 1992.

Starobin, Robert, ed. *Blacks in Bondage: Letters of American Slaves.* Princeton, N.J.: Princeton University Press, 1988.

Starr, Paul. *The Social Transformation of American Medicine.* New York: Basic Books, 1982.

"Two Days at Niagara." *Southern Literary Messenger,* December 1845, 728–33.

Ulrich, Laurel Thatcher. *A Midwife's Tale: The Life of Martha Ballard, Based on Her Diary.* New York: Vintage, 1990.

U.S. War Department. *The War of the Rebellion: A Compilation of the Official Records of the Union and Confederate Armies.* Series 2. Washington, D.C.: Government Printing Office, 1894–99.

Wade, Richard. *Slavery in the Cities: The South, 1820–1860.* New York: Oxford University Press, 1964.

Ward, F. DeW. *Churches of Rochester: Ecclesiastical History of Rochester, New York.* Rochester, N.Y.: Erastus Darrow, 1871.

Watson, Harry. *Liberty and Power: The Politics of Jacksonian America.* New York: Hill and Wang, 1990.

Webster, A. J. "Louisville in the Eighteen Fifties." *Filson Club History Quarterly* 4 (1930): 132–41.

Winks, Robin. *The Blacks in Canada: A History.* Montreal: McGill-Queen's University Press, 1971.

Wright, George. *A History of Blacks in Kentucky.* Vol. 2, *In Pursuit of Equality, 1890–1980.* Frankfort: Kentucky Historical Society, 1992.

———. *Life behind a Veil: Blacks in Louisville, Kentucky, 1865–1930.* Baton Rouge: Louisiana State University Press, 1985.

Yater, George. *Two Hundred Years at the Falls of the Ohio: A History of Louisville and Jefferson County.* Louisville, Ky.: Filson Club, 1987.

Yee, Shirley J. "Gender Ideology and Black Women as Community-Builders in Ontario, 1850–1870." *Canadian Historical Review* 75 (1994): 53–73.

Manuscript Sources

Ballard, Andrew Jackson. Papers, 1848–96. Filson Historical Society. Louisville, Ky.

Ballard Family Files. Filson Historical Society. Louisville, Ky.

Ballard Family Papers, 1840–99. Filson Historical Society. Louisville, Ky.

Census of Canada, 1861. Library and Archives Canada, Ottawa.

Christ Church Cathedral. Registers, 1829–81. Department of Archives and Special Collections. University of Louisville. Louisville, Ky.

Death Books. Louisville, August 1907–December 1910. Louisville Free Public Library. Louisville, Ky.

Fitzhugh, Dennis. Papers, 1802–56. Filson Historical Society. Louisville, Ky.

Janin Family Papers, 1735–1932. Huntington Library. San Marino, Calif.

Jefferson County Marriage Books. Jefferson County Courthouse. Louisville, Ky.

Larrison Pension File. File 631.101. Certificate 485.092. National Archives, Washington, D.C.

Louisville Mortuary Record Books. Filson Historical Society. Louisville, Ky.

Military Service Records. New York State Archives. Albany, N.Y.

State Census of Minnesota, 1875. Minnesota Historical Society. St. Paul, Minn.

Supreme Court of Louisiana Historical Archives. Louisiana and Special Collections Department. Earl K. Long Library. University of New Orleans. New Orleans, La.

Tax Assessment Records. Jefferson County, Kentucky. Filson Historical Society. Louisville, Ky.

Thruston, Charles William. Miscellaneous Papers, 1823–55. Filson Historical Society. Louisville, Ky.

———. Papers, 1777–1865. Filson Historical Society. Louisville, Ky.

Thruston, Rogers Clark Ballard. Papers, 1858–1946. Filson Historical Society. Louisville, Ky.

Thruston Family Files. Filson Historical Society. Louisville, Ky.

Toronto Tax Assessment Rolls. St. John's Ward. Toronto City Archives.

U.S. Bureau of the Census. 1860 Federal Manuscript Census. Slave Schedules. Microfilm Publication M653. National Archives. Washington, D.C.

———. 1870 Federal Manuscript Census. Microfilm Publication M593. National Archives. Washington, D.C.

————. 1880 Federal Manuscript Census. Microfilm Publication T9. National Archives. Washington, D.C.

————. 1900 Federal Manuscript Census. Microfilm Publication T623. National Archives. Washington, D.C.

————. 1910 Federal Manuscript Census. Microfilm Publication T624. National Archives. Washington, D.C.

U.S. Department of Justice. Record Group 60. Records of the Attorney General's Office. General Records. Letters Received, 1809–70. National Archives. College Park, Md.

York County Land Registry Records. Land Registry Office. Toronto.

Index

Index